HEALTH LITERACY AND
SCHOOL-BASED HEALTH EDUCATION

HEALTH LITERACY AND SCHOOL-BASED HEALTH EDUCATION

EDITED BY

RAY MARKS

York College, The City University of New York and Teachers College, Columbia University, NY, USA

United Kingdom – North America – Japan
India – Malaysia – China

Emerald Group Publishing Limited
Howard House, Wagon Lane, Bingley BD16 1WA, UK

First edition 2012

Copyright © 2012 Emerald Group Publishing Limited

Reprints and permission service
Contact: permissions@emeraldinsight.com

British Library Cataloguing in Publication Data
A catalogue record for this book is available from the British Library

ISBN: 978-1-78052-306-4

ISOQAR certified
Management Systems,
awarded to Emerald for
adherence to Quality
and Environmental
standards ISO 9001:2008
and 14001:2004,
respectively

Certificate Number 1985
ISO 9001
ISO 14001

INVESTOR IN PEOPLE

Acknowledgments

Much of what was written here was derived from the observation that the "new medicine" approach which began to emerge in the 1990s might be deleterious, rather than helpful to those with inadequate health literacy. To advance the imperative to address the problem of limited health literacy, giants among others who have identified the school as a crucial venue for building health literacy for some time are Professors Donald Nutbeam and Lawrence St. Leger, in particular. I thank them and others such as Professors Ilona Kickbusch and Rima Rudd and others who have done so much to advance this much-overlooked area of education and citizenship. In particular in this present context, I express my most sincere gratitude to Professor Joan Wharf Higgins, an expert in this and related fields who devoted so much time and energy to advancing this effort. Professor Leger, too, who was so willing to provide direction to us, and to the lecturer innovators Leena Paakkari and Olli Paakkari who have moved the concept of Health Literacy in schools to a very advanced practical level – thank you all. Mr. Chris Hart, from Emerald Books, is to be especially commended for taking on this challenge on a much underreported topic and the volume would not be possible without his continued support, guidance, and interest. It would also not be possible without the dedication, commitment, and editorial expertise of Mrs. Jaya Chowdhury (Project Manager, MPS Limited, Chennai, India) and the helpful assistance of Ms. Sophie Barr.

Contents

List of Contributors

Christine Beer	Department of Curriculum and Instruction, University of Victoria, BC, Canada
Deborah Begoray	Department of Curriculum and Instruction, University of Victoria, BC, Canada
Amy Collins	Department of Curriculum and Instruction, University of Victoria, BC, Canada
Janie Harrison	Department of Curriculum and Instruction, University of Victoria, BC, Canada
Joan Wharf Higgins	School of Exercise Science, Physical and Health Education, University of Victoria, BC Canada
Ray Marks	Department of Health, Physical Education, Gerontological Studies and Services, York College, City University of New York; Department of Health and Behavioral Studies, Teachers College, Columbia University, New York, NY, USA
Leena Paakkari	Department of Health Sciences, University of Jyväskylä, Finland
Olli Paakkari	Department of Health Sciences, University of Jyväskylä, Finland
Lawrence St. Leger	Faculty of Health, Deakin University, Australia

Preface: A Health Literacy Syllabus

Schools face difficult decisions about what subjects and curricula to include during the school day beyond the traditional three 'Rs'. Because children and youth are facing increasingly more challenges to their physical, social and emotional health than previous generations, schools become the 'go-to' place for equitably reaching them with health initiatives. While schools cannot be the sole agent responsible for nurturing healthy citizens, the potential of the classroom as a setting for change cannot be ignored. Yet, can schools accommodate the endless requests from parents and governments to add more content to the school day?

In this book, Marks and colleagues offer a compelling argument for integrating health literacy in schools. As evidenced in the opening chapters, health literacy has become a public health priority. Conceptually and empirically, this book details the import of health literacy not only to individual health, but also to a productive citizenry; it is clear that health literacy is a layered and complex personal attribute that is facilitated or challenged by broader contextual influences. Health literacy today with its wide ranging implications is consequently an important emerging societal issue. But why should schools take on this added role to their already burdened teaching load?

Although distinct from health education and health promotion, health literacy bridges the individually focused learning outcomes of health education with the more emancipatory and collective ideals of health promotion. It captures more than a person being educated or knowledgeable about health. It includes individual interpretive skills, to be sure, but also reflects our ability to interact and succeed in society in a healthy way, to be empowered as an individual, a community and a society. As Marks describes in this book, leading scholars in the field have argued that, with both its individual and community aspects, health literacy is a trait of good citizenry *and* an element of a just society; a health literate citizen possesses 'the skills, capacities and knowledge required to access, understand and interact with social and political determinants of health and their social discourse' (de Leeuw, 2012, p. 2).

In the 21st century, beyond offering a core curriculum, a broad purpose of education is to create a learning environment that 'make[s] a better link between what kids learn at school and what they experience and learn in their everyday lives ... [and where] students can realize their full potential'

(BC Ministry of Education, 2011, p. 2). A broad mission of schools has long been to prepare students to become effective national, and more recently, global citizens (O'Brien & Smith, 2011; Veugelers, 2011). Across the classrooms of Western nations, the primary goals of citizenship education are concerned with instilling skills, attributes and competencies in students to engage critically, not only as civilians of their own country, but also as constituents of planet earth (Nabavi, 2010). For Paakkari and Paakkari (2012), and as discussed in this book, citizenship is a component of health literacy necessary for ' ... the teaching of "survival skills" in preparation for twenty-first century citizenship' (p. 134), including issues of social justice and critical citizenship to create a more equitable and authentic democracy (Van Heertum & Share, 2006).

As Table 1 in the first chapter makes clear, the understanding of health literacy has evolved from a narrow clinical and individually oriented idea to one that reflects a more spacious, multi-faceted and fluid relationship between citizens and society. Consider the shared missions of health literacy and citizenship in terms of enabling people to *reach their full potential*, actively participate in the life of the community and work towards a **healthy, just and fair society** in the *context of everyday life*, first from health literacy and then citizenship literatures:

> ... people cannot *achieve their fullest health potential* unless they are able to take control of those things which determine their health ... this includes a secure foundation in a supportive environment, access to information, life skills and opportunities for making **healthy choices**. (Saan & Wise, 2011, p. 189)

> ... [health literacy] will become a central life skills needed in modern health societies and reflects the capacity to **make sound health decisions** in the *context of everyday life*. (Kickbusch & Maag, 2008, p. 206)

> [a civic orientation to health literacy] ... includes the skills and resources necessary to address health concerns through civic engagement; an individual or group should be able to articulate the **uneven distribution of burdens and benefits of the society**, evaluate who benefits and who is harmed by public health efforts, communicate current public health problems, and address public health problems through civic action, leadership, and dialogue. (Sorenson et al., 2012, p. 14)

> Citizenship — the ability to act in an **ethically-responsible way and take social responsibility** — is the fifth core component of health literacy. (Paakkari & Paakkari, 2012, p. 139)

Citizenship education can '... encourage <u>active and engaged</u> <u>citizens</u> ... and support people in *reaching their full potential*'. (Tonge, Mycock, & Jeffery, 2012, p. 4)

Active engaged citizenship ' ... focuses on those who share a commitment to <u>actively engage in their communities</u> to **build stronger, healthier and safe communities**'. (Zaff, Boyd, Uibing, Lervern, & Lerner, 2010, p. 737)

[citizenship policies must] ... 'aim to provide every citizen regardless of origin ... an equal chance to participate in all aspects of the *country's collective life*'. (Sears, Clarke, & Hughes, 1999, p. 113)

The dimension of citizenship as 'civic literacy' has been identified, at the very least, as part of health literacy competencies (e.g. Kickbush, Wait, & Maag, 2005; Paakkari & Paakkari, 2012; Sorenson et al., 2012), and for Kawachi and Berkman (1999) it serves as a foundation for modern citizenship. As a responsibility for one's health and acting to address health inequities for others, health literacy has been suggested as a duty of a 'good' citizen (Johnson & Morris, 2010). In recognizing these parallels, one solution to addressing the workload of the educational mandate as well as the need to deliver specific lesson plans is by collectively immersing them throughout the curricula in all subject areas. In schools, a health literacy curriculum that is adequately supported and integrated across curricula offers students multiple opportunities to learn about, understand and apply health information in ways that allow them to take more control over their health. They can consequently become adept at appraising the credibility, accuracy and relevance of information and acting on that information to change their own health behaviours and living conditions and that might affect the health of others.

Correspondingly, citizenship education is seen as an important channel to prepare youth for active involvement in a global community (Evans, Ingram, MacDonald, & Weber, 2009; Veugelers, 2011). It includes students learning about the legal rights and responsibilities within the context of civil society. However, the emphasis is on aspects of social citizenship (Evans, 2006) as it seeks to deepen students' understandings of privilege, power, equity, human rights and social justice (Johnson & Morris, 2010) while developing critical civic literacy capacities and competencies for engaging in informed and purposeful civic action (Sears, 2009) for more equal political and social relations (Veugelers, 2011).

Effective teaching strategies for health literacy and citizenship education also share a pedagogical approach that is student centred, grounded in their life experiences and infused through specialized subject areas and integrated across the curriculum, as well as including whole-school and community-based approaches (Nabavi, 2010; OXFAM, 2006; Paakkari & Paakkari, 2012). Doing so allows students to move beyond the acquisition of health and civic knowledge and apply it meaningfully to their lives (Tupper, Cappello, & Sevigny, 2010). Further, scholars from both disciplines note that learning opportunities should follow a 'student-focused approach' (Paakkari & Paakkari, 2012, p. 140), as well as 'cross-disciplinary, participative, interactive, related to life and co-constructed with parents and the community … as well as the school' in order for students to 'shed the passive role of knowledge consumers and assume the active role of meaning makers' (Johnson & Morris, 2010, p. 87). Indeed, there is evidence that citizenship education increases the potential for students to become involved in civic activism, and contributes to a 'healthier polity' (Tonge et al., 2012, p. 22), thus complementing health literacy outcomes of action on the social determinants of health (Mogford, Gould, & Devoght, 2010).

Johnson and Morris (2010) offer a framework for critical citizenship education that has many similarities to health literacy education, and involves progressing the learning from acquisition of knowledge through to empowering the learner to change society. Similarly, Westheimer and Kahne's (2004) categories of 'good citizens' evolve from the personally responsible citizen to the participatory and finally the justice-oriented citizen who is charged with acting on the root causes of problems: 'While the personally responsible citizen would donate food for the hungry, the participatory citizen would be the person who organizes the drive; the justice-oriented citizen asks why people are hunger and act[s] on what they discover' (p. 24). These successions of citizenship mirror Nutbeam's (2000) three dimensions of health literacy, so that the critically health literate citizen will not only take responsibility for eating well themselves but mobilize efforts for structural or policy changes to enhance such opportunities for others: 'Being able to read a food label is one thing, understanding why a Macdonald's is so cheap, filling and ubiquitous is another' (Wills, 2009, p. 4). While there are as many iterations of 'levels of citizenship' as there are dimensions of health literacy, there is a mutual convergence about what constitutes 'critical' health literacy/citizenry: an informed, reflective and engaged individual committed to working collectively to challenge the status quo to address inequities. That health literacy is so strongly, but not always clearly, tied to health behaviours and outcomes, explains why it has joined the long list of factors delineating what makes people healthy. Perhaps unsurprisingly, measures of health and literacy are frequently cited to reflect accomplishments in the social, civic and political arenas (Green, 2007).

Despite the challenges that remain theoretically to capture, measure and design interventions and policies to enhance health literacy, you will read in the pages to follow how critical health literacy is to advancing the health of citizens and communities. As Simonds (1974) suggested almost four decades ago, echoed by St. Leger (2001) in the last decade and this book makes clear today, the classroom provides the setting and opportunity to nurture a health literate constituency. In this book, Marks does her homework to ensure that health literacy fits within the scope of the school's mandate and is aligned with learning outcomes. She makes a compelling argument for the inclusion of health literacy in the classroom and offers practical and tested resources for teachers to adopt and adapt for their own settings and students. In doing so, Marks makes it easier for teachers to assimilate health literacy concepts, content, lesson plans and rubrics into the existing curricula and school day.

Joan Wharf Higgins

References

BC Ministry of Education. (2011). Retrieved from http://www.bcedplan.ca/assets/pdf/bc_edu_plan.pdf

de Leeuw, E. (2012). The political ecosystem of health literacy. *Health Promotion International, 27*(1), 1–4.

Evans, M. (2006). Educating for citizenship: What teachers say and what teachers do. *Canadian Journal of Education, 29*(2), 410–435.

Evans, M., Ingram, L.-A., MacDonald, A., & Weber, N. (2009). Mapping the 'global dimension' of citizenship education in Canada: The complex interplay of theory, practice and context. *Citizenship Teaching and Learning, 5*(2), 17–34.

Green, J. (2007). Health literacy: Socially situating community-based research. *Fine Print, 30*(1), 3–7.

Johnson, L., & Morris, P. (2010). Towards a framework for critical citizenship education. *Curriculum Journal, 21*(1), 77–96.

Kawachi, I., & Berkman, L. F. (1999). Social cohesion, social capital and health. In L. F. Berman & I. Kawachi (Eds.), *Social epidemiology*. New York: Oxford University Press.

Kickbusch, I., & Maag, D. (2008). Health literacy. In K. Heggenhougen & S. Quah (Eds.), *International encyclopedia of public health* (Vol. 3, pp. 204–211). San Diego: Academic Press.

Kickbush, I., Wait, S., & Maag, D. (2005). *Navigating health: The role of health literacy*. Retrieved from http://www.emhf.org/resource_images/Navigating Health_FINAL.pdf. Accessed on May 10, 2012.

Mogford, E., Gould, L., & Devoght, A. (2010). Teaching critical health literacy in the US as a means to action on the social determinants of health. *Health Promotion International, 26*(1), 4–13.

Nabavi, M. (2010). Constructing the 'citizen' in citizenship education. *Canadian Journal for New Scholars in Education [Revue Canadienne des Jeunes Chercheures et Chercheurs en Education]*, *3*(1), 1–10.

Nutbeam, D. (2000). Health literacy as a public health goal: A challenge for contemporary health education and communication strategies into the 21st Century. *Health Promotion International*, *15*(3), 259–267.

O'Brien, J., & Smith, J. (2011). Elementary education students' perceptions of 'good' citizenship. *Journal of Social Studies Education Research*, *2*(1), 21–36.

OXFAM. (2006). *What is global citizenship*. Retrieved from http://www.oxfam. org.uk/coolplanet/teachers/globciti/whatis.htm; http://www.oxfam.org.uk/ coolplanet/teachers/globciti/curric/index.htm. Accessed on May 12, 2012

Paakkari, L., & Paakkari, O. (2012). Health literacy as a learning outcome in schools. *Health Education*, *112*(2), 133–152.

Saan, H., & Wise, M. (2011). Enable, mediate, advocate. *Health Promotion International*, *26*(S2), ii187–ii193.

Sears, A. (Ed.) (2009). Guest editor's introduction. *Citizenship Teaching and Learning*, *5*(2), 1–3.

Sears, A., Clarke, G. M., & Hughes, A. (1999). Canadian citizenship education: The pluralistic ideal and citizenship education for a post-modern state. In J. Torney-Purta, J. Schwille & J.A. Amadeo (Eds.), *Civic education across countries: Twenty-four national case studies from the IEA civic education project* (pp. 111–135). Amsterdam: IEA.

Simonds, S. K. (1974). Health education as social policy. *Health Education Monographs*, *2*(1), 1.

Sorenson, K., Van Den Broucke, S., Fullam, J., Doyle, G., Pelikan, J., Slonska, Z., Brand, H., & the European Health Literacy Project. (2012). Health literacy and public health: A systematic review and integration of definitions and models. *BMC Public Health, 12*(80). doi:10.1186/1471-2458-12-80 (Online).

Tonge, J., Mycock, A., & Jeffery, B. (2012). Does citizenship education make young people better-engaged citizens? *Political Studies*. doi:10.1111/j.1467-9248. 2011.00931.x (Online).

Tupper, J., Cappello, M., & Sevigny, P. (2010). Locating citizenship: Curriculum, social class, and the 'good' citizen. *Theory & Research in Social Education*, *38*(3), 336–365.

Van Heertum, R., & Share, S. (2006). A new direction for multiple literacy education. *McGill Journal of Education*, *41*(3), 249–265.

Veugelers, W. (2011). The moral and the political in global citizenship: Appreciating differences in education. *Globalisation, Societies and Education*, *9*(3-4), 473–485.

Westheimer, J., & Kahne, J. (2004). What kind of citizen? The politics of educating for democracy. *American Educational Research Journal*, *41*(2), 237–269.

Wills, J. (2009). Health literacy: New packaging for health education or radical movement? *International Journal of Public Health*, *54*(1), 3–4.

Zaff, J., Boyd, M., Uibing, L., Lervern, J., & Lerner, R. (2010). Active and engaged citizenship: Multi-group and longitudinal factorial analysis of an integrated construct of civic engagement. *Journal of Youth and Adolescence*, *39*, 736–750.

Introduction

As an important attribute of the ability to function in a changing world as far as health and social issues are concerned, this work describes the concept of health literacy, why it is important, issues related to helping youth develop health literacy skills in the school setting, and potential strategies for classroom and school-wide practices to promote health literacy among pre-kindergarten, elementary, and high school youth. As an offshoot of literacy, this work on the topic of health literacy should be of interest to all educators, as well as school administrators, plus policy makers interested in improving the health and academic performance of youth as well as in fostering successful aging and citizenship across the lifespan.

While still quite limited, research has shown that health literacy is paramount in efforts to maximize the overall well-being of nations world-wide, in efforts to level the playing field as far as health outcomes goes, and in efforts to minimize the growing epidemics of obesity, diabetes, school bullying, and risky behaviors and others that affect young and older citizens, especially among those with poor health literacy. The application of this information remains limited, however, given the present focus on a mode of health delivery that often assumes clients understand and can readily act on health recommendations. This book was written to provide impetus to schools to teach youth to become health literate, and why this is beneficial.

In ordering the flow of information on this topic for the intended audience, the first chapter thus provides a broad introduction to the concept of health literacy, including the various definitions of this. It highlights the rationale for fostering health literacy at the national and global health levels. It discusses who is most affected by limited health literacy, causes of poor health literacy, and the societal costs associated with the problem. In the subsequent chapters the focus is more on the link between health literacy and schools, health and academic achievement, and the specific costs of poor health literacy among classroom youth. This is followed by information on how the teacher and school itself, supported by the community and politicians can help to maximize health literacy learning opportunities in the context of the classroom and what extrinsic resources are desirable to help heighten students' capacities in this regard.

Although health literacy is fundamental to well-being in the 21st century and is supported by the World Health Organization (WHO) Millennium Development project (WHO, 2009) plus the United States Healthy People 2020 goals, it is unlikely these goals can be achieved without significant efforts, since many adults and youth are currently either health illiterate or only marginally "health literate." In this regard, schools have been chosen as the focal point for a discussion on this topic as these are deemed critical in producing, developing, and achieving the goal of an optimally health literate youth (St. Leger, 2001). Alternately, if schools do not equip youth with adequate health literacy skills, including both the knowledge and skills to avoid health risks and to be as healthy as possible, mounting evidence suggests that the academic achievement and health gap between the have and have not's will potentially be increased. As outlined by the WHO (1996), as well as by the World Bank, the link between poverty and poor health status is very strong and poor health literacy due to poor formal education is one of its root causes. Indeed, recent research showing the link between health literacy and education and between education and development provides highly compelling evidence that schools need to do more to promote the health literacy of their students.

However, it is clear very few teachers, administrators, parents, or health professionals are in a position to fully understand the importance of this issue in general, and in the school as a unit of practice, in particular. Even if they do, time and budgetary constraints, and increasing demands to teach "to the tests" set by state and national policy, render opportunities for introducing more work highly limited. A comprehensive work that defines the problem, and presents the research findings as well as the immense benefits of applying solutions to the problem, is possibly extremely timely as there is need to prevent the chronic disease burden, violence, and substance abuse, plus all causes of poverty and poor educational outcomes among youth converge. The economics of health illiteracy and what is needed to prevent or limit health illiteracy and why is specifically discussed.

The book should be helpful to a broad range of readers either unfamiliar with this topic and its relevance, or familiar with the topic, but requiring some up-to-date background information and strategies for addressing health literacy in a school-based setting. These include Health Education Teachers, School Curriculum Developers, School Administrators, Policy Makers, Funders, Politicians, Economists, Medical Professionals, and Teacher Educators across the curriculum, among others.

Ray Marks

References

St. Leger, L. (2001). Schools, health literacy and public health: Possibilities and challenges. *Health Promotion International, 16,* 197–205.

The Millennium Development Goals Report. (2009). Retrieved from http://www.un.org/millenniumgoals/pdf/MDG_Report_2009_ENG.pdf

World Health Report. (1996). Fighting disease, fostering development. Retrieved from http://www.who.int/whr/1996/en/index.html

Chapter 1

Health Literacy: What Is It and Why Should We Care?

Ray Marks

1.1. Background

Derived from the field of education, the term 'health literacy,' first employed by Simonds (1974) in reference to health education as social policy, has been deemed by researchers in the field since that time to represent literacy skills related to vocabulary, materials, and directives employed in health-care settings (Rudd, Moeykens, & Colton, 1999). Health numeracy, defined as those 'skills needed to understand quantitative health information' (Ancker & Kaufman, 2007, p. 713) is another important component within the realm of health literacy and one found lacking in a substantive proportion of adults worldwide (Smith, Wolf, & von Wagner, 2010), especially among those with low incomes and low educational levels. Since adults with limited literacy or numeracy skills or both are likely to have limited functional skills, health literacy is consequently viewed as critical in contemporary efforts to foster the citizen's ability to manage their health and to navigate the increasingly complex health-care system, effectively. It also influences confidence to carry out health recommendations, one's behavioural choices, as well as one's understanding and application of oftentimes complex pieces of health-related information at the individual as well as at the population-wide level (Peerson & Saunders, 2009).

However, although related to the concept of literacy, or one's ability to read and understand written material, health literacy, initially defined by

Seldon, Zorn, Ratzan, and Parker (2000) as the 'currency' patients required to navigate the health-care system, has come to mean much more than being able to read and understand health information (see Table 1.1). Since it is context specific and subject to a variety of external influences including the nature of the health communication, the nature of the associated services, and the nature of related policies (Nutbeam, 2008), being health literate may implicate not only knowledge, but also major psychological, social and environmental constructs that influence peoples' health choices, such as motivation, personal skills, and policy factors (Tones, 2002). Thus despite the challenges involved, given the chasm that now exists between what the public knows and needs to know, targeted efforts to promote health literacy may not only enable people to make effective rather than poor health-related decisions in an era of high health literacy demands, but may also enable them to advocate ably for themselves, acquire the multiple skills needed to successfully negotiate the complexity of the health-care field, as well as to assert their rights to receiving quality health care, including preventive care, more uniformly, where law does not enforce this. The term has thus become one of the central aspirations of citizenship in the post-industrial era.

Moreover, as outlined in Table 1.1, even though the salience of health literacy lies first and foremost in the context of health, which is a highly valued state universally, but one not readily attainable in contemporary societies, health literacy today denotes much more than simply being able to read and act on information. Seen as fundamental to achieving a high personal life quality and an optimal state of individual and societal well-being, along with its profound collective socioeconomic and political implications, being health literate, involves having print literacy (writing and reading), oral literacy (listening and speaking), and numeracy skills (ability to use and understand numbers, such as dosages, body weight), as well as the ability to convey ideas in written and oral formats in pencil and paper and electronic forms.

As health is influenced by the environment, it is consequently of increasing import to be highly health literate in all realms of society, including the home, worksite, and broader cultural domains of life, not only the medical domain (Zarcodoolas, Pleasant, & Greer, 2005). In addition to having better personal health, a person's high health literacy ability can greatly influence the personal health and achievement outcomes of others, for example, in the realm of being a health literate parent or teacher, or an advocate for the health rights of others. Young people who are healthy are also more likely to achieve school-based success than those who are not, while those who succumb to chronic diseases will have better outcomes if they have high level rather than low level health literacy skills. However, even in countries where health is not only valued, but is of high economic and social importance, such as in Ireland, current research reveals epidemic levels of inadequate health literacy exist among its citizens, even though health literacy at its most basic

Table 1.1: Summary of differing definitions of health literacy showing the concept is both multidimensional and is shifting from an individual level to a societal level of ability.

Source	Definition
Adkins and Corus (2009)	'… the ability to derive meaning from the different forms of communication by using a variety of skills to accomplish health-related goals. Health literacy involves a range of practices in the social realm (e.g., language competencies and identity management skills); it is therefore a public act rather than an individual act of decoding forms.'
AMA (1999)	'… the constellation of skills, including the ability to perform basic reading and numerical tasks required to function in the health care environment, including the ability to read and comprehend prescription bottles, appointment slips, and other essential health-related materials.'
IOM Expert Panel	'… encompasses 4 domains: (1) cultural and conceptual knowledge; (2) oral literacy, including speaking and listening skills, (3) print literacy, including writing and reading skills, (4) numeracy.' (Baker, 2006)
IOM + NLM (2000) — Healthy People 2010	'… the degree to which individuals have the capacity to obtain, process, and understand basic health information and services needed to make appropriate decisions.' (DHSS, 2000)
Joint Committee on Health Education Terminology (1991)	'… the continuum of learning, which enables people, as individuals, and as members of social structures, to voluntarily make decisions, modify behaviors and change social conditions in ways that are health enhancing.'
Kickbusch and Maag (2008)	'… will become a central life skill needed in modern health societies and reflects the capacity to make sound health decisions in the context of everyday life — at home, in the

Table 1.1: (*Continued*)

Source	Definition
	community, at the workplace, in the health-care system, in the market place and in the political arena. It is a critical empowerment strategy to increase people's control over their health, their ability to seek out information, and their ability to take responsibility.'
Mancuso (2008)	'... a process that evolves over one's lifetime and encompasses the attributes of capacity, comprehension, and communication. The attributes of health literacy are integrated within and preceded by the skills, strategies, and abilities embedded within the competencies needed to attain health literacy. The outcomes of health literacy are dependent upon whether one has achieved adequate or inadequate health literacy and have the potential to influence individuals and society.'
Peerson and Saunders (2009)	'... includes information and decision-making skills occurring in the workplace, in the supermarket, in social and recreational settings, within families and neighbourhoods, and in relation to the various information opportunities and decisions that impact upon health every day.'
Rootman and Gordon-El-Bihbety (2008)	'The ability to access, understand, evaluate and communicate information as a way to promote, maintain and improve health in a variety of settings across the life course.'
Rubinelli, Schulz, and Nakamoto (2009)	'... reflects the individuals' capacity to contextualise health knowledge for his/her own good health, and to decide on a certain action after full appraisal of what that specific action means for them personally.'
Seldon, Zoorn, Ratzan, Parker, and Ruth (2002)	'... the currency patients need to negotiate a complex health system.'
Stone (2011) — Society for Vascular Surgery	'... includes the ability to understand instructions on prescription bottles, medical

Table 1.1: (*Continued*)

Source	Definition
	education brochures, directions given by your doctor, consent forms, and decisions concerning your own healthcare as well as the healthcare of loved ones.'
United Kingdom National Consumer Council (2004) (cited in Sihota & Lennard, 2004)	'... the capacity of an individual to obtain, interpret and understand basic health information and services in ways that are health-enhancing.'
WHO (Nutbeam, 1998)	'... represents the personal, cognitive and social skills which determine the motivation and ability of individuals to gain access to, understand and use information in ways which promote and maintain good health.'
Zarcodoolas, Pleasant, and Greer (2006)	'... is the wide range of skills, and competencies that people develop to seek out, comprehend, evaluate, and use health information and concepts to make informed choices, reduce health risks, and increase quality of life.'

Note: IOM, Institute of Medicine; NLM, National Library of Medicine; WHO, World Health Organization.

level is known to positively influence compliance, capacity to self-manage, patient's self-esteem, and most importantly patient outcomes and safety (Marshall, Sahm, & McCarthy, 2012). Additionally, while personalized medicine and offering patients opportunities for making informed choices is a currently advocated intervention approach, and there is a hope patients can be encouraged to serve as key decision-makers in their treatment processes in the future (Tattersall, 2002), a recent study by Smith et al. (2012) revealed that adults may vary quite widely in how they understand and integrate quantitative risk information into their decision-making processes; especially if they cannot read sufficiently well or understand numbers. As reported by Nutbeam (2009), although research indicates those who participate actively in health decisions with their providers have better health outcomes than those who do not, many patients report not feeling as involved in the care process to the extent desired in decisions affecting their health (Nutbeam, 2009), and one cause may be low health literacy (Schiavo, 2011). Thus, being health literate, which may not be predicted accurately solely by one's literacy ability or educational attainment, may influence not only people's access to health information quite significantly, but also one's capacity and self-efficacy to use this effectively (Nutbeam, 2008; Paek & Hove, 2012), as well as one's ability to participate in and derive meaning from different forms of communication, and to apply this critically to exert control of controllable life events (Chinn, 2011). Health literacy, which is said to be related to cognitive ability and performance on health-care tasks (Wolf et al., 2012), including those cognitive and social skills that determine the motivation and ability of individuals to access, understand, and apply to promote good health, is also critical to empowerment (Nutbeam, 2008; World Health Organization [WHO], 2010). Thus, not only are individuals with low health literacy less likely to be able to understand medical instructions, educational materials, medical questionnaires, and consent forms (Mayer & Villaire, 1994), but they are less likely to be sufficiently empowered to act assertively in one or more areas of the health-care realm even those paramount to achieving desirable health outcomes for them or their families.

In particular, in addition to basic or functional literacy, the ability to analyze health-related information (critical literacy) as well the ability to actively participate in one's health (communicative/interactive literacy), key components of the tripartite health literacy typology proposed by Nutbeam (1998) is described as being increasingly crucial in the context of preventing and/or managing chronic diseases, which have no known cure, and are increasing in prevalence, worldwide. Given that low literacy, referring to the skills and strategies involved in reading, speaking, writing, and interpreting numbers is but one domain of the four domains considered by Zarcadoolas et al. (2005) that are needed to improve the public's health literacy, including science, civic, and cultural literacy more focused educational inputs in the formative years are clearly needed to avert life negating misunderstandings, miscommunications, and missed opportunities associated with the onset of chronic illness and functional dependence.

In more recent research, and in the context of depression and related disorders alone, mental health literacy, a sub-category of health literacy, has been described as an essential prerequisite for early recognition and intervention of these widespread problems (Pierce & Shann, 2012). Given that mental disorders commonly have an early onset, plus the fact that mental and physical health, as well as mental health and educational attainment cannot be separated, the mental health of young people is correctly receiving increasing global attention, and fostering mental health literacy has been proposed as an appropriate starting point for addressing this widespread issue (Kutcher & Wei, 2012). In this realm, both the role of prevention as well as stigmatization, especially stigmatization of youth suffers of social phobias and other mental illnesses by their peers urgently need to be addressed according to researchers Reavley and Jorm (2011). By contrast, people with mental health challenges who have can face daily exclusion because of stigma can however participate effectively and successfully in their own care, if they have the basic skills (Groleau, 2011).

Consequently, when we consider the societal and personal outcomes widely reported in the face of limited health literacy and its analogues such as more hospitalizations; greater use of emergency facilities; lower receipt of mammography screening and influenza vaccine; poorer ability to demonstrate taking medications appropriately; and to interpret labels and health messages (Berkman, Sheridan, Donahue, Halpern, & Crotty, 2011), as well as excessive social inequalities and social injustices, plus premature mortality and morbidity, which are all issues potentially amenable to improvement (Parker & Ratzan, 2011), there is a clear need for concerted and prolonged action to overcome the foreseeable challenges, both human and economic. Comprehensive efforts to improve health literacy and to thereby encourage proactive rather than reactive health behaviours have consequently become the cornerstone of public health policy and reform in the United States and elsewhere (Parker & Ratzan, 2011).

1.2. Health Literacy Outcomes

Since being health literate is associated with having the capacity to meet the complex demands of modern society (Kickbusch & Maag, 2008), it is not unsurprising that ample research shows people with limited health literacy have far more health challenges and poorer health outcomes than those with adequate health literacy. In addition to the close association between health literacy and health outcomes, low health literacy, a major source of economic inefficiency, potentially poses an immense financial burden for future generations wherever it occurs (Vernon, Trujillo, Rosenbaum, & DeBuono, 2007). As well as being associated with tremendous and excessive health-care costs (Kirsch, Jungebut, Jenkins, & Kolstad, 1993), health illiteracy is closely linked with health disparities, and in absence of carefully designed interventions, culture, and language barriers, as well as low general literacy levels, that can further exacerbate this potentially preventable health gap. Associated problems of lost entitlements, lost rights, and exclusion, resulting in compromised health status can further limit the ability of health illiterate persons to assume the core citizenship value of empowerment, an important priority articulated in the European Commission's Health Strategy 2008–2013 (Sørensen et al., 2012).

In particular, a recent report by the California Family Health Council (2011) detailing the high cost of low health literacy, reported that people who do not read well are not only less likely to seek care and receive treatment, as required, but they may also:

- Make more medication or treatment errors.
- Have less ability to follow treatment instructions.
- Have a higher chance of hospitalization than people with adequate literacy skills.

This group also reported that there may be additional personal costs in terms of diminished self-esteem, and general self-efficacy to care for themselves and family if they have low literacy skills, plus a lower tendency to engage in questioning of health providers and in health decision-making. Finally, their quality of care may suffer because they may not come for needed care, or they may underutilize preventive health-care services (Vernon et al., 2007), simply because they fear having to fill out forms or answer questions regarding their health and health practices. They may also not be able to navigate the health-care system, or understand appointment cards or related instructions, including safety instructions, either.

From a medical practitioner's standpoint, in addition to its direct impact on health status, and health-care costs, low health literacy levels may also impede the attainment of an accurate medical diagnosis, and hence appropriate treatment recommendations, and/or treatment adherence (Peerson & Saunders, 2009), which has immense implications for those at greatest risk for chronic diseases, who are often also those with poor health literacy (Parker, 2000). As recounted by Kickbusch (2001), the educational divide as well as a digital divide that is experienced by those ill equipped to deal with the health challenges and complexities of a rapidly changing societies is a key public health issue today. For example, in light of the world wide obesity epidemic, in terms of efforts to promote physical activity behaviour, individuals with lower levels of health literacy are not only less likely to be informed about the importance of physical activity to overall health (Williams, Baker, Parker, & Nurss, 1998), but more likely to be sedentary (Kim, Quitsberg, Love, & Shea, 2004; Wolf, Gazmararian, & Baker, 2007) than persons with adequate levels of health literacy. Finally, many public health messages and educational materials and screenings that may be helpful to some may be inaccessible cognitively speaking to those with low literacy (Parker, 2000). Another problem, even with a popular technological tool accessible to most, namely the internet, is the finding that more than a third of adolescents have never tried to find online health information. Sixty percent said they found health information, but 14% said they did not think this was important and 46% were unsure of its impor-tance (Paek & Hove, 2012).

This series of intractable overlapping societal and individual problems has consequently encouraged integration of several aspects of health literacy, including education of providers, and shared decision-making into national health policies (Parker & Ratzan, 2011). In addition, to enable all future citizens, to attain the public health goal of active participation and ownership (Lindström & Eriksson, 2011), opportunities to acquire those basic literacy and numeracy skills that equate to being functionally health literate from the earliest possible point in time have been stressed (Protheroe, Nutbeam, & Rowlands, 2009).

As well, the possibility of raising health literacy skills in the classroom, addressing parental literacy and understanding its impact on the school-aged child is becoming increasingly important. For example, having below-basic parental health literacy can significantly lower rates of ensuring health insurance coverage for children in some health systems, thus jeopardizing their health status and exposure to health messages and preventive health care (Rosenbaum & Shin, 2007). The importance of understanding the need for achieving proficient family health literacy for all in the future is further highlighted in multiple studies such as that conducted by Bailey et al. (2009). In this study Bailey et al. set out to determine the level of adult understanding of dosage instructions for a liquid medication commonly prescribed for children. Using structured interviews with 373 adults waiting for an appointment at family medicine clinics serving low-income populations in Chicago and Michigan, they had subjects read a prescription label for amoxicillin and explain how they would take the medication. Correct interpretation was determined by a panel of blinded physician reviewers who coded subjects' verbatim responses. Qualitative methods were used to determine the nature of incorrect responses. Results showed 28% of subjects misunderstood medication instructions. The prevalence of misinterpreting instructions among subjects with adequate, marginal, and low literacy was 18%, 34%, and 43%, respectively. Common causes for misunderstanding included problems with dosage measurement (28%; i.e., tablespoon instead of teaspoon) and frequency of use (33%; i.e., every 3 hours instead of every 6–8 hours). It was concluded misinterpretation of pediatric liquid medication instructions is common. Moreover, it was concluded that limited literacy is a significant risk factor for misunderstanding and could contribute to racial health disparities.

1.3. Persistent Challenges

Although experts agree health literacy is a skill that can be learned (Rosenbaum & Shin, 2007), and an increasing number of children, adolescents, and adults are affected by chronic diseases, which have a tendency to progress and involve increasing numbers of body systems over time, a sizeable volume of research data shows that children, as well as adults caring for them may not have the health literacy skills to effectively enable them to manage or moderate their health conditions, nor prevent premature disability. Instead, those at risk for health conditions may be completely unaware of this risk, and even if they are aware, may not be empowered to form partnerships with providers, interpret information, acquire the support or competencies they need, nor the ability to communicate their needs. As one of the many research examples indicating negative implications that exist where family members who are often the sole source of health information and health decision-making for young people may not have the skills to help youth offset their health risks for one or more of the chronic diseases (Mayer & Villaire, 1994), Freedman, Jones, Lin, Robin, and Muir (2012), found parental health literacy and dosing responsibility on pediatric glaucoma medication adherence, which would markedly influence a child's vision and overall health outcomes, was significantly correlated.

Moreover, as a result of the current focus in the realm of health literacy on secondary and tertiary prevention, 'rather than on primary prevention' (Freedman et al. 2009, p. 447), young immigrants and those whose home language is not English or the first language of the country in question, may not even be aware of salient health messages, nor how their own behaviours may place them at risk for future health problems. As well, even if they understand their risks they may lack access to care and treatment (Freedman et al., 2009), and be unable to use, act on or decipher information that would be helpful to them in offsetting preventable health problems in the future, given that about half of all premature deaths are related to health-risk behaviours often established during youth (Lee, 2009). This 'clinical approach to health literacy' which aims to improve medication adherence and lifestyle changes after the person becomes ill (Freedman et al., 2009, p. 447), may explain why one recent study for example, clearly showed that overweight, a largely preventable health condition, was associated with perceived lack of health information among recently settled Iraqi migrants in Sweden, among other factors (Lecerof, Westerling, Moghaddassi, & Östergren, 2011). Also, although the field has grown immensely over the past decade, most health literacy research does not explicitly focus on food or nutrition, and dietetics practitioners often remain unaware of patients' health literacy level (Carbone & Zoellner, 2012) despite the enormous implications of this in face of the present obesity and diabetes epidemics. Unsurprisingly, additional data reveal that if there is unequal access to high-quality education (Freedman et al., 2009), or the school is not educating its pupils with skills to advance their health literacy, even children with high rankings of cognitive competence may have problems thriving and can exhibit psychosomatic and mental well-being challenges that might otherwise be preventable (Lindström & Eriksson, 2011). Others may be especially challenged to manage prevalent diseases affecting youth today such as type 2 diabetes, a universal health concern, given that the ability to successfully self-manage the disease is strongly and positively associated with the affected individual's health literacy level (McCleary-Jones, 2011).

Other data show that even if health providers are highly educated, many may not always consider their patient's ability to understand or act on their instructions, and commonly assume their patients have the competency to make health-related decisions and carry out recommendations, even though this expectation is often unrealistic (Lukoscheck, Fazzari, & Marantz, 2003), especially for adolescents who are economically and socially marginalized, or where gender-based norms and passive participation rather than active engagement predict health behaviours (Armstrong & Cohall, 2011). In addition, to add to these challenges, health literacy in medical settings is often diminished in the face of illness and complex health instructions (Mayer & Villaire, 1994; Protheroe et al., 2009). All of these issues, plus the fact that adult populations in leading nations of the United States and United Kingdom who must oversee the well-being of most children in their formative years commonly have poor functional literacy, potentially further reduces the likelihood of a young person attaining a high life quality in the future if schools in particular do not take an active role in fostering the health literacy of young people. Finally, recent data reveal youth themselves may adopt negative attitudes toward citizenship and social participation in community life that is potentially relevant in the process of health literacy development. That is, results of three studies that examined generational differences in life goals, concern for others, and civic orientation among American high school seniors and entering college students, civic orientation (e.g., interest in social problems, political participation, trust in government, taking action to help the environment and save energy) declined an average of $d = -.34$, with about half the decline occurring between GenX and the Millennials. Some of the largest declines appeared in taking action to help the environment. In most cases, Millennials slowed, though did not reverse, trends toward reduced community feeling begun by GenX. The results generally support the 'Generation Me' view of generational differences rather than the 'Generation We' or no change views (Twenge, Campbell, & Freeman, 2012). Yet, in a recent Edelman Barometer survey, lifestyle and the environment were among the key factors people globally agreed have the most impact on their health.

It was also shown there is a pervasive knowledge–action gap in health across the globe, meaning people 'know' what they should do in many cases to bolster their health outcomes — but the spirit or action component is weak or absent. The top 10 unhealthy behaviours were unsurprising and included not exercising enough, smoking, poor nutrition, overeating, not getting enough sleep, and consuming alcohol or drugs. Moreover, while 62% stated they had tried to change one of these negative health behaviours or others, fewer than one-half were able to sustain that behaviour change with the main reason being because of the enjoyment of the behaviour, followed by addiction or dependency, or failure to adhere to the changes long enough to show an effect. It is possible having more facility to discuss these issues with parents, teachers, school counselors, and physicians would be helpful and this could be advanced during a child's formative years, along with a self-efficacy building and social skills development approach to changing these behaviours or choosing more favourable behaviours in light of the high risk of chronic health problems as a result of all the behaviours listed above. Since health is a multidimensional concept encompassing mental and emotional health elements, social and emotional health elements, occupational and intellectual elements, balanced and nutritious diet, active and fit lifestyles, a healthy weight, a functioning body, sound financial health, physical appearance, and enough energy, citizens today may feel overwhelmed or not understand what is required to be a healthy citizen and why this is important. With so many competing messages, demands of the social market place, cultural norms that are life negating, and policies that favour marketers, they are clearly in need of much more input during their formative years than the basic 3 Rs. If we want to change the barometer, youth clearly need consistent learning opportunities to enable them to develop self-efficacy skills, and advanced interactive and critical thinking skills that motivate them to build social environments that are life affirming for all.

1.4. Changing the Landscape

Shifts in populations, population aging, and diversity have made it essential for the future citizen to be well armed and informed about their health. To this end, there are enormous imperatives for policy-makers and others to attend to the link between health literacy and overall well-being and health-care costs, especially in the context of promoting an informed citizenry, one that can participate thoughtfully and confidently in ongoing public and private dialogues about health. As a key strategy in the processes needed to foster the urgent development of a health literate citizenry, one potentially able to apply health concepts and information to novel situations (Sørensen et al., 2012), and one that can demonstrate mental health literacy, as well as functional, interactive, and critical health literacy, the importance of placing greater emphasis on health literacy outside of health-care settings has been discussed (Peerson & Saunders, 2009), along with the need to attend to 'upstream' or macro-level determinants of health and well-being (Freedman et al., 2009, p. 447) such as education (Nutbeam, 2008). One such venue, namely the school, has recently received some attention in this regard (e.g., St Leger, 2001; Vardavas, Kondilis, Patelarou, Akrivos, & Falagas, 2009) and only recently, a working conference entitled *Health Literacy and Schools — think global, act local* was conducted in Amsterdam, bringing together leaders in the field from across the globe with discussions that included the prospect of integrating health literacy into school curricula. In fact, in accord with Nutbeam (2000), it seems clear that if schools today fail to provide youth with the skills and knowledge young people need to critically analyze health information, as well as skills to negotiate the modern health environment, where health status is influenced by individual and behavioural patterns, as well as social, economic, and environmental factors (Nutbeam, 2000), youth today may incur heightened or unnecessary health challenges, both while at school, as well as in later life. Not surprisingly, and according to the think tank known as the Education Foundation (2012), '... the urgency to educate children on their bodies has become as critical as improving their minds' (http://www.educationfund. org/programs/collaborativenutritioninitiative/).

Recent research findings by Nicholson, Lucas, Berthelsen, and Wake (2012) confirm the importance of education in early childhood as a key intervention strategy for achieving efficacious health promotion and prevention outcomes, which depend in large measure on the child having the opportunity to attain an adequate level of health literacy (Baur, 2011). In the long term, children who receive school-based health education will undoubtedly have better skills for attaining optimal health, and for working more efficiently and effectively, while requiring fewer medical services or sick days (McGovern, 2010). They will be more likely to undertake informed health actions, and become 'health citizens' who can become involved in planning health care, programs, and policy (Groleau, 2011)

Moreover, in an increasingly technologically dependent environment, becoming critically engaged with information in one's formative years can potentially mediate better health outcomes for all (Chinn, 2011) as citizens today who are both healthy or otherwise, are often expected to assume a highly active role in fostering their well-being and in resolving challenging health decisions. To avert the cycle of costly health 'crisis care' described by Koh et al. (2012), the ability to navigate increasingly challenging avenues of information and diverse communication channels is a vital competency required by today's citizen and must be embedded in the educational system to achieve this health-care-related priority. In addition to matters related to the volume, quality, accuracy, credibility contradictory nature, and completeness of information available on the more than 70,000 health-related, often unregulated, websites (Benigeri & Pluye, 2003; Bernhardt, 2004;

Cline & Haynes, 2001; Grandinetti, 2000; Smith, 2004; Ziebland, 2004), studies have found that the technical terms and medical language displayed required reading skills of high school level, reinforcing the urgent need to improve upon educational efforts to maximize literacy skills in general. While the power of this medium has not gone unnoticed: Davis and Farrell (2001) note that 70% of online consumers report that health information has influenced a decision about treatment, even though the ability to critically evaluate these data sources or act on their information is certainly not uniformly high in any country. The use of English dominates websites (Lazarus & Mora, 2000), further limiting comprehension for citizens whose first language (or second, third) is not English.

Conceivably, therefore, as with literacy in general, strategies to improve health literacy, especially active engagement in personal and societal health issues that are emphasized from the earliest years are imperative, and should not be confined to health-care settings, where most of the prevailing remedial efforts have been implemented. Efforts to appeal to youth insofar as the environment and social issues goes should be stressed, as should efforts to decrease rising rates of youth anxiety, depression, and poor mental health and decreased well-being that appear to correlate with an emphasis on extrinsic rather than intrinsic values (Twenge et al., 2012).

To this end, efforts to raise a nation's health literacy rates embedded both in the classroom as well as across the curriculum and community are strongly viewed as paramount in efforts to combat the many rising and converging problems in health care that pose enormous costly challenges to populations across the globe (Adkins & Corus, 2009). The exponential rise in the number of journal articles published in health literacy in the last decade clearly speaks to the interest and importance of this topic as discussed by Chinn (2011) (see Figure 1.1).

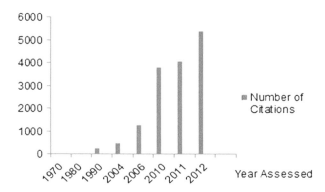

Figure 1.1: Health literacy publication trends during 1970–2012.

1.5. Health Literacy Definitions

In addition to the basic attributes of being able to read, understand, and act on health-care information, Healthy People 2010 (U.S. Department of Health and Human Services [DHSS], 2000) and the United States Institute of Medicine (2004) have defined health literacy in terms of the ability of individuals to access, consider and act accordingly to apply basic information about health issues and related services (Ratzan & Parker, 2006). In the American Medical Association Council of Scientific Affairs definition (Seldon et al., 2000), where the concept of functional health literacy or 'the ability to read simple text and write simple sentences about common events' (Protheroe et al., 2009, p. 721) is the focus, it is argued that a 'functionally health literate' person is one that can read and comprehend prescription-related information, appointment cards, as well as health-related materials. Health literacy has been also been defined in terms of having the cognitive and social skills that can determine the motivation and ability of individuals to gain access to, understand and use information in ways which promote and maintain good health and can also support social and political action (Nutbeam, 2000). Gazmararian, Curran, Parker, Bernhardt, and DeBuono (2005) have drawn attention to the concept of public health literacy as an ethical imperative, and emphasize that a person who is public health literate will be better able to appreciate how health issues influence them, as well as their communities, and society (Freedman et al., 2009). Accordingly, health literacy, is viewed as a crucial factor and as an asset rather than a clinical risk factor (Nutbeam, 2008) in the context of efforts to promote health and to inform, educate and empower the public (Gazmararian et al., 2005), as well as for effective decision-making (Baker, 2006), and according to Ratzan and Parker (2006), the term has now become permanently embedded as a concept in the public health realm.

1.6. Categories of Health Literacy

Below Basic: Can perform tasks involving brief and uncomplicated texts and documents. Adults can generally locate a piece of information in a news story.

Basic: Able to locate information in text, make low-level inferences, and integrate easily identifiable pieces of information.

Intermediate: Able to integrate information from relatively long or dense texts, determine appropriate arithmetic operations, and identify quantities needed to perform the operation.

Proficient: Demonstrates proficiencies associated with long and complex documents and texts (Hauser, 2005).

According to results reported in *The Health Literacy of America's Adults: Results from the 2003 National Assessment of Adult Literacy* (NAAL) (National Center for Educational Statistics [NCES], 2006), and taking the above health literacy dimensions into account, 14% of adults were found to be in the Below Basic category; 22% had Basic Skills; 53% had Intermediate Skills; and only 12% were Proficient. The NAAL also found that 16-year–18-year olds had a relatively low level of health literacy, and although adolescents are generally healthy, research shows that their future health is strongly predicted by the behaviours adopted during youth, such as cigarette smoking (National Institute for Health Care Management [NIHCM], 2011).

Indeed, along with concerted efforts to assess, identify, and promote health literacy in the United States as a result of the NAAL study, the United Kingdom has embraced its own definition of health literacy, and has taken parallel steps to minimize the problems that stem from low or marginal levels of health literacy, as has Australia (Nutbeam, 2009). For example, the U.K. Committee on the Safety of Medicines has specifically highlighted the importance of identifying problems in communicating health information, and the importance of enabling people to use such information for decision-making purposes in the context of medication efficacy and safety (Ratzan & Parker, 2006). One area identified as being highly salient to this body is a component termed 'medication literacy,' which specifically refers to the ability to obtain, comprehend, and use information on medications appropriately (Medicines and Healthcare Products Regulatory Agency, 2005). Another is in the realm of a concept termed Choose and Book, where patients are offered a range of services and can choose their preferred service and make an appointment for this (Protheroe et al., 2009).

Another is the relationship between health literacy and health disparities when considered in terms of 'access and equity,' as well as 'citizenship rights' (Green, 2007). According to Kickbusch, Wait, and Maag (2006), action being taken by European countries to improve health literacy, is being implemented with the dual goal of reducing health disparities, while raising the health status of individuals and populations. This accords comparably with recent research showing that total literacy, health and financial literacy are independently associated with decision-making even accounting for income, depression, and chronic medical conditions (all p values < 0.001. Finally, there was evidence of effect modification such that the beneficial association between literacy and health-care decision-making was stronger among older persons, poorer persons and persons at the lower ranges of cognitive ability and without, suggesting higher levels of health and financial literacy were associated with better decision-making, and that improvements in literacy could facilitate better decision-making and lead to better health and quality of life in later years (James, Boyle, Bennett, & Bennett, 2012).

Unfortunately, those with poor literacy are more likely to obtain health information through potentially less reliable sources such as television and radio, versus brochures, or books, than those with adequate health literacy. As well, providers may not provide the resources these clients need to make informed decisions (Paterson, 2002), due to their own misperceptions and self-assessments (Lukoscheck et al., 2003). Moreover, it is often erroneously assumed by practitioners that an invitation to have patients with chronic illness participate as equal partners is sufficient to assure their empowerment (Paterson, 2002).

Even considering only reading level and no other dimensions of health literacy, much of the health education material disseminated to the public is often produced at or above a ninth grade reading level (Dollahite, Thompson, & McNew, 1996; Greenfield, Sugarman, Nargiso, & Weiss, 2005; Jackson et al., 1991; Neuhauser, Rothschild, & Rodriguez, 2007). Gannon and Hildebrandt (2002) advise that there can be a three-year to six-year difference between the grade completed and reading level. In Canada, new physical activity guidelines have recently been released, and there have been national discussions, led by the Public Health Agency of Canada [PHAC] (2011), as to the best strategies for communicating the new guidelines. While the guidelines are informed by the best available scientific evidence regarding exercise physiology and serve as the key message, it is recognized that a 'one size fits all' approach will not be effective in reaching, informing, and motivating diverse groups of Canadians to be active. Tailored and targeted messages, materials and communication channels are required in order to be perceived as relevant and accessible: 'The guidelines on physical activity should be clear, concise, concrete, and direct; and they should be targeted to specific populations … any targeted messages associated with the guidelines must be simple, specific, non-intimidating and tailored … simple language is an absolute must' (PHAC, 2011, p. 6).

Since over a third of American adults, 50% of older adults, and 75% of high school dropouts along with those 50% who have no health insurance cannot accurately estimate times medications should be taken based on medication labeling, have problems understanding the side-effects of medication or medication interactions, or using written information to determine vaccination schedules for children (Ratzan & Parker, 2006) the importance of promoting and improving health literacy in the context of improving the well-being of children and adults worldwide cannot be underestimated.

Understanding basic health issues such as determining what a healthy weight or diet remains challenging for many, however, because even if a provider is caring and empathetic, as well as knowledgeable, clients today, both young and old, are bombarded by competing media messages, a complex health system, and the requirement they serve as effective self-managers, as well as advocates for their own health (Ratzan & Parker, 2006). In other spheres, recent research shows clinicians to inadequately judge the extent to which pediatric patients are in a state of health literacy-related readiness for transitioning to adult care (Huang, Tobin, & Tompane, 2012). They must therefore not only be able to acquire, and comprehend health-related materials as well understand the extent of their health problems and their role in its treatment and treatment decisions, even if they are not able or ready. They are also obligated as 'consumers' to use information effectively (Rosenbaum & Shin, 2007), and must consequently be able to decipher and navigate complex health messages and systems, even though we know when we enter the world of the health-care system, it expects and assumes we have the knowledge, skills, and capacities to negotiate its byzantine landscape-cluttered with jargon, medical terms, and over-reliance on written information. It is not surprising therefore that clients today are often ill-equipped to meet one or more of these demands and others, however, (Rudd, Colton, & Schacht, 2000), and that they may subsequently cope less well with self-management regimens for chronic conditions than one would anticipate, even in an era of advanced technology and medical science (Schillinger et al., 2002). Indeed, even if we assume young adults can read and understand health information, the health-care environment is often not a user-friendly environment, as the following vignette clearly illustrates.

> Signs and directions posted for employees and visitors outside and within institutions are often inadequate. As Baker and colleagues noted in a study based on patient focus groups at two public hospitals, many of the patients did not benefit from signs indicating that the nephrology unit was straight ahead. The nephrologists, however, most likely knew where to go. (Institute of Medicine, 2004, p. 22)

In addition, once inside the system, individuals seeking or needing health care must be able to engage in effective two-way communications, understand consent forms and their legal implications, as well as medication labels, treatment contra-indications and appointment cards to function successfully in today's health-care environment (Gazmararian et al., 2005). Attributes needed by the consumer in today's health market place that can serve as intervention points are thus numerous as depicted in Box 1.1.

Unfortunately, health literacy rates are generally poor, and are lower than literacy rates due to the added challenges of decoding and acting on health

---

Box 1.1.   Attributes and Abilities Needed to Achieve Optimal, Appropriate and Timely Care and Optimal Health Outcomes that May be Useful for Understanding How to Intervene Early to Promote Health Literacy

- Ability to navigate electronic and structural features of health-care systems.
- Adequate health knowledge.
- Effective communication skills.
- Effective comprehension skills.
- Effective decision-making skills.
- Effective interpretation skills (Kickbusch & Maag, 2008).
- Numeracy skills.
- Reading skills.
- Knowledge of one's rights and responsibilities (Kickbusch & Maag, 2008).
- Knowledge of the health-care system (Parker, 2000).
- Knowledge of appropriate preventive actions (Kickbusch & Maag, 2008).
- Self-management skills.
- Writing skills.

---

information in the real world (Peterson et al., 2011), especially if one is in pain or has some form of mental health or physical health challenge. In the United States, the growing emphasis on consumerism into public health insurance for low income persons has placed a growing emphasis on patient health literacy, even though these individuals may not have the skills or opportunity to make effective use of health care (Rosenbaum & Shin, 2007). As outlined by Protheroe et al. (2009), perhaps even more challenging is the view that health literacy is a critical empowerment strategy in the context of self-care practices and inadequate health literacy can consequently reduce the ability to assert oneself in important health-related contexts, and has a strong negative influence on the ability of the individual to participate in medical decision-making processes (Kickbusch et al., 2006). Yet, even in well-developed countries such as Australia, up to a quarter of the population may have suboptimal health literacy (Barber et al., 2009), even though a moderate level of evidence exists to support a variety of communication/ education interventions employing multiple strategies to advance health literacy as being associated with improved health outcome or health services utilization (John M. Eisenberg Center, Agency for Healthcare Quality and Research, 2012).

In contrast, when viewed through the eyes of the health educator, health literacy is seen as a teachable skill and as the mechanism for enabling individuals to assert control over their health in the context of a variety of personal and societal factors (Nutbeam, 2008). For example, a recent study has shown higher levels of health literacy to increase self-efficacy and utilization of preventive care among older adults (Chen, Hsu, Tung, & Pan, 2012).To date, however, beyond a clinical focus and with the intent of promoting health and preventing disease, health literacy in the last decade has been primarily directed at enhancing knowledge of and skills in nutrition and healthy eating, rather than self-efficacy (Bell, Patel, & Malasanos, 2006; Donovan, 2005; Hartman, McCarthy, Park, Schuster, & Kushi, 1997; Howard-Pitney, Winkleby, Albright, Bruce, & Fortmann, 1997; Kim et al., 2004; Kolasa, Peery, Harris, & Shovelin, 2001; Nimmon, 2007; von Wagner, Knight, Steptoe, & Wardle, 2007; Yajima, Takano, Bakamura, & Wananabe, 2001). Moreover, from results of earlier cross-sectional studies, we know that a poor grasp and application of nutritional information, often an untapped factor, is a remediable one strongly associated with poor nutritional outcomes including malnourishment (Gonzales, Dearden, & Jimenez, 1999), less heart healthy eating (TenHave et al., 1997), lower consumption of the recommended intake of fruits and vegetables (von Wagner et al., 2007), and increased dietary fat intake (Levy, Patterson, Kristal, & Li, 2000), but lessons concerning these topics are not always part of the standard school curriculum. This is unfortunate because adults with low literacy are 1.2–4 times more likely to exhibit negative health behaviours that affect child health, such as dietary behaviours, and are at least twice as likely to exhibit aggressive or antisocial behaviour. As well, chronically ill children who have caregivers with low literacy are twice as likely to use more health services than those with proficient health literacy (Sanders, Federico, Klass, Abrams, & Dreyer, 2009).

1.7. Who is Affected?

Since health literacy depends in part, on one's past education, and ability to deal with complexity, not unsurprisingly, low health literacy tends to affect adults with low incomes and low education, as well as older adults more intently than those who are more affluent or younger than 60 years of age (American Medical Association [AMA], 1999). As outlined by Kickbusch (2001), since approximately 80% of people across the globe live in oral and visual cultures, many are currently severely challenged by systems that use reading and writing to communicate. Communities who are either unable to access key sources of information or have poor ability to decode media messages may be similarly challenged. Non-English speakers may also be less informed by media sources than English speakers, as may those with no access to technology (Kickbusch, 2011). Yet, 60% of Australians are said to lack basic health literacy skills, despite achieving high rates of functional literacy (Nutbeam, 2009).

Sondik (2007) too showed that even though the United States is thought to be a well-developed country, more than a third of its citizens have problems in using charts to complete health-care tasks. Many also have problems following prescriptions or interpreting over the counter medical labels. In addition, many diverse racial and ethnic groups who are non-English-speaking, for example, parents what are recent immigrants are at higher risk for poor health literacy (Dunn-Navarra, Stockwell, Meyer, & Larson, 2012), as are those with low incomes and those over age 65 with limited schooling have health literacy challenges (Center for Health Care Strategies Fact Sheet [CHCS], 2011). The gap between the required skills and actual skills of many Americans is further compounded for persons coming from a non-English speaking household, due to insufficient numbers of appropriately trained interpreters, as well as culturally competent providers who can help assist non-English speaking families of different backgrounds with their health-care needs (Flores & Tomany-Korman, 2008). Public health literacy is also influenced by health-care-related communication materials written at an advanced reading level along with the increasing use of technology in the realm of health communications (Adkins & Corus, 2009; Gazmararian et al., 2005), which remains under-utilized by many of those who have limited literacy (Protheroe et al., 2009) such as those with low economic capital, and poor health status. As outlined below, a number of convergent or overlapping factors at the individual and contextual levels including education, have been discussed as contributory causes of health illiteracy in the burgeoning literature on this topic (Box 1.2).

1.8. Costs of Limited Health Literacy

There is no shortage of examples today in the related research literature highlighting the many highly deleterious individual and systems outcomes in cases where adults are found to have low or marginal health literacy including: problems in applying asthma or other forms of essential knowledge required for self-management purposes (Koh et al., 2012); Williams, Baker, Honig, Lee, & Nowlan, 1998), a limited ability to understand written and oral information (Koh et al., 2012), act appropriately as regards

---

Box 1.2.   Possible Contributory Causes of Poor Health Literacy

Age

Absent or limited school-based health education*
Care fragmentation
Complex health conditions
Complex written materials
Ethnic and racial factors
Health-care systems
Inadequate provider training
Information explosion
Greater reliance on technology
Increased self-care demands
Insurance paperwork
Lack of knowledge on health literacy by clinicians
Lack of provider cultural competence
Limited provision of adequate resources
Limited provider time
Linguistic challenges

Low formal education levels*
Low literacy levels*
Medication complexity
Physicians' attitude
Poor provider communication skills
Poverty
Rural residents

Schooling below college level, short, or incompleted education*
Shame
Short office visits
Stressful environments and illnesses

Undeveloped reading, oral, and numeracy skills*
Unfamiliar concepts and terms, unfamiliar environments, alien vocabulary and concepts

*Specifically where the school is implicated.

Sources: Extracted from CHCS (2011); Ferguson & Pawlak (2011); Kickbusch & Maag (2008); Lukoscheck et al. (2003); McCleary-Jones, 2011; Nutbeam (2008); Paterson (2002); Protheroe et al. (2009).

---

appointment schedules and health recommendations, and difficulties in navigating the health-care system (CHCS, 2011). The literature also reveals less responsiveness, in general, to health education (Nutbeam, 2009), higher health-care costs and poorer health outcomes among those with limited health literacy (CHCS), as well as higher all-cause mortality rates among patients with heart failure (Peterson et al., 2011). These personal costs increase family debt, morbidity, mortality, premature disability, and disproportionately affect minority and immigrant populations, those with low-incomes, and those with chronic mental and/or physical health conditions (Nutbeam, 2008; Pawlak, 2005). Cases with hypertension examined by Williams, Baker, Parker, et al. (1998) for example showed those with limited health literacy were less likely to have knowledge and basic self-management skills than those with adequate health literacy. They are also more likely to be non-adherent in addressing medical therapies and health recommendations (Vernon et al., 2007). Even though we have known about the fact that health literacy is positively related with preventive health behaviours for some time, recent research shows low health literacy continues to impede the extent to which sedentary Latinas — a highly vulnerable group — as far as health challenges go, to adhere optimally to physical activity guidelines (Dominick, Dunsiger, Pekmezi, & Marcus, 2012). Health literacy, which can influence the degree to which informed consent forms are understood, plus the extent of enrolment in insurance programs for which people may be eligible, as well as the extent of services obtained once enrolled (CHCS, 2011), can ultimately have highly adverse bioethical and legal implications, in addition to significant financial implications (Sarasohn-Kahn, 2011).

Not surprisingly, other data show low-literacy diabetes patients are nearly twice as likely as high-literacy patients to have poor control of their blood sugar levels and more serious long-term health consequences (Schillinger et al., 2002). Diabetic children aged 5–17, have also been found to have poorer glycemic control if their parents have low literacy versus high literacy skills (Ross, Frier, Kelnar, & Deary, 2001). Lower physical activity literacy among foster parents, which was associated with greater perceived barriers and less support for physical activity, especially among those with low education, may explain why children in these homes are at high risk for diabetes and other chronic diseases (Dominick, Friedman, Saunders, Hussey, & Watkins, 2012). Yet other data focus on how the lack of functional literacy not only results in an ever widening chasm between what providers intend to convey and what the patient understands (Koh et al., 2012), but drives up health-care costs as a result of poor utilization of services in general (Vernon et al., 2007), as well as among those with poor health literacy (Parker, Ratzan, & Lurie, 2003). Others show low health literacy influences health behaviours, as well as economic, social, personal, and societal health outcomes (Ferguson & Pawlak, 2011). Related data show especially high costs attributable to medication non-adherence, less than optimal preventive care, and reduced ability to make decisions among persons with limited or deficient health literacy skills (Adkins & Corus, 2009).

Sharp, Zurawski, Roland, O'Toole, and Hines (2002) who examined the relationship between health literacy, distress, and cervical cancer risk factors in women at high risk for cervical cancer, found 45% of the sample had low health literacy levels, and that those with lower levels of health literacy were more distressed than those with higher health literacy levels. This was important because 25% of those with cervical abnormalities were found to be severely distressed, a finding consistent with the view that lower health literacy is commonly associated with less health knowledge, as well as less expression of health concerns (Rootman, 2006). There are also assertions that those with lower levels of health literacy may receive less preventive care, (Hibbard, Peters, Dixon, & Tusler, 2007), and they may be less able to describe their health histories and understand explanations concerning diagnoses and treatment (AMA, 1999), even though they may have higher than average usage rates of emergency departments and hospitals, later on.

Miscommunications or failure to communicate health risks can also jeopardize people's safety in addition to their health status and can occur readily if health providers do not take people's cultural beliefs and traditions, educational experiences, linguistic capacities, and numeracy skills into account in the decision-making process (Vahabi, 2007). In an article by Mayer and Villaire (1994) that reviewed the effects of low health literacy on patient care, it was thus no surprise to read that low literacy skills reduced the chance of a good health outcome, as well as appropriate levels of adherence to medical instructions. Mayer also observed lower rates of health seeking early in the course of illnesses, more hospitalizations, more outpatient visits, and higher health-care costs among those with limited or deficient health literacy. Similarly, in their excellent article on the topic of health literacy and its relationship to the need for increasing participation by patients in health care, Protheroe et al. (2009) pointed out that related efforts by the U.K. Health Services to increase patient choice may be less accessible to those with low literacy. They further described research showing those with poor health literacy are less responsive to health education and use of disease prevention services, as well as chronic disease management strategies. As mentioned earlier, people living with low levels of health literacy are less familiar with the importance of physical activity to health and also more apt to live sedentary lives than others with higher levels of literacy. The economic implications of inactive and overweight populations on health care and related productivity and social costs are well documented and significant (Scarborough et al., 2011). Even in countries with self-proclaimed 'universal access to health care,' governments struggle to cope with the rising costs of health-care systems, access to preventing disease and promoting health is becoming increasingly privatized (Kickbusch & Payne, 2003) and relegated to a highly unregulated marketplace. In addition to excess physical health disadvantages, those with low health literacy may also suffer negative psychological consequences, including shame and stigma (Health and Human Services, 2011, Health Literacy and Health Outcomes Fact Sheet). As part of a cycle of deleterious outcomes, it appears plausible to suggest that limited health literacy, leading to health inequalities, as well as economic challenges, will limit the individual's chances for a health productive and empowered life, as well as a country's chances for sustaining and developing a civil society with the potential for future growth when considered collectively.

1.9. Summary

As recounted in the preceding sections, many data sources support the fact that health literacy, a discrete form of literacy, is a key public health issue and one demanding increasing focus of attention by policy-makers worldwide due to its immense ramifications for citizens as well as societies, in general (Martensson & Hensing, 2011). However, while policymakers frequently address education and health separately, many are not aware of the silent epidemic relevant to both spheres of policy, namely health literacy (Parker et al., 2003). Among a multiplicity of factors, an increasing volume of research shows health literacy is central to multiple health system priorities, as well as educational priorities (Parker et al., 2003), plus numerous health-related issues, as well as social and economic issues arising from sectors of the population affected by inadequate health literacy. These include, but are not limited to problems with treatment adherence, medication usage, usage of appointment cards, understanding one's rights, and the ability to seek early directions for care. Moreover, a growing volume of current research attests to the fact that inadequate health literacy compromises participation in the health education process, as well information seeking practices, in addition to limiting an individual's ability to access care by either limiting their ability to navigate the health delivery system as a whole and/or related information resources (Wilson, 2003). Especially disadvantaged are those whose well-being may already be compromised as a result of poverty and lack of education and economic resources, thus contributing to the current 'health divide.' In addition, limited health literacy leading to an inadequate understanding of self-care behaviours

(Heisler, Bouknight, Hayward, Smith, & Kerr, 2002), underutilization of physician visits, dependence on the internet which the undiscerning low literate individual may not be able to decipher at all adequately, misinterpretation of information, and poor parental literacy (NIHCM, 2011), potentially predicts poorer health status, higher health-care expenditures, higher numbers of hospitalizations, legal ramifications, and reduced life quality (Betancourt, Green, & Carrillo, 2000). Inattention to the achievement of health literacy for all, clearly also increases the 'inequalities gap' between the most and least advantaged in society (Protheroe et al., 2009, p. 721) and has thus grown from being an under-recognized phenomenon to a global issue that drives health policy (Parker & Ratzan, 2011).

Since this issue affects everyone, even those with high health literacy, the topic is currently taking center stage in many nation's health-care dialogues and debates, and is becoming an increasingly urgent imperative as patients everywhere are being asked to take a more active and accountable role in their own health care. There is also a great emphasis today on primary prevention, where it is incumbent on young and old to be active players and consumers in the health market place to reduce the chronic disease burden. To provide insight into the challenges faced by society due to low health literacy, as well as to highlight untapped opportunities, this chapter has explored the nature of health literacy, and the manifold costs of low health literacy. These include enormous societal, as well as personal costs. For example, research shows diabetic adults with inadequate health literacy are less likely than those with adequate health literacy to have effective glycemic control, and are also more likely than others to report vision problems caused by their diabetes. Some of the reasons for these findings and why low health literacy raises health-care costs fourfold (Partnership for Clear Health Communication, Steering Committee, 2003) are high-lighted in Box 1.3 and present a multitude of opportunities for improving the delivery of care and reducing numbers of hospital visits, and hospital stays, that in our view should not be limited solely to those being made in the health-care environment itself.

However, if the solutions to some of the above-mentioned problems are not attended to in a concerted way, it appears that despite a recent emphasis in the literature on increasing patient participation in the context of health-care activities (Protheroe et al., 2009), many health tasks will remain daunting for a large majority of today's and tomorrow's populations (Ratzan & Parker, 2006). This is partly owing to the nature of some of the factors listed in Box 1.3, as well as the fact health and its maintenance often involve tasks in more than one domain, require effective interactions in the health-care context, as well as high level cognitive and functional skills to meet the various challenges involved in

---

Box 1.3. Why Low Health Literacy May Affect Health Outcomes — and Possible School-Based Intervention Points

- Individuals with low health literacy may be reluctant to ask questions or participate in the decision-making process — *advance interactive health literacy and communication skills.*
- History-taking may be impacted negatively (Mancuso, 2008) — *advance basic communication skills.*
- Clinicians may not recognize problem of health illiteracy (McCormick & Jain, 2003) — *Intervention = education.*
- Access to insurance + health services may be impeded (Peterson et al., 2011) — *advance critical health literacy.*
- Persons with low/limited health literacy may not adhere to preventive measures such as flu shots (Scott, Gazmararian, Williams, & Baker 2002) — *advance basic + critical health literacy.*
- They may enter the health-care system when they are sicker compared to those with adequate health literacy (Bennet et al., 1998) — *advance basic health literacy.*
- People with low or limited health literacy may be more likely to have chronic health conditions, and be less able to manage these than those with adequate health literacy (Health and Human Services, 2011, Health Literacy and Health Outcomes Fact Sheet) — *advance basic and critical health literacy.*
- Persons with limited health literacy may be unable to carefully evaluate the relevance or truth behind media messages, especially those that market ill health and promote risky behaviours) — *advance media literacy.*
- Individuals with limited literacy may suffer from confusion or misunderstand labels and health risks plus explanations concerning diagnoses and treatment (Mancuso, 2008; Shone, King, Doane, Wilson, & Wolf, 2011).

---

health decision-making and self-management practices at home, work, and in the community (Institute of Medicine, 2004). Conversational competence, plus the ability to listen effectively, articulate health concerns, and explain symptoms accurately are also key components of health literacy, as are the abilities to weigh competing facts and choose the correct solution, and to advocate for one's personal health, as well as one's family, and community's health (Mancuso, 2008). Moreover, finding the right resources, clearly involves more than just locating information, both verbal and written, as does the ability to assess its quality, for example, finding the right foods to eat in light of one's health condition and age, as well as knowing how much food to have, and what not to have are simply not likely to be forthcoming without prior input, despite their great importance to most citizens globally. Economic resources, also of immense import to the self-health-care process may not be available to many, and choices about where to invest one's limited resources may be confusing to those who cannot decipher a menu of options.

Clearly, helping young people to be economically independent as well as reflective consumers will go a long way to improving their ability to translate age-associated health recommendations across the lifespan into practice. Providing them and possibly their parents or caregivers with the tools to foster facility with numbers, such as helping them to be able to carry out simple mathematical calculations, fostering their eHealth literacy (Paek & Hove, 2012), and helping them to be able to judge risk appropriately in light of their age, gender, and educational status are equally essential. Although informed adults and youth have better health outcomes (Parker et al., 2003), in the absence of any prior appropriately planned and organized educational scaffolding and preparation multiple avoidable challenges to achieving optimal wellness may persist given the variety of skills often needed to carry out health recommendations and the dependence on one's ability to read and understand instructions in this respect (Protheroe et al., 2009). Other reasons why so many adults today may experience health literacy challenges, even if they come from progressive societies where literacy is reasonable high, are outlined in Box 1.2 presented in an earlier section.

Hence, even though there is often more than enough information circulating for citizens to master their health care, assuming that this information can be conveniently accessed and easily digested, placing the onus on a generally health 'illiterate' population to be responsible for understanding and acting on health recommendations, must be challenged (Hoffman, 2011). As proposed by Ratzan and Parker (2006), it seems reasonable to suggest that to minimize the detrimental impact of health illiteracy on health outcomes outlined in Box 1.3, and to ensure a high-quality health system characterized by effective use not under use or misuse (Parker et al., 2003), enabling all citizens to maximize their personal health, in addition to improving the delivery of health care, through the insightful application of health and education related policies (Institute of Medicine, 2004) that aim to optimize the individual citizen's health literacy and 'health competence,' from the earliest formative years is imperative (see Figure 1.2).

According to Baker's conceptual model of health literacy (2006), fostering the capacity of tomorrow's youth to read fluently, including prose, and numbers, plus fostering their capacity to retrieve and

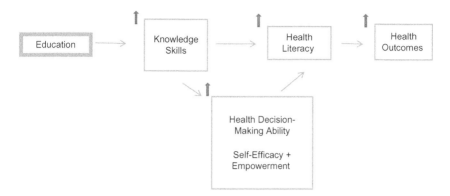

Figure 1.2: Schematic representation of influence of education on health outcomes.

comprehend appropriate materials, and to act on instructions, as well as to question providers is essential to achieving the desired ability to make appropriate health enhancing decisions later on. To develop a health-literate public, oral literacy, media literacy, mental health literacy, science literacy, civic literacy, financial literacy, eHealth literacy, and the ability to communicate across and within the health-care environment are similarly overlapping crucial competencies that can be learned through the educational system. In addition, to counter limited health literacy and promote an empowered citizenry who can confidently assert their rights in the context of health and medicine (Kickbusch, 2009), as well as become involved in medical decision-making (Kickbusch & Maag, 2008), fostering the ability to independently initiate interactions with providers and others (Rosenbaum & Shin, 2007), improving inter-generational health literacy, and directing ongoing policy efforts to address the social determinants of health are critical (Koh, Piotrowski, Kumanyika, & Fielding, 2011).

As the WHO, United Nations, Chinese Ministry of Health, the European Union among others such as Australia (Nutbeam, 2009) are moving toward embracing health literacy as a key policy factor (Parker & Ratzan, 2011), concerted efforts in the educational realm toward improving literacy as the foundation that supports the development of health literacy (McCleary-Jones, 2011) is key to reinforcing positive life-skills and healthy practices across the lifespan. That is, when applied thoughtfully and insightfully as a specific educational topic teaching essential health literacy skills will potentially help all future citizens to be in an equal position to achieve the goal of optimal health, as well as health equalities, rather than perpetuating the present chasm of health and other inequities (Ratzan & Parker, 2006), especially among lower income and minority groups

---

Box 1.4.   Potential Approaches for Improving Health Literacy

Employ a skills-development approach*
Enhance reading, writing, media literacy, and numeracy skills*
Evaluate educational materials for comprehensibility, clarity before using
Improve medical training practices
Improve navigability and reduce complexity of public health systems
Provide shame free environment for consumers (CHCS, 2011)
Simplify health information
Translate materials into language of population(s)
Use plain language for oral and written communications
Use 'surrogate' readers

*Specifically where the school is implicated

(Koh et al., 2011), where 'increasing participation without addressing low health literacy can exacerbate existing health inequalities' (Nutbeam, 2009, p. 3) (Box 1.4).

As outlined so succinctly by Kickbusch (2009, p. 132), to address the new concept of medical delivery, the chronic disease epidemic, as well as economic and social dislocations that prevail worldwide, there is increasing urgency to ensure all children who will become the adults of the future are afforded equal opportunities to acquire a basic set of health and health system understandings, as well as how health is linked to social determinants and community features.

Conversely, when one considers the future costs resulting from taking action or from the lack of action, it is envisioned that lack of action will raise national treatment costs wherever this exists, increase national debt, increase costs for employers, increase national health insurance expenditures, increase utilization of emergency, primary care, hospitals, specialized health facilities as well as vulnerability to bogus, substandard health treatments and therapies (DHSS, 2010, p. 10). It will also maintain or perpetuate the health and socioeconomic gap, and 'misinformation, miscommunication, and mistakes that characterize the health care experience of people with inadequate health literacy' (Parker et al., 2003).

In support of Parker (2000), and from the perspective of health promotion, prevention, or treatment of diseases, knowledge of ways to foster health literacy, as well as efforts to raise awareness about the costs of not addressing health literacy adequately are paramount given the immense encroaching chronic disease threat as populations age, plus the costs of caring for people with these conditions (American College of Physicians,

Table 1.2: Scope of selected health literacy topics covered in PubMed Database, 1970–March 2012, showing potential importance of school-based approaches to achieving health literacy.

Topic	Number of articles
Health literacy + Adults	2281
Health literacy + *Adolescents*	791
Health literacy + *Children*	1090
Health literacy + Health disparities	263
Health literacy + Health outcomes	666
Health literacy + *Empowerment*	111
Health literacy + Cancer	337
Health literacy + *Immigrants*	68
Health literacy + Chronic disease	210
Health literacy + Diabetes	251
Health literacy + Drug use	387
Health literacy + *Media literacy*	259
Health literacy + Mental health	468
Health literacy + HIV	193
Health literacy + Heart disease	100
Health literacy + Oral health	237
Health literacy + *Schools*	234
Health literacy + *Academic achievement*	1488
Health literacy + Parents	356
Health literacy + Print materials	24

2010). As well as strategies focused on the individual, addressing the health literacy needs of the future generations through multi-sector partnerships that go well beyond the health-care providers, and include community, school-based, and individual educational training programs (Kickbusch & Maag, 2008; Mancuso, 2008), formal and informal educational networks (Freedman et al., 2009), are becoming essential (Iwanowicz, 2009). There is thus a renewed call for all school age children to become literate in health, a concept first proposed by Simonds in 1974 (Tones, 2002). This call is also consistent with the long-standing idea that education is an essential component of population wide health promotion and disease prevention strategies as outlined by Nutbeam (2000). It is also consistent with the view that health literacy is a skill that goes beyond individual responsibility and urges citizens to be aware of and address the root causes of health and related inequalities and is a critical capability in modern society (Kickbusch, 2009, p. 132) (Table 1.2).

References

Adkins, N. R., & Corus, C. (2009). Health literacy for improved health outcomes: Effective capital in the marketplace. *The Journal of Consumer Affairs, 43,* 199–221.

American College of Physicians. (2010). Inaugural Pennsylvania Health Literacy Conference. Retrieved from http://www.acpfoundation.org/docs/conferences/2010%20files/PA-HL-10-exsum.pdf

American Medical Association (AMA). (1999). Health literacy: Report of the Council on Scientific Affairs. Ad Hoc Committee on Health Literacy for the Council on Scientific Affairs. *Journal of the American Health Association, 281,* 552–557.

Ancker, J. S., & Kaufman, D. (2007). Rethinking health numeracy: A multi-disciplinary literature review. *Journal of the American Medical Informatics Association, 14,* 713–721.

Armstrong, B., & Cohall, A. (2011). Health promotion with adolescent and young adult males: An empowerment approach. *Adolescent Medicine State of the Art Review, 22,* 544–580.

Bailey, S. C., Pandit, A. U., Yin, S., Federman, A., Davis, T. C., Parker, R. M., & Wolf, M. S. (2009). Predictors of misunderstanding pediatric liquid medication instructions. *Family Medicine, 41*(10), 715–721.

Baker, D. W. (2006). The meaning and the measure of health literacy. *Journal of General Internal Medicine, 21,* 878–883.

Barber, M. N., Staples, M., Osborne, R. H., Clerehan, R., Elder, C., & Buchbinder, R. (2009). Up to a quarter of the Australian population may have suboptimal health literacy depending upon the measurement tool: Results from a population-based survey. *Health Promotion International, 24,* 252–261.

Baur, C. (2011). Calling the nation to act: Implementing the national action plan to improve health literacy. *Nursing Outlook, 59,* 63–69.

Bell, J., Patel, B., & Malasanos, T. (2006). Knowledge improvement with web-based diabetes education program: Brainfood. *Diabetes Technology and Therapeutics, 8,* 444–448.

Benigeri, M., & Pluye, P. (2003). Shortcomings of health information on the internet. *Health Promotion International, 18*(4), 381–386.

Bennet, C. L., Ferreira, M. R., Davis, T. C., Kaplan, J., Weinberger, M., Kuzel, T., … Sartor, O. (1998). Relation between literacy, race, and stage of presentation among low-income patients with prostate cancer. *Journal of Clinical Oncology, 16,* 3101–3104.

Berkman, N. D., Sheridan, S. L., Donahue, K. E., Halpern, D. J., & Crotty, K. (2011). Low health literacy and health outcomes: An updated systematic review. *Annals of Internal Medicine, 155,* 97–107.

Bernhardt, J. (2004). Communication at the core of effective public health. *American Journal of Public Health, 94*(12), 2051–2052.

Betancourt, J. R., Green, A. R., & Carrillo, J. E. (2000). The challenges of cross-cultural healthcare: Diversity, ethics, and the medical encounter. *Bioethics Forum, 16,* 27–32.

California Family Health Council. (2011). Health education and health information. Retrieved from http://www.cfhc.org/health-education/Consulting/Articles/2006 0518HealthLit.htm

Carbone, E. T., & Zoellner, J. M. (2012). Nutrition and health literacy: A systematic review to inform nutrition research and practice. *Journal of Academic Nutrition and Diet, 112,* 254–265.

Center for Health Care Strategies Inc. (2011). Fact sheet. Retrieved from http://www.chcs.org. Accessed on September 2011.

Chen, J. Z., Hsu, H. C., Tung, H. J., & Pan, L. Y. (2012). Effects of health literacy to self-efficacy and preventive care utilization among older adults. *Geriatric Gerontology International.* doi: 10.1111/j.1447-0594. 2012.00862.x

Chinn, D. (2011). Critical health literacy: A review and critical analysis. *Social Science and Medicine, 73,* 60–67.

Cline, R., & Haynes, K. (2001). Consumer health information seeking on the internet: The state of the art. *Health Education Research, 16,* 671–692.

Davis, J., & Farrell, M. (2001). eHealth initiative applauds new study by California healthcare foundation and Rand health on quality of health information on the internet. Retrieved from http://www.ehealthinitiative.org. Accessed on November 14, 2004.

Department of Health and Human Services, Office of Disease Prevention and Health Promotion (DDHS). (2010). *National action plan to improve health literacy.* Washington, DC: United States Printing Office.

Dollahite, J., Thompson, C., & McNew, R. (1996). Readability of printed sources of diet and health information. *Patient Education and Counseling, 27,* 123–134.

Dominick, G. M., Dunsiger, S. I., Pekmezi, D. W., & Marcus, B. H. (2012, June 26). Health literacy predicts change in physical activity self-efficacy among sedentary Latinas. *Journal of Immigrant and Minority Health.*[Epub ahead of print] PubMed PMID: 22733230.

Dominick, G. M., Friedman, D. B., Saunders, R. P., Hussey, J. R., & Watkins, K. W. (2012). Factors associated with physical activity literacy among foster parents. *American Journal of Health Behavior, 36,* 179–192.

Donovan, O. (2005). The carbohydrate quandary: Achieving health literacy through an interdisciplinary webquest. *Journal of School Health, 75,* 359–362.

Dunn-Navarra, A. M., Stockwell, M. S., Meyer, D., & Larson, E. (2012, June 16). Parental health literacy, knowledge and beliefs regarding upper respiratory infections (URI) in an Urban Latino Immigrant population. *Journal of Urban Health.* [Epub ahead of print] PubMed PMID: 22707307.

Ferguson, L. A., & Pawlak, R. (2011). Health literacy: The road to improved health outcomes. *The Journal for Nurse Practitioners, 7,* 123–129.

Flores, G., & Tomany-Korman, S. C. (2008). The language spoken at home and disparities in medical and dental health, access to care, and use of services in US children. *Pediatrics, 121,* e1703–e1714.

Freedman, D. A., Bess, K. D., Tucker, H. A., Boyd, D. L., Tuchman, A. M., & Wallston, K. A. (2009). Public health literacy defined. *American Journal of Preventive Medicine, 36,* 446–451.

Freedman, R. B., Jones, S. K., Lin, A., Robin, A. L., & Muir, K. W. (2012). Influence of parental health literacy and dosing responsibility on pediatric glaucoma medication adherence. *Archives of Ophthalmology, 130,* 306–311.

Gannon, W., & Hildebrandt, E. (2002). A winning combination: Women, literacy, and participation in health care. *Health Care for Women International, 23,* 754–760.

Gazmararian, J. A., Curran, J. W., Parker, R. M., Bernhardt, J. M., & DeBuono, B. A. (2005). Public health literacy in America: An ethical imperative. *American Journal of Preventive Medicine, 28,* 317–322.

Gonzales, F., Dearden, K., & Jimenez, W. (1999). Do multi-sectoral development programmes affect health? A Bolivian case study. *Health and Policy Planning, 14,* 400–408.

Grandinetti, D. (2000). Doctors and the web: Help your patients surf the net safely. *Medical Economics, 63*(8), 28–34.

Green, J. (2007). Health literacy: Socially situating community-based research. *Fine Print, 30*(1), 3–7.

Greenfield, S. F., Sugarman, D. E., Nargiso, J., & Weiss, R. D. (2005). Readability of patient handout materials in a nationwide sample of alcohol and drug abuse treatment programs. *American Journal of Addictions, 14,* 339–345.

Groleau, D. (2011). Embodying 'health citizenship' in health knowledge to fight health inequalities. *Revista Brasiliera de Enfermagem, 64*(5), 811–816.

Hartman, T., McCarthy, P., Park, R., Schuster, E., & Kushi, L. (1997). Results of a community-based low-literacy nutrition education program. *Journal of Community Health, 22,* 325–341.

Hauser, M. R. (2005). *Measuring literacy: Performance levels for adults* (National Research Council of the National Academies). Washington, DC: National Academies Press.

Health and human services. (2011). Fact sheet: Health literacy and health outcomes. Retrieved from http://www.health.gov/communication/literacy/quickguide/factsliteracy

Healthy People 2010. Focus area 11. *Health Communications.* Retrieved from http://www.healthypeople.gov/Document/HTML/Volume1/11HealthCom.htm. Accessed on August 11, 2012.

Heisler, M., Bouknight, R. R., Hayward, R. A., Smith, D. M., & Kerr, E. A. (2002). The relative importance of physician communication, participatory decision making, and patient understanding in diabetes self-management. *Journal of General Internal Medicine, 17,* 243–252.

Hibbard, J. H., Peters, W. E., Dixon, A., & Tusler, M. (2007). Consumer competencies and the use of comparative quality information: It isn't just about literacy. *Patient Care Research and Review, 64,* 379–394.

Hoffman, K. D. (2011). Low literacy may lead to poorer health. Retrieved from http://healthchange4you.blogspot.com/2011/08/low-literacy-may-lead-to-poorer.html

Howard-Pitney, B., Winkleby, M., Albright, C., Bruce, B., & Fortmann, S. (1997). The Stanford nutrition action program: A dietary fat intervention for low-literacy adults. *American Journal of Public Health, 87,* 1971–1976.

Huang, J. S., Tobin, A., & Tompane, T. (2012). Clinicians poorly assess health literacy-related readiness for transition to adult care in adolescents with inflammatory bowel disease. *Clinics in Gastroenterology and Hepatology, 10,* 626–632.

Institute of Medicine. (2004). *Health literacy: A prescription to end confusion.* Washington, DC: Board on Neurosciences and Behavioural Health, Committee on Health Literacy, Institute of Medicine.

Iwanowicz, E. (2009). Health literacy as one of the contemporary public health challenges. *Medycyna Pracy, 60,* 427–437.

Jackson, R., Davis, T., Bairnsfather, L., George, R., Crouch, M., & Gault, H. (1991). Patient reading ability: An overlooked problem in health care. *Southern Medical Journal, 84,* 1172–1175.

James, B. D., Boyle, P. A., Bennett, J. S., & Bennett, D. A. (2012, June 22). The impact of health and financial literacy on decision making in community-based older adults. *Gerontology.* [Epub ahead of print] PubMed PMID: 22739454.

John M. Eisenberg Center for Clinical Decisions and Communications Science. Mitigating the effects of low health literacy: A brief of the research evidence for health communicators and educators. (2012). Comparative effectiveness review summary guides for clinicians [Internet]. Rockville (MD): Agency for Healthcare Research and Quality (US); 2007-. Retrieved from http://www.ncbi.nlm.nih.gov/books/NBK95340/

Joint Committee on Health Education Terminology. (1991). Report of the joint committee on health education terminology. *Journal of Health Education, 22,* 97–108.

Kickbusch, I. (2001). Health literacy: Addressing the health and educational divide. *Health Promotion International, 16,* 289–297.

Kickbusch, I. (2009). Health literacy: Engaging in a political debate. *International Journal of Public Health, 54,* 131–132.

Kickbusch, I. (2011). Global health diplomacy: How foreign policy can influence health. *BMJ, 10,* 342:d3154. doi: 10.1136/bmj.d3154

Kickbusch, I., & Maag, D. (2008). In K. Heggenhougen & S. Quah (Eds.), *International encyclopedia of public health* (Vol. 3, pp. 204–211). San Diego, CA: Academic Press.

Kickbusch, I., & Payne, L. (2003). Twenty-first century health promotion: The public health revolution meets the wellness revolution. *Health Promotion International, 18*(4), 275–276.

Kickbusch, I., Wait, S., & Magg, D. (2006). *Navigating health: The role of health literacy.* London: International Longevity Center.

Kim, S., Quitsberg, A., Love, F., & Shea, A. (2004). Association of health literacy with self-management behaviour of patients with diabetes. *Diabetes Care, 27,* 2980–2982.

Kirsch, I. S., Jungebut, A., Jenkins, L., & Kolstad, A. (1993). *Adult literacy in America: A first look at the results of the National Adult Literacy Survey.* Washington, DC: Department of Education.

Koh, H. K., Berwick, D. M., Clancy, C. M., Baur, C., Brach, C., Harris, L. M., & Zerhusen, E. G. (2012). New federal policy initiatives to boost health literacy can help the nation move beyond the cycle of costly 'crisis care'. *Health Affairs (Millwood), 31,* 434–443.

Koh, H. K., Piotrowski, J. J., Kumanyika, S., & Fielding, J. E. (2011). Healthy people: A 2020 vision for the social determinants approach. *Health Education and Behavior, 38*, 551–557.

Kolasa, K., Peery, A., Harris, N., & Shovelin, K. (2001). Food literacy partners program: A strategy to increase community food literacy. *Topics in Clinical Nutrition, 16*, 1–10.

Kutcher, S., & Wei, Y. (2012). Mental health and the school environment: Secondary schools, promotion and pathways to care. *Current Opinion in Psychiatry, 25*, 311–316.

Lazarus, W., & Mora, F. (2000). *Online content for low-income and under-served Americans: The digital divide's new frontier.* Children's Partnership Report. Retrieved from http://childrenspartnership.org/pub/pub.html. Accessed on August 21, 2004.

Lecerof, S. S., Westerling, R., Moghaddassi, M., & Östergren, P. O. (2011). Health information for migrants: The role of educational level in prevention of overweight. *Scandinavian Journal of Public Health, 39*, 172–178.

Lee, A. (2009). Health-promoting schools: Evidence for a holistic approach to promoting health and improving health literacy. *Applied Health Economics and Policy, 7*, 11–17.

Levy, L., Patterson, R., Kristal, A., & Li, S. (2000). How well do consumers understand percentage daily value on food labels? *American Journal of Health Promotion, 14*, 157–160.

Lindström, B., & Eriksson, M. (2011). From health education to healthy learning: Implementing salutogenesis in educational science. *Scandinavian Journal of Public Health, 39*(Suppl 6), 85–92.

Lukoscheck, P., Fazzari, M., & Marantz, P. (2003). Patient and physician factors predict patient's comprehension of health information. *Patient Education and Counseling, 50*, 201–210.

Mancuso, J. M. (2008). Health literacy: A concept/dimensional analysis. *Nursing and Health Sciences, 10*, 248–255.

Marshall, S., Sahm, L., & McCarthy, S. (2012). Health literacy in Ireland: Reading between the lines. *Perspectives in Public Health, 132*, 31–38.

Martensson, L., & Hensing, G. (2011). Health literacy-a heterogeneous phenomenon: A literature review. *Scandinavian Journal of Caring Sciences, 25*(3), 1–10.

Mayer, G., & Villaire, M. (1994). Low health literacy and its effects on patient care. *Journal of Nursing Administration, 34*, 440–442.

McCleary-Jones, V. (2011). Health literacy and its association with diabetes knowledge, self-efficacy and disease management among African Americans with diabetes. *The ABNF Journal, 22*, 25–32.

McCormick, J., & Jain, R. (2003). Who actually has the 'low health literacy'? *Archives of Internal Medicine, 163*, 1745–1746.

McGovern, E. (2010). Health literacy: Our children and the future. Tallahasse, FL: Institute for America's Health. Retrieved from http://healthy-america.org/?p = 616. Accessed on June 13, 2012.

Medicines and Healthcare Products Regulatory Agency. (2005). *always read the leaflet: Getting the best information with every medicine.* Report of the Committee on Safety and Medicines Working Group on Patient Information. London: The Stationary Office.

National Institute for Health Care Management (NIHCM). (2011). Recent presentations on adolescent health literacy. Retrieved from http://www.nihcm. org/about-us. Accessed on June 23, 2012.

Neuhauser, L., Rothschild, R., & Rodriguez, F. (2007). MyPyramid.gov: Assessment of literacy, cultural and linguistic factors in the USDA food pyramid web site. *Journal of Nutrition Education and Behaviour, 39,* 219–225.

Nicholson, J. M., Lucas, N., Berthelsen, D., & Wake, M. (2012). Socioeconomic inequality profiles in physical and developmental health from 0–7 years: Australian National Study. *Journal of Epidemiology and Community Health, 66,* 81–87.

Nimmon, L. (2007). Within the eyes of the people. *Canadian Journal of Public Health, 98,* 337–340.

Nutbeam, D. (1998). Health literacy as a public health goal: A challenge for contemporary health education and communication strategies into the 21st century. *Health Promotion International, 15,* 259–267.

Nutbeam, D. (2000). Health literacy as a public health goal: A challenge for contemporary health education and communication strategies into the 21st century. *Health Promotion International, 15,* 259–267.

Nutbeam, D. (2008). The evolving concept of health literacy. *Social Science and Medicine, 67,* 2072–2078.

Nutbeam, D. (2009). Building health literacy in Australia. *Medical Journal of Australia, 191,* 525–526.

Paek, H. J., & Hove, T. (2012). Social cognitive factors and perceived social influences that improve adolescent eHealth literacy. *Health Communications,* March 27, 1–11. doi: 10.1080/104102235.2011.616627

Parker, R. (2000). Health literacy: A challenge for American patients and their health care providers. *Health Promotion International, 15,* 277–283.

Parker, R., & Ratzan, S. C. (2011). Health literacy: A second decade of distinction for Americans. *Journal of Health Communication, 15,* 20–33.

Parker, R. M., Ratzan, S. C., & Lurie, N. (2003). Health literacy: A policy challenge for advancing high-quality health care. *Health Affairs, 22,* 147–153.

Partnership for Clear Health Communication, Steering Committee. (March, 2003). Eradicating *low health literacy: The first public health movement of the 21st century overview* (White Paper). Retrieved from http://www.aameda.org/MemberServices/ Exec/Articles/sum03/EradicatingLowHealthcareLiteracy.pdf. Accessed on June 22, 2012.

Paterson, B. (2002). Myth of empowerment in chronic illness. *Evidence Based Nursing, 5,* 62.

Pawlak, R. (2005). Economic considerations of health literacy. *Nursing Economics, 23,* 170–180.

Peerson, A., & Saunders, M. (2009). Health literacy revisited: What do we mean and why does it matter. *Health Promotion International, 24,* 285–296.

Peterson, P. N., Shetterly, S. M., Clarke, C. L., Bekelman, D. B., Chan, P. S., Allen, L. A., … Masoudi, F. A. (2011). Health literacy and outcomes among patients with heart failure. *JAMA, 305,* 1695–1701.

Pierce, D., & Shann, C. (2012). Rural Australians: Mental health literacy: Identifying and addressing their knowledge and attitudes. *Community Medicine & Health Education, 2*, 4.

Protheroe, J., Nutbeam, D., & Rowlands, G. (2009). Health literacy: A necessity for increasing participation in health care. *British Journal of General Practice, 59*, 721–723.

Public Health Agency of Canada. (2011). National consultation of physical activity guidelines. Retrieved from http://www.phac-aspc.gc.ca/hp-ps/hl-mvs/pa-ap/index-eng.php

Ratzan, S. C., & Parker, R. M. (2006). Health literacy-identification and response. *Journal of Health Communications, 11*, 713–715.

Reavley, N. J., & Jorm, A. F. (2011). Young people's stigmatizing attitudes towards people with mental disorders: Findings from an Australian national survey. *Australia and New Zealand Journal of Psychiatry, 45*, 1033–1039.

Rootman, I. (2006). Health literacy: Where are the Canadian doctors? *Canadian Medical Association, 175*, 606–607.

Rootman, I., & Gordon-El-Bihbety, D. (2008). *A vision for a health literate Canada (Report of the expert panel on health literacy)*. Ottawa: Canadian Public Health Association.

Rosenbaum, S., & Shin, P. (2007). *Achieving family health literacy: The case for insuring children*. Washington, DC: Department of Health Policy, George Washington University School of Public Health and Health Services.

Ross, L. A., Frier, B. M., Kelnar, C. J., & Deary, I. J. (2001). Child and parental mental ability and glycaemic control in children with Type 1 diabetes. *Diabetic Medicine, 18*, 364–369.

Rubinelli, S., Schulz, P., & Nakamoto, K. (2009). Health literacy beyond knowledge and behaviour: Letting the patient be a patient. *International Journal of Public Health, 54*, 307–311.

Rudd, R., Colton, T., & Schacht, R. (2000). *An overview of medical and public health literature addressing literacy issues: An annotated bibliography*. The National Center for the Study of Adult Learning and Literacy, World Education. Retrieved from http://www.ncsall.net/fileadmin/resources/research/report14.pdf. Accessed on June 2004.

Rudd, R. E., Moeykens, B. A., & Colton, T. C. (1999). *Health and literacy. A review of medical and public health literature* (Chapter 5). New York, NY: Jossey-Bass.

Sanders, L. M., Federico, S., Klass, P., Abrams, M. A., & Dreyer, B. (2009). Literacy and child health: A systematic review. *Archives of Pediatric Adolescent Medicine, 163*, 131–140.

Sarasohn-Kahn, J. (2011). *The Edelman health barometer: Health is a team sport*. Retrieved from http://careandcost.com/2011/10/07/the-edelman-health-barometer-health-care-is-a-team-sport/. Accessed on June 23, 2012.

Scarborough, P., Bhatnagar, P., Wickramasinghe, K. K., Allender, S., Foster, C., & Rayner, M. (2011). The economic burden of ill health due to diet, physical inactivity, smoking, alcohol and obesity in the UK: An update to 2006–07 NHS costs. *Journal of Public Health, 33*(4), 527–535.

Schiavo, J. H. (2011). Oral health literacy in the dental office: The unrecognized patient risk factor. *Journal of Dental Hygiene*, *85*, 248–255.

Schillinger, D., Grymbach, K., Piette, J., Wang, F., Osmond, D., Daher, C., ... Bindman, A. B. etal. (2002). Association of health literacy with diabetes outcomes. *Journal of the American Medical Association*, *288*(4), 475–482.

Scott, T. L., Gazmararian, J. A., Williams, M. V., & Baker, D. W. (2002). Health literacy and preventive health care use among medicare enrolees in a managed care organization. *Medical Care*, *40*, 395–404.

Seldon, C., Zorn, M., Ratzan, S. C., & Parker, R. M. (Eds.). (2000). Health literacy, January 1990 through 1999 (LM Pub. No. CBM 2000-1). Maryland National Institutes of Health, National Library Medicine, Washington, DC.

Seldon, C., Zoorn, M., Ratzan, S. C., Parker, R. M., & Ruth, M. (compilers). (2002). Health literacy (bibliography online). National library of Medicine, Bethesda, MD. Retrieved from http://www.nlm.nih.gov/pubs/resources.html. Accessed on September 2011.

Sharp, L. K., Zurawski, J. M., Roland, P. Y., O'Toole, C., & Hines, J. (2002). Health literacy, cervical cancer risk factors, and distress in low-income African-American women seeking colonoscopy. *Ethnic Diseases*, *12*, 541–546.

Shone, L. P., King, J. P., Doane, C., Wilson, K. M., & Wolf, M. S. (2011). Misunderstanding and potential unintended misuse of acetaminophen among adolescents and young adults. *Journal of Health Communication*, *16*(Suppl 3), 256–267.

Sihota, S., & Lennard, L. (2004). *Health Literacy: Being able to make the most of health.* London: National Consumer Council.

Simonds, S. K. (1974). Health education as social policy. *Health Education Monograph*, *2*, 1–25.

Smith, B. (2004). Health literacy: A new perspective on an old problem. *Social Marketing Quarterly*, *X*(3-4), 69–72.

Smith, S. G., Wolf, M. S., & von Wagner, C. (2010). Socioeconomic status, statistical confidence, and patient-provider communication: An analysis of the Health Information National Trends Survey (HINTS 2007). *Journal of Health Communications*, *15*, 169–185.

Smith, S. K., Kearney, P., Trevena, L., Barratt, A., Nutbeam, D., & McCaffery, K. J. (2012, April 19). Informed choice in bowel cancer screening: A qualitative study to explore how adults with lower education use decision aids. *Health Expect.* doi: 10.1111/j.1369-7625.2012.00780.x. [Epub ahead of print] PubMed PMID: 22512746.

Sondik, E. (2007, April 19). *Healthy People 2010 Focus Area 11: Health Communication. Progress Review.* Retrieved from http://www.cdc.gov/nchs/hphome.htm

Sørensen, K., Van den Broucke, S., Fullam, J., Doyle, G., Pelikan, J., Slonska, Z., & Brand, H., Consortium Health Literacy Project European (HLS-EU). (2012). Health literacy and public health: A systematic review and integration of definitions and models. *BMC Public Health*, *12*, 80.

St Leger, L. (2001). Schools, health literacy and public health: Possibilities and challenges. *Health Promotion International*, *16*, 197–205.

Stone, D. H. (2011). Health literacy. Society for Vascular Surgery, Chicago, IL. Retrieved from http://www.VascularWeb.org

Tattersall, R. L. (2002). The expert patient: A new approach to chronic disease management for the twenty-first century. *Clinics in Medicine, 2*, 227–229.

TenHave, T., Van Horn, B., Kumanyika, S., Askov, E., Matthews, Y., & Adams-Campell, L. (1997). Literacy assessment in a cardiovascular nutrition education setting. *Patient Education and Counseling, 31*, 1139–1150.

Tones, K. (2002). Health literacy: New wine in old bottles? *Health Education Research, 17*, 287–290.

Twenge, J. M., Campbell, W. K., & Freeman, E. C. (2012). Generational differences in young adults' life goals, concern for others, and civic orientation, 1966–2009. *Journal of Personality Social Psychology, 102*, 1045–1062.

U.S. Department of Health and Human Services. (2000). *Healthy People 2010*. Washington, DC: U.S. Government Printing Office. Originally developed for Ratzan S. C., & Parker R. M. (2000). Introduction. In *National Library of Medicine Current Bibliographies in Medicine: Health Literacy*. In C. R. Selden, M. Zorn, S. C. Ratzan & R. M. Parker (Eds.), NLM Pub. No. CBM 2000-1. Bethesda, MD: National Institutes of Health, U.S. Department of Health and Human Services.

Vahabi, M. (2007). The impact of health communication on health-related decision making: A review of the evidence. *Health Education, 107*, 27–41.

Vardavas, C. I., Kondilis, B. K., Patelarou, E., Akrivos, P. D., & Falagas, M. E. (2009). Health literacy and sources of health education among adolescents in Greece. *International Journal of Medical Health, 21*, 179–186.

Vernon, J. A., Trujillo, A., Rosenbaum, S., & DeBuono, B. (2007). Low health literacy: Implications for national health policy. Retrieved from http://www.gwumc.edu/sphhs/departments/healthpolicy/CHPR/downloads/LowHealth-LiteracyReport10_4_07.pdf

von Wagner, C., Knight, K., Steptoe, A., & Wardle, J. (2007). Functional health literacy and health-promoting behaviour in a national sample of British adults. *Journal of Epidemiology and Community Health, 61*, 1086–1090.

Williams, M. V., Baker, D. W., Honig, E. G., Lee, T. M., & Nowlan, A. (1998). Inadequate literacy is a barrier to asthma knowledge and self-care. *Chest, 114*, 1008–1015.

Williams, M. V., Baker, D. W., Parker, R. M., & Nurss, J. R. (1998). Relationship of functional health literacy to patient's knowledge of their chronic disease: A study of patients with hypertension and diabetes. *Archives of Internal Medicine, 158*, 166–172.

Wilson, J. F. (2003). The crucial link between literacy and health. *Annals of Internal Medicine, 139*, 875–878.

Wolf, M. S., Curtis, L. M., Wilson, E. A., Revelle, W., Waite, K. R., Smith, S. G., Weintraub, S., …, Baker, D. W. (2012, May 8). Literacy, cognitive function, and health: Results of the LitCog Study. *Journal of General Internal Medicine, 27*(10), 1300–1307.

Wolf, M. S., Gazmararian, J., & Baker, D. (2007). Health literacy and health risk behaviours among older adults. *American Journal of Preventive Medicine, 32*, 19–24.

World Health Organization. (2010). Health literacy and health behaviour. Retrieved from http://www.who.int/healthpromotion/conferences/7ghp/track2/en/. Accessed on December 9, 2010.

Yajima, S., Takano, T., Bakamura, K., & Wananabe, M. (2001). Effectiveness of a community leaders' programme to promote healthy lifestyles in Tokyo, Japan. *Health Promotion International, 16*, 235–243.

Zarcodoolas, C., Pleasant, A., & Greer, D. S. (2005). Understanding health literacy: An expanded model. *Health Promotion International, 20*, 195–203.

Zarcodoolas, C., Pleasant, A., & Greer, D. S. (2006). *Advancing health literacy: A framework for understanding and action.* San Francisco, CA: Jossey-Bass.

Ziebland, S. (2004). The importance of being expert: The quest for cancer information on the internet. *Social Science & Medicine, 59*, 1783–1793.

Chapter 2

Health Literacy, Health and Academic Status

Ray Marks and Joan Wharf Higgins

2.1. Role of Schools in Promoting Health Literacy

As outlined in Chapter 1, health literacy, a significant global problem impacting health outcomes, as well as overall citizenship, has tremendous implications for all citizens, especially those with limited literacy. As recently noted by Ferguson and Pawlak (2011), health literacy, a significant predictor of health outcomes is markedly impacted by low formal education levels, with knowledge gaps that can extend from childhood through parenthood (Sanders, Shaw, Guez, Baur, & Rudd, 2009), among other factors. Since data in the United States has shown 7,000 students drop out of school each day, and that even among those who remain in school, the lack of consistent health curricula across grades K-12 may produce students with low levels of health literacy (National Action Plan to Improve Health Literacy, 2010), it is not surprising that 65% of young people, ages 16–24 have difficulty reading and processing everyday health information (Kansas Head Start Association, 2012). Because health is a highly valued state and the key to personal and social well-being of individuals and society (McGovern, 2010), there are increasing calls across the globe for early interventions to foster health literacy, so youth will have a better chance of becoming healthier adults (Kickbusch, 2008; Manganello, 2008; McGovern, 2010).

Since graduating from high school is no longer sufficient to guarantee an adult will be able to read materials at a 12th grade level and most health materials are written above the 8th grade level (Ferguson & Pawlak, 2011), the failure of schools to foster basic literacy and skills that are paramount in the context of health literacy, may predictably have far-reaching personal and collective health consequences (see Box 2.1). At a minimum, basic literacy problems that occur during the school years usually persist throughout an adolescent's lifetime (e.g. Fletcher et al., 1994) and are related to broad health issues such as delinquency (e.g. Waldie & Spreen, 1993), homelessness (e.g. Barwick & Siegel, 1996), loneliness (Sabornie, 1994), substance abuse (e.g. Beitchman, Wilson, & Douglas, 2001) and suicide (e.g. McBride & Siegel, 1997), in addition to poor physical and mental health (Gans, Kenny, & Ghany, 2003; Rootman & Ronson, 2005). These consequences may also prevail among students who remain in schools which do not provide for basic health literacy development in a consistent manner across grades K-12. They may prove especially problematic, however, for those who do not complete high school since research shows literacy levels in general, are commonly comparable to those attained in classrooms three to five grades below the highest grade of school completed (Kansas Head Start Association, 2012). We know that reading and comprehending material is necessary but not sufficient for impacting health decisions and health behaviours. Thus, in addition to effective health promotion and disease prevention strategies in later life and skills to communicate effectively about health, more practical ways of improving health literacy early on in life, even at the toddler stage, are strongly warranted (Sanders, Federico, Klass, Abrams, & Dreyer, 2009).

Indeed, among the extrinsic factors identified as highly influential for the attainment of the health literacy skills required by the contemporary child, adolescent and adult, health education in the formative years (McGovern, 2010) appears to be especially salient as proposed by Ferguson and Pawlak

---

Box 2.1.   Health Literacy Related Skills Known to be Impacted Though Well-Coordinated Comprehensive Classroom and/or Experiential Educational Approaches

- Ability to *access* valid sources of information, products, and services.
- Ability to *analyse* factors that influence responsible health decisions.
- Ability *to make sound choices* and *set health-affirming goals* based on these decisions.
- Ability to *communicate* with others.
- Ability to *read* and *understand* health information.
- Ability to *use* health information in health enhancing ways.
- Ability to *advocate* (Benham-Deal & Hodges, n.d).
- Ability to *weigh* the validity of health claims.

in their causal model of the determinants of health literacy, as well as by the Institute of Medicine in the United States (2004). This idea that initial efforts to achieving a health literate populace rests with formal educational systems, including elementary, and high schools (Freedman et al., 2009), is supported by related research in the United States that shows that health literacy varies directly with level of education, in that over three-quarters of adults with less than a high school degree are found to have below basic level or basic level health literacy, and this percentage decreases markedly as education level increases. Moreover, even though higher education is more favourable than not, 44% of high school graduates and 12% of college graduates were found to have below basic or basic health literacy (America's Health Literacy, United States Department of Health and Human Services, http://www.health.gov/communication/literacy/issuebrief/#lower).

Because of the growing importance of health as an important value and one that influences academic attainment significantly, plus the evidence that a multitude of factors influence health literacy, including education, schools have consequently become an essential component in efforts to achieve the goal of health literacy for all (St. Leger, 2001).

2.1.1. Why is the School Venue so Important?

The school is a fundamental institution in building both the wealth and the health of citizens, and countries, where youth spend more time in schools in their formative years than any other venue, and are thus likely to be affected considerably by this institution (Begoray, Wharf Higgins, & MacDonald, 2009). Yet, in an advanced nation such as the United States, national standards to improve primary and high school students' health literacy skills have not been widely adopted. Given that health instruction K-12 that includes the teaching of age-appropriate, personnel and social skills, along with other strategies not only improves health literacy (Society for Public Health Education Fact Sheet, 2011), and reduces risky behaviours (Ghadder, Valerio, Garcia, & Hansen, 2011) that greatly impact the risk for future chronic disease as adults (NIHCM Foundation, 2011), optimally designed and delivered health education units can significantly improve students' academic behaviours and academic achievement as well as their health skills for wellness (Flay, Allred, & Ordway, 2001; Zins, Bloodworth, Weissberg, & Walberg, 2004).

Because the health issues today are quite different from those of past decades and are predominantly lifestyle related, and paediatricians are aware of health literacy-related problems and the need for good communication with families, but struggle with time demands to implement these skills (Turner et al., 2009), educating children to make healthy life choices through the teaching of age-appropriate health lessons as a component of formal education, promises to improve students' ability to access and interpret health information as an important step in the process of achieving lifelong wellness, foster their academic ability, in general (St. Leger, 2001; Wharf Higgins, Begoray, & MacDonald, 2009). That is, coupled with appropriate basic literacy and numeracy skills, enhancing health literacy through school-based strategies has the potential to significantly improve both the health and the educational outcomes of the child (Wharf Higgins et al., 2009), including how to solve problems and arrive at critical decisions, while lowering the long-term health-care costs and societal burden attributable to health illiteracy (Lee, 2009). It also seems crucial to acknowledge the high prevalence of childhood health concerns in today's classroom. Specifically, there is evidence that young adults with diabetes, which is becoming an epidemic involving youth in their formative years, have been found to report a higher rate of negative health behaviours than their counterparts who are healthy insofar as physical activity, weight control behaviours, binge eating, is concerned. They can also experience lower self-esteem, body satisfaction, depressive symptoms and teasing that may warrant classroom discussion and attention among other approaches to preventing negative health outcomes (Berge, Bauer, Eisenberg, Denny, & Neumark-Sztainer, 2012).

Furthermore, because many school aged children may have cognitive, social and emotional challenges that impact health, the school is well poised to assist children with a special health-care requirement to develop health knowledge and self-care skills so they can become effective independent self-managers. This may be especially salient for those living with limited cognitive abilities (DeWalt & Hink, 2009). This opportunity to optimize the opportunities for challenged youth, whether as a result of a chronic physical or mental illness, or multiple health challenges, is of great import, because research shows without consistent school-based efforts to foster a level of adequate health literacy among this group of youth, adolescents with special health-care needs will experience a heightened risk for adverse health outcomes, which require at a minimum, the achievement of an adequate level of health literacy (Betz, Ruccione, Meeske, Smith, & Chang, 2008).

Yet, even though knowledge on health and disease prevention and adolescent satisfaction with the health-care system affect the adolescent's health status, Vardavas, Kondilis, Patelarou, Akrivos, and Falagas (2009), found a large percentage of adolescents, especially boys, to be insufficiently informed on major health issues in the context of the Greek school. Astonishingly, the case for promoting youth health literacy was made more than 10 years ago by St. Leger (2001) who acknowledged that most effectively schools should address health literacy at the basic level. Nonetheless, there remain very few interventions in the related research realm that depict any form of intervention specifically designed to improve child health outcomes by focusing on their health literacy development (DeWalt & Hink, 2009), and few that appear to promote critical health literacy or examine its effect on empowerment (St. Leger, 2001). Because ample research has shown that literacy levels that are below grade level in adolescence are related to an increase in risk-taking or violent behaviours later on (Diamond, Saintonge, August, & Azrack, 2011), health education programming for all youth, including those in Greek schools, would appear imperative in efforts to promote healthier lifestyles and to prevent chronic and infectious diseases, as well as the gap in outcomes between individuals with low and higher literacy (DeWalt & Hink, 2009).

Results of a study by Davis, Byrd, Arnold, Auinger, and Bocchini (1999) that found those with low literacy to report higher rates of violence either as an instigator or as a victim than those with better literacy, arguably supports this view. Also affected detrimentally by low literacy was weapon carrying, the tendency to become embroiled in a fight, and the need for treatment for an injury incurred as a result of a fight. Although health literacy was not assessed directly, low literacy is a strong predictor of poor health literacy, and again suggests a crucial role for the school in helping children develop appropriate health-related behaviours. It has also been argued that among the many perceived needs associated with promoting mental health in the school environment, an appropriate starting point might involve efforts to promote mental health literacy (Kutcher & Wei, 2012).

In addition to the above-mentioned arguments, as outlined by the Institute of Medicine, the education system is one of three key points of intervention deemed necessary or essential in efforts to develop a health literate society (Institute of Medicine, 2004), and is a key factor among those system factors that affect health literacy as outlined by Paasche-Orlow and Wolf (2007). To this end, growing evidence suggests formal educational systems, including elementary and high schools that aim to prepare youth to become informed members of the public, in multiple ways, including work, and parenting (Freedman et al., 2009) are good investments (Nutbeam, 2009). Moreover, classroom-based health education, in particular comprehensive school health education or the Coordinated School Health model (discussed below in more detail), can significantly impact student's health literacy through its processes of consistent instruction and formative assessments (Benham-Deal & Hodges, n.d.), and by improving the desired health knowledge, skills and attitudes inherent in the concept of being a health literate individual.

National health education standards for classroom-based health education have thus been developed to establish what students should understand and be able to do so in order to be deemed health literate

(Benham-Deal & Hodges, n.d.). As well, the Joint Committee on National Health Education Standards in the United States (2007) and the American Association for Health Education (2008) have identified health literacy as the desired outcome of these criteria. Kickbusch (2008) is a strong advocate in favour of the school as a key resource for providing youth with the knowledge needed to make appropriate health-affirming decisions.

Nutbeam (2009), another long-time leader and visionary in the educational and health field, has similarly affirmed that health literacy, a vital 21st century skill, is best developed through education. As a venue, schools have long been deemed an effective setting in which to promote health behaviours of youth (Lee, 2009). We recognize that schools cannot realistically prepare the individual for all the challenges they may face, but recommendations that health literacy be incorporated into National Curricula, such as that conducted in Australia, are laudable first steps. Similarly, the concept and growing impact of the 'health-promoting school' (also referred to as a Coordinated School Health model) that fosters a broad approach to promoting healthy behaviour has been identified as 'an imperative strategy' (Cale & Harris, 2006; Naylor & McKay, 2009; Lee, 2009) that can facilitate the achievement of higher levels of health literacy by both providing a positive culture for health and by helping youth, especially youth from disadvantaged backgrounds, to tackle determinants of chronic diseases and health risks more ably (Lee, 2009). Informed by social ecological ideas of systems context and interconnectedness, and empowering students to have a voice and choice in shaping school-wide initiatives, whole or comprehensive school models that address changes to the school environment and school policies, in addition to curricula, and support learning about and practicing healthy behaviours are advocated for advancing the well-being of young learner (Beaudoin, 2011). It appears feasible to suggest that schools offering comprehensive curricula, as well as healthy physical and social environments, can foster all levels of health literacy, including the more important interactive and critical levels of health literacy needed in today's health-care environment (Deaton, 2002) (see Box 2.1). Conceivably, therefore, by providing children with knowledge as part of the regular curriculum, as well as practical opportunities to shop, cook, exercise and use the health-care system and learn to care for others, the development of a health literate population is more likely to be achieved than not, and to foster a populace that can think critically, problem solve, as well as access and analyse information, plus collaborate, all skills strongly predictive of healthy choices, as well as health status (Kickbusch, 2009; Wharf Higgins et al., 2009) (see Box 2.1). Among older youth, this translates into having skills to organize and apply health knowledge, as well as attitudes and practices relevant to managing their health in the health-care environment (Massey, Prelip, Calimlin, Quiter, & Glik, 2012).

2.2. Does This Idea Work?

2.2.1. Case Examples

To reduce the asthma burden, one of the most common causes of school absenteeism, 15 teachers were recruited from the St. Louis, MO, USA area during the 2006–2007 school year to assess an integrated curriculum that presents asthma as a real world example with the aim of raising all children's awareness and understanding of asthma, not just those with the condition. A 15-lesson, asthma-based curriculum was developed to integrate with and enhance the core subjects of math, science and communication arts. A pilot test was performed in fourth- and fifth-grade classes to assess student asthma knowledge gain, teacher acceptance and grade appropriateness of the curriculum. Paired t tests were used for each lesson taught, to evaluate pre-/post-test and classroom differences and focus groups were used for qualitative evaluation. Results showed a post test increase in asthma knowledge in both grades, individually and combined ($p < 0.001$) and intervention post-test scores were higher than four comparison classroom scores ($p < 0.001$). Teacher feedback indicated the lessons enhanced previously learned skills and increased students' overall understanding of the topic. It was concluded that the classroom activities provided an opportunity for all students to gain asthma knowledge and build health literacy about a leading chronic disease (Pike et al., 2011).

In their study, Naito, Nakayama, and Hamajima (2007) examined the acceptability and effectiveness of a new type of health literacy program for children. The program was organized in the form of a workshop by a dentist. Sixty-three students ranging in age from 11 to 12 years were divided into 14 groups. The discussion topic focused on the effectiveness of toothbrushing for preventing oral health problems. After a group discussion, participants received a lecture on appraising the quality of health information. Pre- and post-program questionnaire surveys were administered to assess the program. The post-program questionnaire survey revealed that 89% of participants easily understood the content of the program, and 76% found the program to be useful. These findings demonstrate the feasibility of using health literacy programs for schoolchildren. It was concluded health literacy programs for children can be developed and administered through collaborations between education and health professionals.

In a more recent classroom-based activity, Katz et al. (2011) employed a curriculum called Nutrition Detectives™. This program, designed to teach elementary school students and their parents to distinguish between more healthful and less healthful choices in diverse food categories was assessed in three schools. A sample of 1180 second, third and fourth grade students, 628 in the experimental group and 552 in the control group were studied.

The program, delivered by physical education instructors over several for a maximum of two hours involved learning how to identify and choose healthful foods. Results showed that the program increased nutrition label literacy significantly, especially among third graders. Parents too improved their ability to identify more nutritious foods. Since food intake is considered one of the most important risk factors underlying obesity and chronic health problems, this school-based effort, which was not time consuming seems to be a promising one to emulate.

2.2.2.   *Current Barriers to Achieving Optimal Health Literacy Among School-Aged Youth*

Although primary prevention that is achieved through health literacy instruction and practice in the classroom through health education may improve educational and social outcomes of today's children (Benham-Deal & Hodges, n.d.), among the various reasons why the problem of low health literacy prevails and cannot be readily resolved relate to the following issues:

1. The nature of traditional instructional units in the health realm that commonly focus on risky behaviours such as drugs, family life and sexuality may not necessarily help the student to develop the capacity to obtain, interpret and use this information competently to access services.
2. The reported widespread use of television as a means of entertainment, a medium that widely and routinely advertises unhealthy lifestyles to youth who often cannot readily discriminate healthy from unhealthy messages and behaviours, especially in the absence of any well-designed counter messages (Willeden et al., 2006) or media literacy skills may prove very potent.
3. The possibility that current school education programs are not developmentally appropriate, or tailored to accommodate the student's everyday lived experiences, their views and their social norms and areas of interest, and thus these do not engage them sufficiently or make them able or motivated to enact responsible choices (Gibbons & Naylor, 2007; Naylor & McKay, 2009).
4. The possibility of encountering poor role models in schools, the low focus on health as a priority subject area in the school, the use of non-health teachers to teach health, plus a broader environmental policy and infrastructure setting that does not support healthy decisions.
5. The possible assumption by school personnel that children are receiving health instruction in the home even though this may not be the case.

Research shows the low or limited health literacy skills of many caregivers today has a strong direct negative impact on many children's health (Abrams, Klass, & Dreyer, 2009), further limiting opportunities to acquire basic health-related skills needed to assure optimal health literacy, health behaviours and use of preventative care services across the lifespan (Sanders et al., 2009).

6. The reliance of youth, especially adolescents on technology for communication, accessing information, and generally adopting lifestyles exposed to on social media sites, which may or not provide credible or healthful sources of information or being (Ghadder et al., 2011).
7. The lower than average literacy levels of ethnic youths or minority populations (Ghadder et al., 2011), who are often difficult to reach with health services because of economic and socio-political barriers (Lee, 2009).
8. The failure of teachers to focus on developing their student's self-efficacy so that they can confidently be empowered to make healthy choices (Benham-Deal & Hodges, n.d.).
9. Instructional units do not offer a skills-based approach (Benham-Deal & Hodges, n.d.).
10. Evidence that young people are less willing to overcome barriers to health access than older people (Lee, 2009).

Unfortunately, too, educators or educational administrators may not be aware of the importance of health literacy, or the need to redesign curricula and methods of instruction delivery in school settings, along with paediatricians who are unaware of these health-literacy-related problems and the need for effective communication with families, and teachers themselves who are not health literate. Those who are aware or have the desired skills, in turn, may struggle to do anything about this due to the time demands required to implement such skills (Turner et al., 2009), particularly when entrenched institutionalized practices and policies pose obstacles to changing curricula and medical protocols.

As a result of the low priority placed on health education by policy makers and administrators, media exposure, socio-economic disadvantages and parental misconceptions about health, it is unsurprising that children today do not always have sufficient knowledge and the understandings needed to enable them to make wise personal healthy choices. Thus, despite much evidence that health literacy is a fundamental skill needed by the contemporary citizen, society may not be able to meet the health literacy needs of young people in the 21st century without making concerted efforts in this realm to mobilize policy makers and education administrators to implement comprehensive evidence-based programs that can help students access, understand and make appropriate science based and value judgments about health-related issues.

According to Nutbeam (2008), health literacy should be viewed as an asset that can be built and as an important outcome of health-related education. In addition, the ability to communicate one's health needs and issues affords greater empowerment in the context of decision-making. The ability to govern one's behaviour and make healthy choices requires teachers recognize the hierarchical and synergistic nature of health literacy and provide the means to achieve this through basic skills development, followed by interactive applications, and analysis.

2.2.3.   Are There Solutions to Meet This Set of Challenges?

In light of the overlapping barriers to fostering the health literacy of youth in the school setting, and that a positive culture for health would facilitate higher levels of health literacy (Lee, 2009), leading national education organizations are being urged to recognize the close relationship between health and education, as well as the need to foster health and well-being within, as well as beyond, the educational environment for all students. That is, effective multi-pronged strategies that have been evaluated indicate that if implemented strategically, these can provide the future adult with tools and skills to maximize their health and citizenship attributes. Indeed, multi-dimensional programs designed to improve academic performance are increasingly recognized as important public health interventions, and schools that can tailor health education instruction along with basic reading, writing, math and science skills to meet the developmental needs and challenges of students (Benham-Deal & Hodges, n.d.) can thus play a critical role in promoting the optimal health status and lifelong health behaviours that can impact health and productivity in highly positive ways (Centers for Disease Control and Prevention, Health and Academics, http://www.cdc.gov/HealthyYouth/health_and_academics/index.htm).

According to Abrams et al. (2009), helping children grow up with good general literacy skills will improve their health literacy and chance of effectively understanding and managing their own health and care, especially dietary behaviours (Reinaerts, Nooijer, Kar, & Vries, 2006). As well, school-oriented interventions can serve as an important upstream strategy to help prevent or attenuate the adoption of high risk health behaviours (Marks, 2009). Since health behaviours such as smoking often adopted during adolescence greatly impact the risk of future ill health as an adult (NIHCM, 2011), a strong imperative prevails for introducing interventions that can foster life-long literacy during critical developmental periods through exposure to research-based programs such as Reach Out and Read, early Head Start and universal preschool. Other ideas include:

- The creation of schools where all students are encouraged and enabled to read proficiently at their prevailing grade level.
- The creation of schools where those with reading and learning disabilities are identified early on and treated accordingly.
- The creation of schools where resources for fostering literacy and numeracy are made available and are offered as indicated.
- Improving the preparation of teachers, as well as school health instruction (Peterson, Cooper, & Laird, 2001), as well as recognizing the hierarchical nature of health literacy identified by Nutbeam (Benham-Deal & Hodges, n.d.).

In light of the growing importance of health literacy as a basic adult competency, as others before them have argued, Abrams et al. (2009) call for incorporating health literacy-related skills into standard kindergarten through 12th grade curricula. For Ghadder et al. (2011), advocating adolescent health literacy can serve to address and minimize current inequities and disparities in health outcomes, because youth constitute a group of dependent health-care system users who will eventually become independent users of the system. The goal of achieving critical health literacy is also consistent with those skills students need to master in order to succeed in work and life in the 21st century (Benham-Deal & Hodges, n.d.).

2.2.4. *Promoting School-Based Health Literacy*

As outlined in the preceding paragraphs, increasing research suggests that to attain the goal of achieving a more health literate populace, promoting the health literacy of younger generations is critical (Ghadder et al., 2011). To this end, one strategy for advancing this goal involves a collaboration between researchers, educators, school administrators and policy makers as well as parents, school health counsellors and nurses. Working together these stakeholders can help identify: the health literacy skills vital to their communities and community members, what can be taught through the educational system, where current curricular approaches in health education and other subjects need to be updated to account for newer dimensions of health-seeking behaviours, as well as local health issues among adolescents (Ghadder et al., 2011). The appropriate use of evidence-based strategies to develop efficacious lesson plans and curricula that can help advance critical personal, cognitive, social and analytic skills necessary for understanding their bodies and how their behaviours influence their health is recommended. Because there is a wide gap between the current presentation of most school-based health lessons in the classroom and the health information seeking behaviours of youth (Ghadder et al., 2011), opportunities for learning how to obtain and evaluate the accuracy and trustworthiness of health information is critical in a world where access to information is less of a problem than understanding what is being written or discussed. Moreover, as outlined by Abrams et al. (2009) such efforts are likely to work most effectively if they begin with preschool curricula that can reinforce health promotion activities among toddlers and their caregivers, rather than later on. Hence standardizing kindergarten through 12th grade curricula to teach health literacy competencies across all educational disciplines including science, mathematics, reading, social studies, health and physical education is deemed crucial and highly recommended. Adult-education modules that teach health literacy skills in environments that are designed to foster general educational development (GED) and English-as-a-second-language curricula are strongly indicated as well to enhance the literacy skills of those adults who have trouble reading. As supplemental strategies, health literacy activities integrated into after-school, camp, literacy programs, community centres, health-care centres, home-visiting and community-based parenting programs can potentially help reinforce the novice learner to appreciate and act on the manifold attributes of health and related competencies that lead to the development of health literacy.

Sanders et al. (2009) have specifically proposed a developmental model for attaining health literacy skills that suggests school age children be able to apply adequate reading, verbal and expressive skills as well as numeracy and navigational skills. Similarly because adolescents and young adults are also expected to be able to understand and act on complex health information, including decisions that impact them personally, they indicate adolescents too require these skills albeit at a more advanced level. Accordingly, in maintaining that schools have a fundamental role to play in the develop-ment of health literate populations, Benham-Deal and Hodges (n.d.) suggest classroom-based health education as a specific discipline be supplemented by mathematics, arts, science, social studies, language arts, as well as physical education and nutrition services.

Donald Nutbeam has proposed a three tier model of health literacy development involving basic or functional literacy, communicative or interactive literacy and critical literacy. Since considerable research points to the importance of health and health promotion in maximizing learning outcomes, St. Leger and Nutbeam (St. Leger, 2001) proposed the health promoting school or whole school approach to addressing health and social issues because these can potentially provide youth with adequate building blocks to achieve both health and educational outcomes that are fundamental to health literacy.

These four school-related learning outcomes include the acquisition of (a) lifelong learning skills; (b) appropriate health-related competencies and behaviours; (c) adequate knowledge and skills; and (d) self-attributes and self-efficacy. These are all said to be dependent on students attaining all three levels of health literacy as proposed by Nutbeam. Adhering to national and state health education standards, as well as collaborations across the school sectors, educators can specifically foster the student's competencies to become active members of society, members who are empowered to act autonomously, rather than those who commonly only help students develop very basic reading and writing skills, or knowledge, alone.

Given their heightened vulnerability to poor health literacy, children living in poverty who are found to acquire language and reading skills more slowly (Aikens & Barbarin, 2008; Wyner, Bridgeland, & Dilulio, 2007) should be specifically targeted, and their early participation in quality childhood education programs, plus placing emphasis on contemporary evidence-based health education classroom curricula and basic literacy skills development is especially recommended (Benham-Deal & Hodges, n.d.; Zaza, Briss, & Harris, 2005). As with more able youth, all should be afforded opportunities to participate and learn more about their own health (Zaza et al., 2005).

Teaching the elements of health and literacy in schools, and focusing on lessons that evoke higher order thinking, communication, problem solving and decision-making skills, children can succeed more ably, and they may experience better health. Likewise, the intentional, meaningful, and continuous involvement of young people in well-designed programs from Pre K-12 will help youth to develop the confidence to participate as thoughtful active partners in decisions that affect them individually and collectively. This 'life-course' approach to promoting health behaviour should begin early in life, and include the inputs of the health promoting school or school structures such as food services, and counselling services.

Helping youth to keep up with evolving health issues, plus current technological advances is also a crucial aspect of the education process. For example, given that technologies that are currently in the pipeline will vastly advance the field of personal genetics, Kung and Gelbart (2012) suggest we do all we can to ensure our current and future generations of students will be well informed about the science, benefits, risks and ethical issues related to genetic testing. At a more basic level, recent qualitative research has shown the need to address low levels of oral health literacy among young boys ages 5–7 by developing their functional health literacy, and schools were implicated as the ideal site in which such an initiative could occur with the added benefit of concomitant knowledge transfer back to the family home (Drummond & Drummond, 2012).

In contrast to the detrimental impact of limited health literacy on long-term outcomes shown in Box 2.2, the role of education in attenuating these

---

Box 2.2.   Health-Associated Impact of Health Illiteracy

- Low adherence to medical regimens (DeWalt & Hink, 2009).
- Health risk behaviours are increased (DeWalt & Hink, 2009).
- Child depressive symptoms and withdrawn behaviour problems are rife (DeWalt & Hink, 2009).
- Child diabetes control is suboptimal (DeWalt & Hink, 2009).
- Enormous societal and medical costs are incurred.
- Higher incidence of emergency department visits, hospitalizations and missed school days are reported (DeWalt & Hink, 2009).
- Health disparities are magnified.
- Optimal educational attainment may be impeded.
- Preteenaged tobacco usage (DeWalt & Hink, 2009), associated with dropping out of high school, low commitment to school, academic failure and poor achievement (Townsend, Flisher, & King, 2007) may increase.
- Students' health, well-being and quality of life may be lowered (St. Leger, 2001; Wharf Higgins et al., 2009, p. 352).

---

outcomes may yield students who are not only educated about health and healthy lifestyle choices but also may grow into happier, healthier and more productive adults. Because those who are health literate are more likely to have the skills to better achieve and maintain their physical, social and emotional health, they will be better able to contribute to the nation's economic competitiveness by working more effectively, missing fewer days from work due to injury and illness, and by using fewer medical services, and health insurance benefits. They may also be more empowered on behalf of themselves and others (McGovern, 2010).

To summarize, related studies in the United States and elsewhere (e.g. Carlson et al., 2008) provide increasing evidence that health-related instruction, which can foster health literacy, can significantly improve academic achievement. In addition, youth exposed to health-associated instructions may exhibit heightened motivation for schooling, reduced absenteeism and suspensions. Not surprisingly, initiatives that foster health-related personal and social skills are found to yield improved test scores, grades and graduation rates. In turn, academic success, a predictor of the overall well-being of youth, is a primary predictor and determinant of adult health status (Eggert, Thompson, Herting, Nicholas, & Dicker, 1994; Flay et al., 2001; Hawkins, Catalano, Kosterman, Abbott, & Hill, 1999).

To achieve a desirable outcome for future, citizens St. Leger (2001) believed good schools that apply quality teaching and learning approaches will foster the achievement of the three levels of health literacy proposed by Nutbeam (2000). As indicated by St. Leger, schools that work diligently towards the goal of helping their students to become critical thinkers and provide a participatory collegial support system for students will build a strong basis for attaining both functional and interactive and critical health literacy. The latter component of health literacy is deemed especially crucial for enabling the student leaving the school to become a member of society that can help him or herself to improve opportunities for health for themselves as well as for others.

St. Leger (2001) described three challenges to schools embracing critical health literacy that remain relevant in this decade: (a) the school structure; (b) teachers, practices and skills; (c) time and resources. According to Benham-Deal and Hodges (n.d.), emphasizing 21st-century instructional skills, practice and assessment, in the health class, as well as in mathematics, science, social studies, English language arts and involving all academic disciplines can enhance the health literacy skills of youths and future adults both within and beyond the educational system. Indeed, without a well-developed health curriculum, administrative support for its implementation, knowledgeable staff, plus an appropriate evaluation component (Ghadder et al., 2011), schools are likely to produce less than optimal educational and health outcomes for their students.

As this chapter has discussed, among the many domains where improvements can be made to foster health literacy, the educational system, schools and continuing education institutes play a major role (Kickbusch & Maag, 2008) in teaching children to make healthy choices on a daily basis. As such, and following in the leadership of Nutbeam and St. Leger, Kickbusch and Maag argue health literacy must become a focus or central element of school agendas (2008, p. 204). The health promoting school approach, similar to the Coordinated School Health Program approach, can undoubtedly empower students quite markedly to develop optimal health and critical thinking related skills, to respond to health challenges with confidence and to achieve beneficial societal outcomes, and consequently this approach appears strongly encouraged.

References

Abrams, M. A., Klass, P., & Dreyer, B. P. (2009). Health literacy and children: Recommendations for action. *Pediatrics, 124*, S327–S331.

Aikens, N. L., & Barbarin, O. (2008). Socioeconomic differences in reading trajectories: The contribution of the family, neighbourhood, and school contexts. *Journal of Educational Psychology, 100*, 235–251.

American Association for Health Education. (2008). *Health literacy: A position statement of the American Association of Health Education.* HExtra. Reston, VA: author.

Barwick, M. A., & Siegel, L. S. (1996). Learning difficulties in adolescent clients of a shelter for runaway and homeless street youths. *Journal of Research on Adolescence, 6,* 649–670.

Beaudoin, C. (2011). Twenty years of comprehensive school health: A review and analysis of Canadian research published in refereed journals (1989–2009). *PHENex Journal, 3*(1), 1–17.

Begoray, D. L., Wharf Higgins, J., & MacDonald, M. (2009). High school health curriculum and health literacy: Canadian student voices. *Global Health Promotion, 16,* 35–42.

Beitchman, J. H., Wilson, B., & Douglas, L. (2001). Substance use disorders in young adults with and without LD: Predictive and concurrent relationships. *Journal of Learning Disabilities, 34,* 317–332.

Benham-Deal, T. B., & Hodges, B. (n.d.). Role of 21st Century Schools in Promoting Health Literacy. National Education Association Health Information Network. Retrieved from http://www.neahin.org/educator-resources/health-literacy/benhamdeal-hodges-paper.pdf. Accessed on June 9, 2012.

Berge, J. M., Bauer, K. W., Eisenberg, M. E., Denny, K., & Neumark-Sztainer, D. (2012). Psychosocial and health behavior outcomes of young adults with asthma or diabetes. *Community Medicine and Health Education, 2,* 4.

Betz, C. L., Ruccione, K., Meeske, K., Smith, K., & Chang, N. (2008). Health literacy: A pediatric concern. *Pediatric Nursing, 34,* 231–239.

Cale, L., & Harris, J. (2006). School-based physical activity interventions: Effectiveness, trends, issues, implications and recommendations for practice. *Sport, Education and Society, 11*(4), 401–420.

Carlson, S. A., Fulton, J. E., Lee, S. M., Maynard, M., Drown, D. R., Kohl, H. W., III., & Dietz, W. H. (2008). Physical education and academic achievement in elementary school: Data from the Early Childhood Longitudinal Study. *American Journal of Public Health, 98,* 721–727.

Davis, T. C., Byrd, R. S., Arnold, C. L., Auinger, P., & Bocchini, J. A. (1999). Low literacy and violence among adolescents in a summer sports program. *Journal of Adolescent Health, 24,* 403–411.

Deaton, A. (2002). Policy implications of the gradient of health and wealth: An economist asks, would redistributing income improve population health? *Health Affairs, 21,* 13–30.

DeWalt, D. A., & Hink, A. (2009). Health literacy and child health outcomes: A systematic review of the literature. *Pediatrics, 124,* S265–S274.

Diamond, C., Saintonge, S., August, P., & Azrack, A. (2011). The development of building wellness™, a youth health literacy program. *Journal of Health Communication, 16*(Suppl 3), 103–118.

Drummond, M., & Drummond, C. (2012). Boys and their teeth: A qualitative investigation of boys' oral health in early childhood. *Journal of Child Health Care.* Epub ahead of print, May 7.

Eggert, L. L., Thompson, E. A., Herting, J. R., Nicholas, L. J., & Dicker, B. G. (1994). Preventing adolescent drug abuse and high school dropout through an intensive school based social network development program. *American Journal of Health Promotion*, *8*, 202–215.

Ferguson, L. A., & Pawlak, R. (2011). Health literacy: The road to improved health outcomes. *The Journal for Nurse Practitioners*, *7*, 123–129.

Flay, B., Allred, C. G., & Ordway, C. (2001). Effects of the positive action program on achievement and discipline: Two matched-control comparisons. *Prevention Science*, *2*, 71–89.

Fletcher, J., Shaywitz, S., Shankweiler, D., Katz, L., Liberman, I., Stuebing, K., ... Shaywitz, A. (1994). Cognitive profiles of reading disability: Comparisons of discrepancy and low achievement definitions. *Journal of Educational Psychology*, *86*, 6–23.

Freedman, D. A., Bess, K. D., Tucker, H. A., Boyd, D. I., Tuchman, A. M., & Wallston, K. A. (2009). Public health literacy defined. *American Journal of Preventive Medicine*, *36*, 446–451.

Gans, A. M., Kenny, M. C., & Ghany, D. L. (2003). Comparing the self concept of students with and without learning disabilities. *Journal of Learning Disabilities*, *36*, 287–296.

Ghadder, S. F., Valerio, M. A., Garcia, C. M., & Hansen, L. (2011). Adolescent health literacy: The importance of credible sources for online health information. *Journal of School Health*, *82*, 28–36.

Gibbons, S., & Naylor, P. J. (2007). Whole school obesity prevention models: Considerations for secondary schools. *Physical and Health Education Journal*, *72*(4), 8–13.

Hawkins, J., Catalano, R., Kosterman, R., Abbott, R., & Hill, K. (1999). Preventing adolescent health-risk behaviors by strengthening protection during childhood. *Archives of Pediatric Adolescent Medicine*, *153*, 226–234.

Institute of Medicine. (2004). *Health literacy: A prescription to end confusion*. Washington, DC: National Academic Press.

Joint Committee on National Health Education Standards. (2007). *National health education standards: Achieving excellence*. Atlanta, GA: American Cancer Society.

Kansas Head Start Association. (2012). Health Literacy. Retrieved from http://www.kheadstart.org/node/90

Katz, D. L., Katz, C. S., Treu, J. A., Reynolds, J., Njike, V., Walker, J., ... Michael, J. (2011). Teaching healthful food choices to elementary school students and their parents: The Nutrition Detectives™ program. *Journal of School Health*, *81*, 21–28.

Kickbusch, I. (2008). Health literacy: An essential skill for the twenty-first century. *Health Education*, *108*, 101–104.

Kickbusch, I. (2009). Health literacy: Engaging in a political debate. *International Journal of Public Health*, *54*, 131–132.

Kickbusch, I., & Maag, D. (2008). Health literacy. In K. Heggenhougen & S. Quah (Eds.), *International encyclopedia of public health* (Vol. 3, pp. 204–211). San Diego: Academic Press.

Kung, J. T., & Gelbart, M. E. (2012). Getting a head start: The importance of personal genetics education in high schools. *Yale Journal of Biology and Medicine*, *85*, 87–92.

Kutcher, S., & Wei, Y. (2012). Mental health and the school environment: Secondary schools, promotion and pathways to care. *Current Opinion in Psychiatry, 25*(4), 311–316.

Lee, A. (2009). Health promoting schools: Evidence for a holistic approach to promoting health and improving health literacy. *Applied Health Economics and Health Policy, 7*, 11–17.

Manganello, J. (2008). Health literacy and adolescents: A framework and agenda for future research. *Health Education Research, 23*, 840–847.

Marks, R. (2009). Schools and health education: What works, what is needed, and why? *Health Education, 109*, 4–8.

Massey, P. M., Prelip, M., Calimlin, B. M., Quiter, E. S., & Glik, D. C. (2012). Contextualizing an expanded definition of health literacy among adolescents in the health care setting. *Health Education Research*. Epub ahead of print, May 21.

Mayer, A. B., Smith, B. J., & McDermott, R. J. (2011). Health education: Always approved but still not always on schools' radar. *American Journal of Health Education, 42*, 349–359.

McBride, H., & Siegel, L. S. (1997). Learning disabilities and adolescent suicide. *Journal of Learning Disabilities, 30*, 652–659.

McGovern, E. (2010). *Health literacy: Our children and the future.* Institute for America's Health. Retrieved from http://healthy-america.org/?p = 616. Accessed on June 13, 2012.

Naito, M., Nakayama, T., & Hamajima, N. (2007). Health literacy education for children: Acceptability of a school-based program in oral health. *Journal of Oral Science, 49*, 53–59.

National Action Plan to Improve Health Literacy. U.S. Department of Health and Human Services, Office of Disease Prevention and Promotion. (2010). Retrieved from http://www.health.giv/communication/HLActionPlan/

National Institute for Health Care Management. NIHCM Foundation. (2011, October). The case for investing in youth health literacy: One step on the path to achieving health equity for adolescents. NIHCM Foundation Issue brief, Washington, DC. pp. 1–15.

Naylor, P. J., & McKay, H. (2009). Prevention in the first place: Schools a setting for action on physical inactivity. *British Journal of Sports Medicine, 43*(1), 10–13.

Nutbeam, D. (2000). Health literacy as a public health goal: A challenge for contemporary health education and communication strategies into the 21st century. *Health Promotion International, 15*, 259–268.

Nutbeam, D. (2008). The evolving concept of health literacy. *Social Science in Medicine, 67*, 2072–2078.

Nutbeam, D. (2009). Building health literacy in Australia. *Medical Journal of Australia, 191*, 525–526.

Paasche-Orlow, M., & Wolf, M. (2007). The causal pathways linking health literacy to health outcomes. *American Journal of Health Behavior, 31*, 19–26.

Peterson, F. L., Cooper, R. J., & Laird, J. M. (2001). Enhancing teacher health literacy in school health promotion: A vision for the new millennium. *Journal of School Health, 71*, 138–144.

Pike, E. V., Richmond, C. M., Hobson, A., Kleiss, J., Wottowa, J., & Sterling, D. A. (2011). Development and evaluation of an integrated asthma awareness curriculum for the elementary school classroom. *Journal of Urban Health*, *88*(Suppl 1), 61–67.

Reinaerts, E., Nooijer, J. D., Kar, A. V. D., & Vries, N. D. (2006). Development of a school-based intervention to promote fruit and vegetable consumption: Exploring perceptions among 4-to-12-year old children and their parents. *Health Education*, *106*, 345–356.

Rootman, I., & Ronson, B. (2005). Literacy and health research in Canada: Where have we been and where should we go? *Canadian Journal of Public Health*, *96*, S62–S77.

Sabornie, E. J. (1994). Social-affective characteristics in early adolescents identified as learning disabled and nondisabled. *Learning Disabilities Quarterly*, *17*, 268–279.

Sanders, L. M., Federico, S., Klass, P., Abrams, M. A., & Dreyer, B. (2009). Literacy and child health: A systematic review. *Archives of Pediatric and Adolescent Medicine*, *163*, 131–140.

Sanders, L. M., Shaw, J. S., Guez, G., Baur, C., & Rudd, R. (2009). Health literacy and child health promotion: Implications for research, clinical care, and public policy. *Pediatrics*, *124*, S306–S314.

Society for Public Health Education. (2011). *health instruction K-12 improves academic achievement and health literacy while reducing risk behaviors that interfere with achievement*. Fact Sheet for School and Public Health Administrators. Retrieved from http://www.sophe.org

St. Leger, L. (2001). Schools, health literacy and public health: Possibilities and challenges. *Health Promotion International*, *16*, 197–205.

Townsend, L., Flisher, A. J., & King, G. (2007). A systematic review of the relationship between high school dropout and substance abuse. *Clinical Child and Family Psychology*, *10*, 295–317.

Turner, T., Cull, W. L., Bayldon, B., Klass, P., Sanders, L. M., Frintner, M. P., … Dreyer, B. (2009). Pediatricians and health literacy: Descriptive results from a National Survey. *Pediatrics*, *124*, S299–S305.

Vardavas, C. I., Kondilis, B. K., Patelarou, E., Akrivos, P. D., & Falagas, M. E. (2009). Health literacy and sources of health education among adolescents in Greece. *International Journal of Adolescent Medicine and Health*, *21*, 179–186.

Waldie, K., & Spreen, O. (1993). The relationship between learning disabilities and persisting delinquency. *Journal of Learning Disabilities*, *6*, 417–423.

Wharf Higgins, J., Begoray, D., & MacDonald, M. (2009). A social ecological conceptual framework for understanding adolescent health literacy in the health education classroom. *American Journal of Community Psychology*, *44*, 350–362.

Willeden, M., Taylor, R. W., McAuley, K. A., Simpson, J. C., Oakley, M., & Mann, J. I. (2006). The APPLE project: An investigation of the barriers and promoters of healthy eating and physical activity in New Zealand children aged 5–12 years. *Health Education Journal*, *65*, 135–148.

Wyner, J. S., Bridgeland, J. M., & Dilulio, J. J. (2007). *Achievement trap: How America is failing millions of high-achieving strudents from lower-income families*. Landsdowne, VA: Jack Kent Cooke Foundation.

Zaza, S., Briss, P., & Harris, K. W. (Eds.). (2005). *The guide to community preventive services: What works to promote public health?* New York, NY: Oxford University Press.

Zins, J. E., Bloodworth, M. R., Weissberg, R. P., & Walberg, H. J. (2004). The scientific base linking social and emotional learning to school success. In *Building academic success on social and emotional learning: What does the research say?* New York, NY: Teachers College Press.

Chapter 3

Healthy Literacy Skills Needed by Children, Teachers and Parents

Ray Marks and Joan Wharf Higgins

> *Developing health literacy will empower children and students to make informed choices and decisions about their health and wellbeing.*
>
> Tricia Knott, Program and Policy Officer, H&PE, DECS

As recounted in the preceding chapters, health literacy is a discrete form of literacy (Kickbusch, 2001), fundamental to wellbeing in the 21st century. Encompassing the cognitive and social skills which determine the motivation and ability of individuals to gain access to, understand and use information in ways which promote and maintain good health, health literacy is increasingly crucial for ensuring optimal social, economic, and health development. To paraphrase the oft cited quote of Nutbeam (2000), health literacy is more than the simple ability to read pamphlets and successfully make appointments, it influences behavioural choices and health-related decisions, and is one of the many skills needed by today's adult in order to function effectively in any society. Health literacy is especially critical to empowerment (WHO, 2010) and the ability to carry out informed decisions that influence health status.

Children, along with most adults, may currently experience large gaps in their understanding of health-related issues even though, according to Dr. Frank Keil at Yale University, research strongly suggests children of all ages have the potential to understand a great deal about health and about how to access health information. In as much as health literacy helps

Health Literacy and School-Based Health Education
Copyright © 2012 by Emerald Group Publishing Limited
All rights of reproduction in any form reserved
ISBN: 978-1-78052-306-4

people to access, utilize and comprehend messages related to self-care (Paasche-Orlow & Wolf, 2007), Keil argues that more attention should be paid to the ways in which children can grasp cause–effect relationships in the world around them and how they can use these relationships to reason more powerfully and effectively, both about health and about providers of health information (Proceedings, http://www.ncbi.nlm.nih.gov/books/NBK44263/).

Indeed, given that half of all premature deaths are related to health-risk behaviours often acquired during youth (Lee, 2009), where an array of risky behaviours commonly prevails (Paek, Reber, & Larsy, 2011), particularly among low literate youth (DeWalt & Hink, 2009), it is thus unsurprising that schools have been deemed as critical in producing, developing and achieving the goal of an optimally health literate youth (St. Leger, 2001). As well as strong evidence that low literacy/health literacy is associated with risky behaviours and lower levels of health-promoting behaviours (Ghaddar, Valerno, Garcia, & Hansen, 2011), there are also strong links between learning and health, and evidence that better learning and being 'health literate' results in better health and wellbeing. Alternately, if schools do not equip youth with health literacy skills, including the knowledge and skills to avoid health risks and to be as healthy as possible, the academic achievement and health gap between the haves and have-nots will be likely to increase, rather than decrease.

As outlined by the World Health Organization (WHO) in 1996, as well as by the World Bank, the link between poverty and poor health status is very strong and poor health literacy (due to poor formal education) is one of its root causes (Flecha, Garcia, & Rudd, 2011). Evidence of the link between health literacy and education, between education and development, and that lack of health care literacy leads to health care access and outcome inequalities (Volandes & Paasche-Orlow, 2007), speaks to the strength of the calls for promoting health literacy during formative learning years. As Dr. Keil and colleagues from Yale University have argued 'that from preschool years onward, there are tremendous benefits to be gained from teaching health-related concepts in ways that connect that information to coherent causal biological accounts' (Keil, 2006, Proceedings, Panel 2, http://www.ncbi.nlm.nih.gov/books/NBK44263/).

However, it is clear very few teachers, administrators, parents or health professionals are in a position to fully understand the importance of health literacy in general, and in the school as a unit of practice, in particular. They may also lack time and resources, or desired competencies needed to promote all three aspects of health literacy and their core constructs (see Table 3.1).

In addition, children living in poverty, whose parents may lack formal or complete education and/or low literacy and confidence to make appropriate

Table 3.1: Summary of the three core aspects of health literacy.

Basic literacy including:
  Ability to read
  Ability to interpret numbers and instructions
  Ability to comprehend health information
Interactive and participatory literacy including:
  Ability to participate in health discussions
  Ability to act on information
Critical literacy
  Ability to weigh scientific facts and assess
  Competing alternatives

Source: Adapted from Marks (2009).

health care decisions for themselves and their children are further disadvantaged (Kansas Head Start Association, 2012). This is compounded by a lack of time and exposure to health-related books at home, second language problems, the changing family structure and the failure of schools to focus on health issues in an era of competing classroom topics. Consequently, it is extremely unrealistic to expect all children will become sufficiently empowered to make healthy choices across the lifespan and have skills to take greater control of their lives in general, solely on the basis of their family-based influences.

At a more macro level, consistent exposure to environmental and social factors that foster poor health and mixed messages about health, a medical environment that focuses on curative rather than preventive medicine, a medical model that focuses on physical well being rather than on holistic health, among other factors, further stymies efforts to both address as well as achieve those skills youth need currently to become health literate without considerable thought, energies and resources. Unfortunately, although there are now many thousands of publications that discuss adult health literacy, literacy challenges and their solutions, very limited attention has been devoted to understanding the effects of health literacy on child health outcomes (DeWalt & Hink, 2009) and adolescent health literacy and its unique determinants (Paek et al., 2011), especially within the school environment (Ghaddar et al., 2011)

If as Ilona Kickbusch (2001, p. 2) states, health literacy is about the life skills needed to navigate modern society, and the choices we make in everyday life that influence our health and wellbeing, it is clear that the outcome of health literacy is not likely to occur automatically. Rather, it needs to be fostered by systematic measures which can increase individual knowledge and skills, as well as by policies and environments that encourage healthy choices, and includes basic literacy skills related to reading, writing, speaking and listening. Basic mathematical skills and conceptual knowledge skills are also components of health literacy (Rudd, 2006).

This process of enabling individuals to read, understand and act on health formation in daily life, often discussed solely in the context of the adult health care environment, must clearly start from the earliest years, and follow a hierarchical process (Nutbeam, 1998) embedded in the classroom, and in the school as a whole in order to improve both personal health and health outcomes in later life. As discussed in Chapter 2, as a place where young people spend considerable time during their formative years, schools offer an ideal setting for helping youth to become health literate through well-designed curricula and the provision of a holistic supportive environment (Lee, 2009). This chapter focuses on topics that need to be covered as well as broad strategies that might be helpful in any effort to promote school-based health literacy and children's confidence to critically evaluate health information, as well as teachers and family members' needs in this respect.

According to Begoray, Wharf Higgins, and MacDonald (2009), society believes being knowledgeable and health literate is a critical skill needed by all future citizens. As such, today's youth need to be efficacious in both in accessing health information, as well as in navigating an increasingly complex, constantly changing, and dense health information landscape. Specific health issues they need to understand include, but are not limited to, diabetes; asthma; tobacco usage and smoking, drug use and abuse; risky sexual behaviours; bullying; overweight/obesity, and physical inactivity (Marx, Hudson, Deal, Pateman, & Middleton, 2007).

Yet, even though healthy living, health information, healthy relationships and effective health decisions are deemed important health-related topics by youth (Begoray et al., 2009), today's youth may not be able to acquire these skills without the concerted efforts of policy makers, as well as educators and school administrators. Unlike students in past decades who were recipients of health messages deemed sufficient to arm them as adults against risky health practices, today's youth who may be insufficiently informed on major health issues (Vardavas, Kondilis, Patelarou, Akrivos, & Falagas, 2009). Such generational differences may be accounted for by increased exposure to complex competing messages, a dizzying array of accessible and affordable unhealthy choices, and adverse peer, parental and multiple environmental influences that can all impact their ability to make sound health decisions, or to act on these, or both in the absence of appropriate school-based educational efforts. In addition to the glamorizing of unhealthy behaviours and images, such as being excessively thin, challenges imposed by the strong influence of social media, and time spent on sedentary activities involving media, youth are consistently exposed to media marketing of unhealthy products and practices. Access to media marketing has never been as effortless and portable, inviting youth to engage with it anywhere, anyway and anytime. Lacking access to health information through the media is not the issue, rather it is youths' critical ability to sift through the good, the bad and the ambiguous (Begoray, Cimon, & Wharf Higgins, 2010). At the same time, youth may not be able to discuss sensitive issues in a family context, may not be able to access or decode, or act on positive public health media, in addition to not having a regular health provider, or a health literate parent or caregiver. Additionally, while teachers and the curricula they implement are not the only determinants of health literacy among students (Wharf Higgins et al., 2009), challenges to achieving this goal exist given that teacher health literacy may be limited (Peterson, Cooper, & Laird, 2001). Current health curricula in schools may lack developmental specificity, personal and/or cultural relevance or are taught in isolation in an environment that is itself not considered health promoting.

To prevent the onset of one or more preventable chronic health conditions, and health risk behaviours that impair health, young people must clearly not only be able to access appropriate sources of health information, resources and services, but must be able to appraise these as well as discriminate between health-promoting and health-negating messages and practices, in the face of a multitude of competing health-related claims and practices continuously generated via the internet, printed or television-related media sources (Harris & Bargh, 2009). They must also be able to act on the information they receive, and be able to communicate effectively with their teachers, coaches, counsellors, parents, peers and physicians regarding health-related issues.

At the same time, new health challenges, such as childhood obesity have reached unprecedented proportions, and warrant the insightful development of strategies including health literacy to prevent this costly universal epidemic. Yet, it is clear from the research that societies have not adequately predicted the need to prepare citizens for this or how to deal effectively with other health-related issues such as the effect on health of biohazards, depression, anorexia, cancer, HIV/Aids, and how to best access medical assistance (Begoray et al., 2009). Formal programmes on health literacy in schools have also reportedly failed because they have not taken into account the teachers' and family members' needs (Flecha et al., 2011).

Adding to the challenges that need to be overcome to successfully foster student's health literacy in the context of classroom-based health education and other related sites, is the perceived need to enhance the capacity of teachers to obtain, interpret and understand health information in a way that will enhance students' learning (Peterson et al., 2001). In addition, a more inclusive approach involving families in health discussions that affect children from vulnerable groups, and empowering them to make appropriate decisions about their health, affords the school an opportunity to become an active partner in local efforts to overcome health inequalities and to strengthen social cohesion (Flecha et al., 2011). Some of the numerous issues children, teachers and parents need to be discerning about in this realm and others are:

- What websites and information are trustworthy?
- What other sources of information are there?
- What is the nature of the information being imparted and who is responsible for the content? They also need to understand if the health-related information is complete, science-based, unbiased and up to date.

Unsurprisingly, Brown and Witherspoon (2002) wonder why

> Given the ubiquity of unhealthy behavior presented in teen's media and the accumulating evidence that these portrayals and images do have an effect on those who read, view, and listen to them, we might well wonder why adolescent are as healthy as they are. Why are they not all drunk, chain-smoking, anorexic, fat, or pregnant gun-toters? Of course, the answer is the media are not the sole cause of the health status of our youth. Adolescents come to the media with individual characteristics, and from families and communities that already have pushed them in certain directions and that have provided models of healthy and unhealthy behavior. Those perceptions and experiences will influence what effect the media have on their health in the future (p. 165).

Yet as Kickbusch reports, despite a growing list of critical literacies needed for 21st century societies — such as media, consumer and financial literacy, digital literacy and information society literacy and health and environmental literacy — none of them currently feature very prominently in the school curriculum. There are also gaps in basic literacy and numeracy skills between students from more versus less advantaged families that impact their health status as well as their ability to become health literate. Mental health literacy, a possible factor in the early detection and prompt treatment of mental, emotional and behavioural disorders among young people, has been found to be limited among adolescents in classrooms in a small town in the eastern United States as well as in Australia (Olsson & Kennedy, 2010). Similarly, limited e-literacy, as represented by difficulties regarding functional, critical, and interactive skills, was found among 157 adolescent students, aged 11–19, in diverse geographical and socioeconomic settings in the United Kingdom (UK) and United States (Gray, Klein, Noyce, Sesselberg, & Cantrill, 2005). Difficulties in accessing online information, not knowing which search engines to trust, and how to decode health-related information if one can access this are further documented challenges (Gray et al., 2005).

Consequently, the ability to make choices, absolutely relevant to health in some way — in terms of what we eat, how much we should move, what products we should buy or not buy — whether we should take action or not — and many other day to day questions linked to health, are not generally taught in any systematic or effective way from the earliest years, despite adequate long-term research to support this approach. Thus, even though health literacy entails the ability to make sound health decisions in the context of everyday life — at home, in the community, at school, at the workplace, in the health care system, in the market place and in the political arena — it cannot be assumed young people today will simply absorb these skills and attributes over time in today's highly health negating social, economic, technological and cultural context without any intervention. For example, despite widespread access and usage of electronic resources by adolescents, youth will clearly only derive maximum benefit from this information resource if they are able to search for, evaluate and use its online information effectively (Gray et al., 2005), and of course have equal access to the technology and language-based information pieces. Moreover, since health is a multi-dimensional construct with physical, mental, and social wellbeing components, among others, and many youth today are already in a health-compromised state, advancing health literacy among youth, while imperative, is consequently a multi-layered task where basic competencies and resources may not be well correlated, and variation, rather than uniformity may preside. As a result it appears reasonable to suggest that a broad range of health, media, internet, digital and related literacy learning objectives and appropriate lesson plans that are sequential and action oriented need to be embedded in the context and curricula of a health promoting school environment (Lee, 2009) and supported by integrative approaches that are cohesive and culturally adapted (Flecha et al., 2011, p. 216). In Chapter 4, Wharf Higgins, Begoray and colleagues share their experiences in high-school and middle-school classrooms with media and health literacy and confirm recommendations for early intervention and curricula integration.

In this regard, as well as educating children and adolescents who will constitute the future generation, teachers and administrators, like parents, need to be similarly informed about aspects of their day to day school-based classroom practices and environment, as well as the home and cultural environment, that can jeopardize a child's health, or promote lifelong unhealthy behaviours. Both teachers and parents may not realize:

- Soft drinks at school can be as dangerous and habit forming as cigarettes;
- Getting children to move is as important as their cognitive development; and
- Teaching them to respect one another has important mental health dimensions.

Teachers may not realize that their own behaviours can be noticed and modelled readily, and that they can influence better health choices through their own actions in the classroom, school, community and home settings. They themselves might therefore benefit from some form of education in this regard.

Parents, as well as policy makers and administrators, may also not fully appreciate that school settings are particularly effective sites for enhancing health literacy, as well as basic literacy and numeracy skills, plus opportunities for imparting consistent health messages and the means to increase other critical literacies. Schools help youth to develop life skills, skills for making effective judgments and choices, as well as offering supportive and safe environments that make the healthier choice the easier choice. If given the opportunity, children can learn about what creates health and what are the most important health determinants of chronic non-communicable diseases, as well as communicable diseases, violence and injuries associated with premature disability and death.

An improvement in health literacy can not only reduce the health burden presently affecting people globally, but can also contribute to lowering and overcoming inequalities in health, while empowering motivation and interest, self esteem, critical thinking abilities and perceived control and intentions to act.

In terms of the obesity epidemic alone, schools can play a critical role in developing students' health literacy in this area, by improving their understanding of messages about food they see in the media and in the marketplace. For example, as discussed in Chapter 4, teaching youth the truth about TV food ads, and critically appraising the marketing techniques used and information provided, will potentially help children make more informed choices about the foods advertised, and hence about their own food choices. This topic, which has many determinants, can be potentially be more successfully addressed through the combined lessons embedded in English, Health and Physical Education, Mathematics, Science, Biology, and Technology Learning Areas, among others, than in Health Education alone.

For example, collaborative teaching about TV food ads and how foods cause obesity and diseases can:

- Help youth develop critical literacy skills;
- Develop an understanding of the types of foods promoted in TV food ads;
- Develop an understanding of the marketing techniques used in TV food ads; and
- Learn about healthy eating, how to measure obesity, how to evaluate food labels, how foods affect biology and how and why one should make healthful food choices.

Developing children's health literacy in the school setting in a holistic manner, rather than solely relying on traditional Health and Physical Education classes, strengthens and reinforces health literacy strategies and is likely to impact more readily on reducing the global disease burden than not. The more youth are exposed to similar aspects of key topics and have a chance to apply these, the more opportunities they will have to become health literate. As well as being consistently exposed to a comprehensive science-based curriculum, schools, preschools and childcare sites can all play a part in developing health literacy in children and young people by creating safe and healthy environments, and by providing a source of positive role models.

To this end, teachers from different learning areas including both health and education areas, plus personnel from school health services, as well as administrators and others might work collaboratively to develop a cross curriculum approach as well as a positive health promoting school environment that can effectively foster health literacy and wellbeing of children and adolescents. Topics that address a range of issues including: physical activity, relationships, growth and development, safety, nutrition and violence that employ a range of learning strategies in and out of the classroom can all help to encourage the development of health literate youth, and it is highly recommended individuals teaching these topics and who are part of the system should be as health literate as possible (Benham-Deal & Hodges, n.d.). Hobbs (2004) argues that 'Teachers must design learning experiences that help students, as quickly as possible, to stand on their own two feet — able to critically analyse messages in a culture that is densely saturated with an ever-changing array of media messages and technology tools' (p. 56). Finally, as mentioned earlier integrative approaches that yield cohesive and coherent messages are especially critical (Buijs, 2009), as are culturally appropriate and sensitive collaborations with families, in light of their knowledge, circumstances, traditions and world views.

Several reports suggest health literacy learning can be further enhanced when schools and preschools work in partnership with health professionals, health organizations, family and relevant community members. Involving government and non-government agencies and organizations to work in partnership with teachers and schools to enhance the health and wellbeing of students and teachers in schools is also recommended.

In this regard, focusing on issues relevant to youth (Flecha et al., 2011), and offering them a chance to demonstrate their learning through engagement is likely to be more effective than passive learning (Begoray et al., 2009). Hence, the ability of youth to practice health literacy in relevant and authentic situations is clearly indicated. For example, students involved in designing posters and brochures, writing reports, surveys and articles for school newsletters and local newspapers, performing plays, debating, and developing videos and films about health-related issues are likely to demonstrate higher levels of health literacy than those who do not.

Setting up displays and health information rooms and websites within their school and community, establishing a health and wellbeing committee which includes representatives of students and parents, and developing a range of healthy initiatives related to school canteens and occupational health and safety may be helpful strategies as well.

Based on the recent observation of adolescents in Taiwan, those with low health literacy are less likely to report good perceived health status and less likely to exhibit health-promoting behaviours compared to those with high health literacy (Chang, 2011), it is anticipated that school-based efforts to develop health literacy and that teach them how to access, understand, evaluate and communicate health information (Begoray et al., 2009), will empower children to make more informed choices and decisions about their health and wellbeing. It will also assist them to clarify and better understand the health, social, ethical and environmental issues that exist within their communities, and this appears especially beneficial in the context of nutrition and interpersonal relations (Chang, 2011).

Furthermore, designing well-planned school-based health education programmes, especially for those at highest risk, will prepare youth more ably for effective participation in their local, national and global environments and will enable them to successfully seek out and negotiate appropriate pathways and support for their own and others' health and wellbeing. Supporting teachers professional development is an additional crucial key to solving this worldwide challenge, and should be integral to both health education and elementary teacher education programmes (Benham-Deal & Hodges, n.d.).

To create an environment in the home that is supportive of healthy food and other choices, it is recommended parents understand the need to reduce the amount of commercial television and other media their children consume. In addition, helping young people to develop critical media literacy skills may help them become more aware of the messages they are

Box 3.1.   Key Attributes of School-Based Health Education to Promote Critical Health Literacy Should:

✔ Involve appropriate sequencing of health topics that meet national standards.
✔ Encompass culturally sensitive reading level appropriate lessons.
✔ Apply developmentally appropriate lessons.
✔ Involve effective use of media, classroom discussions and meaningful activities.
✔ Focus on the development of self-efficacy.
✔ Involve collaboration between the learner, family and teachers across disciplines.
✔ Use practice or skills-based curricula (Benham-Deal & Hudson, 2006).
✔ Use science-based curricula and lesson plans.
✔ Involve repetition across pre-school, kindergarten, primary and secondary school.
✔ Have available time and resources to carry out effective learning (St. Leger, 2001).
✔ Teachers conversant with facts about health use challenging instructional approaches and formative assessments.

Basic elements needed are reading, writing and numeracy literacy.

Desirable health literacy competencies are:

– Analytic and decision-making skills.
– Communicative or interactive skills.
– Computer-based skills.
– Content literacy skills.
– Critical thinking skills.
– Information seeking and decoding skills.
– Media literacy skills.
– Mental health literacy.
– Transfer skills.

Additional components needed to acquire health literacy proficiency include:

– Access to reliable information and resources.
– Exposure to effective role models.
– Healthy, safe school and community environments.
– Opportunities to learn and practice health skills and have healthy behaviours reinforced (see Chapter 6, this volume).

To reduce problems associated with low health literacy teachers need:

- Adequate preparation time.
- Adequate classroom time.
- Knowledge of health and/or related subject issues.
- Support to develop expertise in various topic areas (Wharf Higgins, Begoray, & MacDonald, 2009).
- Training in curriculum design, instruction and implementation, as indicated.
- Resources including human resources, as indicated.
- Technical, organizational, policy, community-based and parental support
- Access to comprehensive school health curricula.
- An understanding of the structure of the young persons' social worlds.
- An understanding of the developmental and cultural appropriateness of available curricula (Wharf Higgins et al., 2009).
- An understanding of role of culture and cultural norms in mediating health and health literacy.
- An understanding that some youth cannot read at the grade level assigned and that health information is often written or presented at an advanced level.
- A favourable school climate.

Families and parents need:

- Appropriate knowledge and skills.
- Resources that can foster healthy lifestyles.

Benefits of Intervening to Improve Health Literacy of Youth

- ✔ Lower risk taking or violent behaviours.
- ✔ Fewer missed school days.
- ✔ Reduced knowledge and health gap.
- ✔ Correct dosing and ability to get and take medicines.
- ✔ Better academic performance of children with chronic medical needs.
- ✔ Better ability to address controllable situations that affect health.

exposed to and how to interpret these messages to achieve better health outcomes (Begoray et al., 2009)

In sum, to assist the developing child, especially those who live in poverty who are found to acquire language skills more slowly, and are at higher risk for reading difficulties (Aikens & Barbarin, 2008; Wyner, Bridgeland, & Dilulio, 2007) to develop health literacy skills, concerted efforts embedded in the classroom, and across curricula that employ a developmentally appropriate skills-based approach are indicated. In addition to recommendations that schools improve the curricula of both language arts and health education courses at all levels in order to improve the health literacy skills of children and the adults they will become (Society for Public Health Education [SOPHE], 2011), these efforts must also extend beyond the boundaries of the school to involve the surrounding community as a whole.

Further, the application of effective learning theories (St. Leger, 2001), commitment of school authorities as well as teachers to professional development (St. Leger, 2001) and the provision of a holistic supportive environment (Lee, 2009; St. Leger, 2001) is necessary to ensure that schools provide favourable opportunities for nurturing health literacy. The role of parents, peers, traditional and non-traditional media, and the school itself as a socializing agent must be also considered in the context of trying to meet the health literacy needs of youth in the context of the school setting (Paek et al., 2011).

To foster these ideas, this chapter has focused on some topics that need to covered, as well as on some broad strategies that might be helpful in any effort to promote school-based health literacy. Attributes of effective programmes are listed in Box 3.1.

References

Aikens, N. L., & Barbarin, O. (2008). Socioeconomic differences in reading trajectories: The contribution of family, neighborhood, and school contexts. *Journal of Educational Psychology, 100*, 235–251.

Begoray, D., Cimon, M., & Wharf Higgins, J. (2010). *MEDIAting health: The powerful role of media.* New York, NY: NovaScience.

Begoray, D. L., Wharf Higgins, J., & MacDonald, M. (2009). High school health curriculum and health literacy: Canadian student voices. *Global Health Promotion, 16*, 35–42.

Benham-Deal, T. B., & Hodges, B. (n.d.). *Role of 21st century schools in promoting health literacy.* Washington, DC: National Education Association Health Information Network. Available online at: http://www.neahin.org/educator-resources/health-literacy/benhamdeal-hodges-paper.pdf

Benham-Deal, T. B., & Hudson, N. (2006). Are health educators in denial or facing reality? Demonstrating effectiveness within a school accountability system. *American Journal of Health Education, 37*(3), 154–158.

Brown, J., & Witherspoon, E. (2002). The mass media and American adolescents' health. *Journal of Adolescent Health, 31*, 153–170.

Buijs, G. J. (2009). Better schools through health: Networking for health promoting schools in Europe. *European Journal of Education, 44*, 507–520.

Chang, L.-C. (2011). Health literacy, self-reported status and health promoting behaviours for adolescents in Taiwan. *Journal of Clinical Nursing, 20*, 190–196.

DeWalt, D. A., & Hink, A. (2009). Health literacy and child health outcomes: A systematic review of the literature. *Pediatrics, 124,* S265–S274.

Flecha, A., Garcia, R., & Rudd, R. (2011). Using health literacy in school to overcome inequalities. *European Journal of Education, 46,* 209–218.

Ghaddar, S. F., Valerno, M. A., Garcia, C. M., & Hansen, L. (2011). Adolescent health literacy: The importance of credible sources for online health information. *Journal of School Health, 82,* 28–36.

Gray, N. J., Klein, J. D., Noyce, P. R., Sesselberg, T. S., & Cantrill, J. A. (2005). The internet: A window on adolescent health literacy. *Journal of Adolescent Health, 37,* 243.

Harris, J. L., & Bargh, J. A. (2009). Television viewing and unhealthy diet: Implications for children and media interventions. *Health Communications, 24,* 660–673.

Hobbs, R. (2004). A review of school-based initiatives in media literacy education. *American Behavioral Scientist, 48,* 42–59.

Kansas Head Start Association. (2012). Health literacy. Retrieved from http://www.kheadstart.org/node/90

Keil, F. C. (2006). Proceedings of the surgeon general's workshop on improving health literacy, September 7, 2006, National Institutes of Health, Bethesda, MD. Panel 2: Meeting the health literacy needs of special populations. Retrieved from http://www.ncbi.nlm.nih.gov/books/NBK44263/. Accessed on June 14, 2012.

Kickbusch, I. S. (2001). Health literacy: Addressing the health and education divide. *Health Promotion International, 16,* 289–297.

Knott, T. (2006). Health literacy in SA school settings: Much more than H&PE. *Virtually Healthy, 41*(Term 3), 1. Retrieved from http://www.healthpromotion. cywhs.sa.gov.au/library/vh41.pdf

Lee, A. (2009). Health-promoting schools: Evidence for a holistic approach to promoting health and improving health literacy. *Applied Health Economics and Health Policy, 7,* 11–17.

Marks, R. (2009). Ethics and patient education: Health literacy and cultural dilemmas. *Health Promotion Practice, 10,* 328–332.

Marx, E., Hudson, N., Deal, T., Pateman, B., & Middleton, K. (2007). Promoting health literacy through the health education assessment project. *Journal of School Health, 77,* 157–163.

Nutbeam, D. (1998). Health promotion glossary. *Health Promotion International, 13,* 349–364.

Nutbeam, D. (2000). Health Literacy as a public health goal: A challenge for contemporary health education and communication strategies into the 21st century. *Health Promotion International, 15,* 259–267.

Olsson, D., & Kennedy, M. G. (2010). Mental health literacy among young people in a small U.S. town: Recognition of disorders and hypothetical helping responses. *Early Intervention in Psychiatry, 4,* 291–298.

Paasche-Orlow, M. K., & Wolf, M. S. (2007). The causal pathways linking health literacy to outcomes. *American Journal of Health Behavior, 31,* S19–S26.

Paek, H.-J., Reber, B. H., & Larsy, R. W. (2011). Roles of interpersonal and media socialization agents in adolescent self-reported health literacy: A health socialization perspective. *Health Education Research, 26,* 131–139.

Peterson, F. L., Cooper, R. J., & Laird, J. M. (2001). Enhancing teacher health literacy in school health promotion: A vision for the new millennium. *Journal of School Health, 71*, 138–144.

Rudd, R. (2006). Proceedings of the surgeon general's workshop on improving health literacy: Panel 1. Retrieved from http://www.surgeongeneral.gov/healthliteracy/pdf/panel1.pdf

Society for Public Health Education (SOPHE). (2011). *Society for public health education.* Washington, DC. Retrieved from http://www.sophe.org/

St. Leger, L. (2001). Schools, health literacy and public health: Possibilities and challenges. *Health Promotion International, 16*, 197–205.

Vardavas, C. I., Kondilis, B. K., Patelarou, E., Akrivos, P. D., & Falagas, M. E. (2009). Health literacy and sources of health education among adolescents in Greece. *International Journal of Adolescent Medicine and Health, 21*, 179–186.

Volandes, A. E., & Paasche-Orlow, M. K. (2007). Health literacy, health inequality, and a just healthcare system. *American Journal of Bioethics, 7*, 5–11.

Wharf Higgins, J., Begoray, D., & MacDonald, M. (2009). A social ecological conceptual framework for understanding adolescent health literacy in the health education classroom. *American Journal of Community Psychology, 44*, 350–362.

World Health Organization. (2010). Health literacy and health behaviour. Retrieved from htpp://www.who.int/healthpromotion/conferences/7ghp/track2/en/. Accessed on December 9, 2010.

Wyner, J. S., Bridgeland, J. M., & Dilulio, J. J. Jr. (2007). Achievement trap: How America is failing millions of high-achieving students from low income families. A report by the Jack Cooke Foundation & Civic Enterprises with original research by Westat. Retrieved from http://www.civicenterprises.net/pdfs/jkc.pdf

Chapter 4

Strategies for Measuring and Maximizing Health Literacy of Youth

Joan Wharf Higgins, Deborah Begoray, Christine Beer, Janie Harrison and Amy Collins

The last decade has witnessed considerable concern about adolescents' health around the globe (WHO, 2008), including for example Canada (Shields & Tremblay, 2010), the United States (Kaiser Family Foundation, 2010), Australia (Cinelli & O'Dea, 2009), the United Kingdom (Stamatakis, Zaninotto, Falaschetti, Mindell, & Head, 2010), Egypt and China (Fisher et al., 2011), Sweden (Kelly, 2007) and Singapore (Lay, Ang, Chong, & Huan, 2007). Issues primarily related to unhealthy body weight, poor nutrition, sedentary activity and lack of exercise, as well as substance use and abuse, have contributed to the early onset of chronic diseases in adolescence, most notably diabetes (Amed, Daneman, Mahmud, & Hamilton, 2010; Van Cleave, Gortmaker, & Perrin, 2010; Zimmet, 2011). Because health behaviours formed during adolescence often persist into adulthood (Marx, Hudson, Deal, Pateman, & Middleton, 2007), it becomes increasingly difficult to change and sustain healthy living patterns as people get older and their habits more entrenched (Pietilainen et al., 2008). Such behavioural patterns are not just the result of individual choices but in fact are significantly influenced by the broader living conditions and circumstances (Daniel, Moore, & Kestens, 2007; Marmot, 2007).

In the current urgent debate about how to address issues related to physical inactivity, body weight and early onset of chronic diseases in adolescents (Tremblay et al., 2010), as this book makes clear, health education both during school (Nutbeam, 2000) and in after school programs (Diamond, Saintonge, August, & Azrack, 2011) has been promoted as a possible vehicle of change. Health education teaches adolescents to plan, think critically about and cope with these and other outcomes, in order to promote health literacy (Flecha, Garcia, & Rudd, 2011) and health enhancing behaviours (Brey, Clark, & Wantz, 2007) and skills (Kickbusch, 2008) essential for well-being. Educational settings — and the health education curricula within — have an unparalleled (and perhaps the only) opportunity to positively influence the health literacy of youth. Moreover, schools can mitigate health inequities as they serve adolescents from diverse race and socio-economic backgrounds, providing fair distribution of resources during the time they are on campus (Institute of Medicine of the National Academies, 2009), which provides a synergistic effect: improving health literacy has been identified as an approach to reduce health inequities (Ghaddar, Valerio, Garcia, & Hansen, 2012) and address social exclusion (European Commission, 2010).

Health education has been defined as 'the continuum of learning, which enables people, as individuals, and as members of social structures, to voluntarily make decisions, modify behaviors and change social conditions in ways that are health enhancing' (Joint Committee on Health Education Terminology, 1991, p. 105). We recognize that health education is a necessary component of behaviour change, but is insufficient without resources and supportive environments to facilitate change (Kupersmidt, Scull, & Weintraub Austin, 2010). While there is an impressive amount of scholarly work on Health Promoting Schools (e.g. de Leeuw, 2012; McCuaig, Coore, & Hay, 2012; Simovska, 2012) or Comprehensive School Health (e.g. Haerens et al., 2006; Naylor & McKay, 2008; van Sluijs, McMinn, & Griffin, 2007), initiatives modifying physical, social and cultural contexts of school and nearby environments to improve student health outcomes, our focus remains within the classroom on teaching and learning. In keeping with the logic that priming health behaviours early in life will improve health outcomes in adulthood, we might expect a similar succession with health literacy skills (Chang, 2011; Ghaddar et al., 2012), and suppression of differences in health inequities (Paakkari & Paakkari, 2012) although to date there is no research linking health literacy to improved health outcomes or equities (Diamond et al., 2011). Progressing from a transmission to a more dialogic and student-centred approach, effective health education nurtures health literacy by 'offering a more nuanced approach to building and strengthening the competencies needed by all people and communities to achieve and maintain good health across their lives' (Saan & Wise, 2011, p. ii192).

Beyond clinical settings, health literacy is a relatively new concept in Canada unlike the United States experience, when in 1974 National Health Education Standards described the knowledge and skills essential to the development of health literacy (Speros, 2005). Our work in health literacy reflects the Canadian definition 'to access, understand, evaluate, and communicate information as a way to promote, maintain, and improve health in a variety of settings across the life-course' (Rootman & Gordon-El-Bihbety, 2008, p. 3). In doing so, we embrace the work of conceptual leaders in the field (e.g. Abel, 2008; Kickbusch, 2008; Nutbeam, 2008; von Wagner, Steptoe, Wolf, & Wardle, 2009) in understanding health literacy as an empowerment strategy in line with the principles of health promotion to reduce health inequities (de Leeuw, 2012). Health literate students are able to understand and apply health information in ways that allow them to take more control over their health through, for example, appraising the credibility, accuracy and relevance of information and acting on that information to change their health behaviours or living conditions. For example, Chang (2011) found Taiwan students with better health literacy scores to engage in significantly higher health promoting nutrition behaviours and report better health status than their counterparts with lower health literacy scores.

To date, measures of health literacy draw heavily on literacy assessment tools and fail to capture its broader definition and multiple dimensions and levels (Nutbeam, 2008). Further, health literacy has been most often measured in adults, especially in a clinical context, for example: the Rapid Estimate of Adult Literacy in Medicine (REALM) (Murphy, Davis, Long, Jackson, & Decker, 1993), the Test of Functional Health Literacy in Adults (TOFHLA) (Parker, Baker, Williams, & Nurss, 1995) and the National Assessment of Adult Literacy (NAAL), and the Health Activity Literacy Scale (Kutner, Greenberg, & Baer, 2006). TOFHLA has been modified for younger populations (Test of Functional Health Literacy in Adolescents (TOFHLAd) (Chang, 2011), but nevertheless remains focused on clinical disease rather than health promotion concepts. Recently, Begoray and Kwan (2012) investigated self-reporting of health literacy skills, and while they found no correlation of self-reported scores to those measured from task-oriented performance measures (e.g. REALM), they caution against assuming that 'self-report items are inherently less valid than task performance items' (p. 30). Context — other than clinical ones — and populations — other than seniors or patients — are largely missing from measures of health literacy (Manganello, 2008), a critical flaw for Abel (2008). While there is no shortage of definitions and conceptual frameworks of health literacy in the literature (Begoray & Kwan, 2012; Frisch, Camerini, Diviani, & Schulz, 2011; Paakkari & Paakkari, 2012; Sorenson et al., 2012), the field has not agreed upon a 'gold standard' for measuring health literacy (Berkman, Davis, & McCormack, 2010). Further inhibiting the state of health literacy research is the lack of translational studies; most investigations to date have focused on issues of internal validity and failed to adequately address generalizability and external validity (Allen, Zolellner, Motley, & Estabrooks, 2011).

Thus, over the past few years, we have studied the development and measurement of adolescent health literacy, conducting our research in the classroom as part of existing curricula in order to ground our findings in real world practice and maximize their utility for uptake; we refer to these research studies as Projects A, B and C. In particular, in Project A we have examined the implementation of the British Columbia, Canada health curriculum for grade 10 students (e.g. Begoray, Cimon, & Wharf Higgins, 2010; Begoray, Wharf Higgins, & MacDonald, 2009; Wharf Higgins, Begoray, & MacDonald, 2009), and in Project B developed a health literacy measurement tool specific to high school students (Wu et al., 2010). As part of the development of the measurement tool, students were presented with a 'scenario' and then asked a series of questions designed to measure their ability to understand and evaluate the health information presented in each scenario. In an effort to ensure that completing the assignment was as compelling as possible, we conducted focus groups with students to identify their top health concerns. The most popular included: diabetes, physical inactivity, energy drinks, ecstasy, crystal meth, and depression. Appendix A shares lesson plans developed through our research designed to engage students in learning activities for energy drinks in the health education classroom.

In addition to sharing our developed health literacy resources, the primary purpose of this chapter is to discuss our experiences with our third instalment of our research agenda, Project C, where we added a media literacy component to our investigations of adolescents' health literacy. This decision was influenced by three factors: (1) Primarily, we were informed by our findings from Project B where media emerged as a prominent influence on students' health literacy. The literature confirms that 'media use' is a situational determinant of health literacy (Sorenson et al., 2012). (2) This turned our attention towards what Biesta (2010) has dubbed 'reconnecting and updating' our educational research. (3) Lastly, our knowledge of the literature which, despite the soaring popularity of and conceptual development in health literacy, did not offer validated and standardized measures of its constructs, dimensions, domains, levels or skills. As such, we heeded the advice of Frisch et al. (2011) that borrowing efforts from other literacy domains may advance our work. In their review of published literacy domains, the latter authors found media literacy to emerge as the frontrunner. Clearly, there was much we could learn from this discipline.

4.1. Our Conceptual Orientation

Because adolescents make decisions about their behaviours on the basis of their understandings of the world around them, the best theoretical perspective to explain learning and change in the health context is a social ecological one; that is, a model that takes into account the interrelationships among individuals and groups in a broad social network or ecology (Stokols, 2000), and a social constructivist one (e.g. Vygotsky, 1978). Our work from Projects A and B has confirmed the utility of a social ecological and social constructivist framework to generate a theoretical and applied understanding of the influence of health education on health literacy. We also found that classroom instruction that motivates students to learn, often characterized by purposeful strategies of active/experiential learning, reflection, and perspective taking, is important for both health and media literacy (Brey, Clark, & Wantz, 2008; Collins, Doyon, McAuley, & Quijada, 2011; Hill & Lindsay, 2003; Paakkari & Paakkari, 2012; von Wagner et al., 2009). Thus, an educational agenda must be broad enough to enhance not only students' knowledge, literacy, social and civic skills, but also strengthen their motivation and commitment to lifelong learning and enable them to practice healthy behaviours (Friedman & Hoffman-Goetz, 2008; Greenberg et al., 2003; von Wagner et al., 2009).

4.2. Critical Media Health Literacy: Project C

Working with students in Projects A and B, we learned that their health literacy is an especially important skill when applied to media messages. We found that adolescents need to become actively engaged in considering the direct and indirect messages from the media — both the more obvious advertisements and the less obvious product placement embedded in, for example, a television program — in order to be empowered to make their own consumption decisions. Thus, we set out to work in grade 10 health education classrooms to determine whether students could benefit from a media health literacy curriculum. Below we describe our experiences including both encouraging and discouraging findings. We are reminded that sharing our modest results offers instructive implications for future practice and research (Pettman et al., 2012) since 'it is more important to examine what works for whom and under what conditions than trying to determine "what works"'(Metropolitan Area Child Study Research Group, 2002, p. 190). Our rather eye-opening initial findings with grade 10 students are presented first, followed by our work with grade 7 students which offers more hopeful results.

4.2.1. *The Grade 10 Health Education Curriculum*

Informed and inspired by the work of media literacy researchers and educators (e.g. Buckingham, 2003; Collins et al., 2011; Hobbs & Frost, 2003;

Potter, 2004), we initially worked in the grade 10 classroom ($n = 74$) to blend media and health literacy goals and pedagogies in a series of three, 80 minute lessons over six classes (Appendix B). In keeping with our community-based research principles (Montoya & Kent, 2011), interest in establishing ecological validity (Trickett, 2011), and following the advice of McCuaig et al. (2012) to overcome the challenges teachers face when implementing health programs designed by outsiders, we engaged teachers in reviewing our lesson plans and utilized their feedback to ensure that the materials contributed to the educational outcomes were relevant for their students and classroom practice.

In a pre-test/post-test design, we assessed media health literacy prior to and two weeks' following the lessons as a way to gauge the potency of the lessons, and compared the test scores to grade 10 students attending a demographically matched control school ($n = 51$). After viewing a commercial selling a popular soft drink (http://www.youtube.com/watch?v = Bmc1 f-J3jKQ), students completed an 11-item 'quiz' (Appendix C) about the commercial based on existing media literacy measurement tools (Hobbs & Frost, 2003). The lessons were taught by trained teachers on our research team well versed in both media health literacy knowledge and classroom pedagogy. Two additional teachers, blinded to whether students were in the intervention or control condition, graded all the tests based on a marking key developed by our research team. Observational records of how the lessons unfolded and review of students' final assignment (a Public Service Announcement of a health issue of their choice) completed our data collection in the classroom. We also conducted a focus group with students receiving the media health literacy lessons a few weeks after the lessons concluded to gather more in-depth information about their learning.

Our findings were at first glance disappointing despite their statistical significance: the pre-test scores were on average very low (mean score of 22%), and students' scores barely inched upwards after receiving the lessons (mean score of 26%). Exploring these differences with a Wilcoxon Signed Ranks Test showed that the CMHL lessons did elicit a statistically significant change in test scores among intervention classroom of grade 10 students ($Z = -2.264$, $P = 0.024$). Median test scores increased from 6.0 to 7.5. Analysis of the scores for the close-ended questions found no change from pre to post. It was in students' improvement of scores for open-ended questions, most notably for recognition of marketing techniques used to attract and hold the interest of viewers, and for who was missing from the advertisement, that accounted for the changes in overall survey scores. We also found that control school students' scores increased from 24% to 28% ($Z = -2.234$, $P = 0.025$); median test score increased from 6.62 to 8.75 even with instructions to continue with their usual health education lessons. It may be that the existing high school health curriculum does serve to improve media health literacy skills albeit very modestly. Most glaringly of all were the low levels of media health literacy assessed in all 125 students, and the fact that adding 6 hours of curriculum emphasizing media health literacy for 74 of the students translated into humbling (even with significance) differences in their ability to critically deconstruct media messages. Perhaps the test, based on one minute commercial, did not accurately capture students' improved knowledge.

In search of explanations, we consulted our observational data which confirmed that the implementation of the lessons had, in fact, occurred as intended. A review of the assignments by the students in the intervention school similarly revealed a general lack of critical or evaluative stance of health information. Much of their 'public health message' communicated a patho-physiological or behavioural intent to avoiding disease, rather than a more sophisticated portrayal of a health issue, and were informed by a limited number of sources, primarily internet based.

Turning to our focus group data further confirmed the limited skills students possessed. For example, when responding to how they assess the accuracy of health information disseminated through media, students describe themselves as being critical: 'And I'd probably say I'd be a little more critical, not too much, but like I will raise an eyebrow when an ad [comes] on.' This is in keeping with the well documented 'third person effect' in the communications literature where teenagers perceive everyone but themselves to be vulnerable to the persuasive effects of the media (Paul, Salwen, & Dupagne, 2007). In fact, their comments explaining their online search strategies actually revealed how shallow their skills were, as they relied on the popularity of a site as evidence of its trustworthiness:

> Also [internet] forums are really good because that gives everyone's opinions expressed and so if you ask a question … like Wiki answers is a good source I know and Yahoo answers also a very good source I know. Uh, because people can vote which ones are the best. [student focus group]
>
> Usually it's pretty simple for me 'cause Google, I know everyone uses Google to search for anything and the first one page usually have the best sites, because they are the best well known, that most, most people have most viewed it probably that's why they always have it on the first page … [student focus group]

The real epiphany for us, however, emerged from an off-hand comment by one of the students referring to his lifelong consumption of Pepsi when talking about the specific commercial used in the pre- and post-tests. When asked by the focus group facilitator if this enduring familiarity of the product made it difficult to tease out the specific message and isolate it from his cumulative knowledge of the product, he concurred and insightfully noted that 'They [advertisers] are very clever, they mix in like Pepsi with World Cup or something. You tend to forget more about the actual Pepsi and focus on the soccer. So, [I look at the ad] remembering all the other ads ... always in the back of your mind is your previous knowledge, the other things you know about it.'

We were initially attracted to the grade 10 curriculum because it offered students their final opportunity to receive health education in BC classrooms, and it was often at this point that their health practices began to decline. Yet, was grade 10 too late in the educational and developmental lifespan to provide the skills necessary to navigate through a consumer society? Cognitive developmental theory argues that children younger than eight years do not have the capacity to discern persuasive media manipulations, and by the teen years media often serve as the 'super peer' best friend that normalizes risky and unhealthy behaviours (Strasburger, Wilson, & Jordan, 2009). Were grade 10 students already 'branded' by their years of media consumption? Media education and literacy interventions in the literature appear across a variety of school years (Kupersmidt et al., 2010), while health literacy initiatives have most often been directed towards adults — particularly in clinical settings (Allen et al., 2011) and less so with adolescents and children (e.g. Ghaddar et al., 2012).

4.2.2.   The Grade 7 Language Arts Curriculum

Thus, we cast our attention back to the middle school years, integrating critical media health literacy into the language arts curriculum and extending the duration to 10 hours over a 5-week period. Building on the Media Detective initiative (Kupersmidt et al., 2010) and adapting it to reflect Canadian content for an older age group for three grade 7 classrooms ($n = 31$), we developed a critical media health literacy module complete with lesson plans matched to provincial standard learning outcomes, class activity materials and teaching tools (Appendix D). The Media Detective program is a theory- and evidence-based series of 10 media literacy education lessons intended to be integrated into existing curricula. Media Detective is framed as building students' investigative skills to decode media by searching for 'clues' to identify the intended product, audience, ad hooks, and uncover 'hidden messages' and presentation of one-sided information. In a rigorous experimental design, Kupersmidt et al. (2010) demonstrated significant differences between elementary school children receiving the Media Detective lessons and a wait-listed control classroom on measures of critical thinking, self-efficacy and intentions to use alcohol and tobacco. The study also documented a high level of implementation fidelity and teacher and student satisfaction with the program.

For Collins and colleagues (2011), aligning subject content with learning outcomes represents a best practice and presents a natural opportunity to integrate media literacy into the existing curricula without creating an additional burden on the academic schedule. Because neither health nor media are defined subject content areas in teachers' professional training and few have the luxury of time to prepare lesson units (Diamond et al., 2011), and given that literacy is one of the primary goals of the education system (Manganello, 2008), we used the grade 7 language arts curriculum as our intervention context taking care to develop lesson plans in parallel with the provincial performance learning outcomes identified for this grade and subject. The younger ages of the students and the integration of the critical media health literacy emphasis into the existing language arts curriculum necessitated that the lessons were taught by the classroom teachers rather than members of our research team.

Data collection methods included the pre- and post-test used with grade 10 students (adapting for plainer language for grade 7 students), classroom observations of all lessons by three members of the research team (one per classroom), review of five assignments and one class project, and focus groups with teachers and students at the completion of the unit. Grade 7 students in a demographically matched second school ($N = 30$) served as our comparison, and also received the pre- and post-test while continuing with their standard language arts curriculum.

4.3. Results

Scores from the pre- and post-test were once again modest: the average pre-test scores were 23% and 28% for the intervention and control schools respectively, and post-test scores 28% and 27%. A Wilcoxon Signed Ranks Test showed that the 10 lessons improved intervention students' CMHL scores slightly, although not significantly ($Z = -1.787$, $P = 0.074$). Analyzing the scores for the close-ended questions found no change from pre to post for questions one ($Z = -.302$, $P = 0.763$) or two ($Z = -.577$, $P = 0.564$). It was in students' improvement of scores for open-ended question (Q.7 — what is not mentioned in the advertisement?) that significantly accounted for most of the changes in overall survey scores ($Z = -2.552$, $P = 0.011$). At post-test, 77% of students' answers included references to nutrition, sugar, caffeine and/or caloric content as missing information from the commercial, compared to 47% doing so at pre-test. For one of the students who could not identify what was missing at the pre-test and left the question unanswered, wrote at post-test: 'Coca Cola does not make your life better. Coca Cola is full of sugar.'

Grade 7 girls in the intervention classrooms performed statistically better at post-test than boys, with a mean score improvement of 2.5 marks ($Z = 2.120$, $P = .034$); there were no significant differences between girls and boys at pre-test. CMHL scores among the control school students decreased slightly ($Z = -.301$, $P = 0.763$); median test scores fell from 7.0 to 6.8 almost equal to that of students who received the 10 lessons.

It seems that students' learnings are not well captured through the use of the pre- and post-test relative to the other assessment tools. It may be that the format of the test does not reflect typical test formats for this subject and age nor was it treated as a traditional subject in terms of assessment strategies (e.g., teachers told us they typically use more multiple choice questions and set aside time to purposefully study for a test). To best serve students' learning, critical media health literacy needs to be seen as a legitimate and foundational subject area, along with other forms of prose, numeracy, and document literacy, and not merely an 'add on' for fun Friday afternoons or when a substitute teacher is present. Further, it may be that the popularity and familiarity of the product at the focus of the commercial may have also distracted students from critically viewing the message, but certainly reflects the real world context in which they would be exposed to such marketing.

Our analysis of the qualitative data, that is focus groups with teachers, students, and student assignments, revealed improvements in students' knowledge and ability to interpret media messages in terms of health concepts, more so than students' test scores. Because teachers recognized that twelve-year-olds were highly sought after as consumers, they identified this age group as an important one for helping them to understand the manipulative nature of marketing and instilling critical literacy interpretive skills:

> It's a good age [for marketers] to target them because they are developmentally trying to find themselves in terms of their values. They are trying to figure themselves out and their brains are just rubber balls — a perfect age for anyone to start buying their brands and [establishing] brand loyalty. [teacher focus group]
> I think they are aware of branding, of advertising, but I think they need to be taught it in school. Without having someone to teach them [about media health literacy] they would just get swept up by it. [teacher focus group]
> Kids this age are just working through their own values and understanding that most are intrinsic values that are

important for them. Helping them to have the knowledge that marketing ... takes advantage of their insecurity at this age ... [and] is trying to shift their values toward extrinsic ones is important. [teacher focus group]

Yet, teachers wondered if their grade 7 students were still too young to fully develop Nutbeam's (2000) more advanced interactive and critical health literacy skills: 'I don't know if they would think to apply that knowledge beyond the specific product that they learned about. You know, the group that made a counter-ad about energy drink kids now knows about energy drinks, and the group that made a Splenda counter-ad knows about Splenda, but I don't quite know if they would transfer that knowledge to another product.'

Our field notes suggested that the lesson plan introducing 'ad hooks' resonated strongly with students as the level of interest in and engagement with the activity was high. Students' journal entries confirmed our observations. When asked to write about which strategies appealed to them, they were able to connect their experience to commonly used ad hooks:

> The ad I liked most was the Facebook ad where the dog is on Facebook. I like that ad because I have Facebook, I really enjoy Facebook, plus the humour is good. [student journal entry]
>
> The ad I liked best was the iTunes ad because it was cool, colourful; it made it seem that if you listen to music it will be fun. They made it look awesome, fun and if you listen to music you will be popular. [student journal entry]
>
> They try and go with something that is popular at the moment-like Justin Bieber or Taylor Swift-that they know girls will like, so they put it in their ad. [student focus group]

After successfully identifying ad hooks, teachers facilitated students to search for hidden messages in advertisements by completing 'If ... then statements' after viewing a number of different ads (lesson #6 'Real World versus Ad Land'). Although the teachers acknowledged that most students had difficulty uncovering the deeper meanings in advertisements ('To have the ability to see those hidden messages was very difficult. It was just like a shift in paradigm for them to try to think in that way'), it began the process of empowering students to become aware of marketers' ulterior motivations:

> That one activity they did, [where they completed] the 'If ... then' sentences, that was a good one, and played right into all

sorts of critical literacies. If this happens, then what? Trying to get them to think how it's all going to fall into place. [teacher focus group]

Now I know what I see in ads is often a lie. [student journal entry]

I think they try to disguise [what they are selling] with something that catches your eye and gets you distracted from the message. [student focus group]

I think it's just important to know what the hidden message is ... you really want to know what they are trying to [not] tell you about the product. [student focus group]

Students went on to acknowledge — both in their journals and focus group discussions — the effects of such marketing strategies on their purchasing behaviours:

I like the ads that have a lot of action! The movements and explosion make the ad more amusing [to me]. I will probably buy the product if my favourite ad hooks are in the ad. [student journal entry]

We have further summarized our qualitative findings in Table 4.1. It is organized according to the antecedents, critical attributes and outcomes that we suggest comprise a CMHL concept model (Wharf Higgins & Begoray, 2012). Briefly, our CMHL concept model was developed in order to explain our empirical evidence from our previous research; therefore, a framework was largely missing in the literature. Following the conceptual analysis process guided by Rodgers' (1993) work, we conducted a scoping review (Arksey & O'Malley, 2005) of the literature using the terms health literacy, critical health literacy, media literacy, critical media literacy, media activism, critical viewing among others. From this search, 442 articles were identified, 126 located and read, 61 of which were selected for analysis. In keeping with Rodgers' guidelines, articles were examined for excerpts describing or explaining: defining attributes, surrogate terms, related concepts, antecedents and consequences related to our 'concept of interest', and then colour coded and extracted for conceptual overlap, distinctions and synthesis. From this, a working definition was proposed: *Critical Media Health Literacy (CMHL) is a right of citizenship and empowers individuals, in a 'risky consumer society', to critically interpret and use media as a means to: engage in decision-making processes and dialogues, exert control over their health and everyday events, and make healthy changes for themselves and their communities.* CMHL comprises three main elements: (1) a skill set that includes personal, cognitive, social and reflective analytical skills which

Table 4.1: CMHL in the Grade 7 Language Arts Curriculum.

Antecedents	Critical Attributes	Outcomes
Student-centred, discovery-based learning environment.	A Skill Set: reflective, discriminating and interpretive abilities.	Personal, cognitive and social abilities combined with reflective interpretive skills to critically interact with media.
Lesson plans allow for student choice in selecting ads to dissect and create counter-ads. Teaching strategies were interactive and relevant, for example showing current ads for video games and sports drinks, and how ad hooks of star power, humour, sound, colour etc. are used to attract the audience.	'*At our age, with these new techniques you've taught us, I think that we would be a little bit more cautious. I actually think about the commercials and think if they're actually telling something that you want to learn, or just something that they want to make money off of.*' [student focus group]	'*Ads always trick you into thinking their product is the best. After today's lesson on ads I will definitely look at advertisements differently. If I see an ad that makes [someone] look really good, then I will remember that they might have used "photoshop". Another thing is I will make sure when I'm watching something about burgers, and the burger they show looks really good, then I will remember that that's now how they really look, because the one they show isn't edible. So, after today's lesson, I will definitely remember that things aren't always what they seem.*' [student journal entry]
'*Students loved the hands on stuff — creating the counter-ads and dissecting the ads. I think the more hands on things, the better.*' [teacher focus group]	'*My favourite ad hook is comedy. Comedy is a very effective ad hook. Ad hooks definitely contribute to a product's success.*' [student journal entry]	

Table 4.1: (Continued)

Antecedents	Critical Attributes	Outcomes
Dialogical reflection and Socratic questioning; critically negotiate meanings and analyse media culture.	Empowerment.	Making individual and collective healthy and productive decisions across the lifespan.
'Student journals encouraged reflective learning. For example, after the lesson on ad hooks, students were asked to think about how the ad hooks attracted their attention: "How to be an ad detective helped and still helps me figure out the true meaning of an ad. What I thought was best for me was the ad hooks, because now I know what to watch for."' [student journal entry]	*'The media investigator was a good strategy for media and commercial understanding. My favourite part was making our counter-ads! One of the most important strategies was identifying the ad hooks. I think this is because people need to know that they are being convinced or tricked into buying the product.'* [student journal entry]	*'Sometimes ads have very disturbing details that the ad doesn't actually tell you, for example, like McDonald's [burger] is tasty, it's big, it's juicy, but it can get you overweight; it just does bad things to you and that's not what they show to you.'* [student focus group]
'I sometimes think it's [commercials] kind of really silly because athletes don't drink like Coca Cola and then go and [play a game].' [student focus group]	*'In this unit I liked how we learned the hidden messages of ads and how we got to find out some pretty neat stuff about what ads aren't telling you. I liked how now I can realize what ads are really trying to hide — the stuff they don't want you to know.'* [student journal entry]	

Engaged Citizenship.	Recognition that media portray selective ideas and values; active authors of media for social activism to address social determinants of health.	Informed, involved, and included citizens effectively participate in the complexities of modern life.
	'The most important thing I learned was about values. That there are intrinsic and extrinsic values and most ads are targeting extrinsic values, but show in the ads intrinsic values.' [student focus group] 'I think the exercise that was really helpful was when they had to design the product and think about how it would appeal to their own age group and started thinking about the target audience, marketing, what kind of hooks they were going to use. They got quite excited about it. Putting them on the marketing side helped them develop critical thinking skills around the products that are being sent their way.' [teacher focus group] 'I liked making the counter-ads best. I liked that we could make [the products] look silly and inappropriate.' [student journal entry]	

when developed leads to (2) empowerment at the individual and community levels thereby creating (3) a competency of engaged citizenship of informed and critical media consumers.

4.4. Implications for Classroom Teaching and Assessment

Reflecting on their past opportunities to enhance students' critical media health literacy, teachers in our focus group admitted that 'if teachers want to do media awareness, then they do. But it's not something that crops up regularly in the curriculum.' Those who have included media into their classrooms acknowledged that 'I've never really taken the health swing of it. It's been more the message and the critical thinking, but not so much the health spin. Even in the health curriculum, media is a suggestion that you could choose to cover, but it isn't stated clearly.' Moving forward with integrating CMHL into their language arts curriculum must include '... more critical reading. We did writing and we did representing, and we did a lot of speaking, and viewing definitely, but not so much the reading piece, and I think that would have been helpful. And that's where we are going to go from now.'

In keeping with recommendations in the literature (Diamond et al., 2011), our teachers advised integrating CMHL lessons throughout multiple curricula (e.g. math, science, PE) and extending the unit throughout the school year, as well as scaffolding concepts and strategies into ongoing curricula through to graduation.

> [Teachers] could do quite an integrated unit with this [critical media health literacy] ... with Home Economics and the cooking aspect; with mathematics. And, it would have to be school wide and make it across the grades. Try to pull the curriculum elements out for each grade level. [teacher focus group]
> It has to be ongoing. I prefer it if we could teach this throughout the whole year, maybe a weekly class so that they are getting all the information and skills that they need throughout the year, and not just during one unit. [teacher focus group]

Integrating and extending media and health literacy throughout the curricula and grades would maximize the opportunities for students to become fully health literate with the ability to access, understand, evaluate, and communicate health information. Because teachers in our focus group acknowledged that 'the media isn't going to teach them how to make healthy choices ... and some of their parents have been programmed by the media too, so their parents aren't making healthy choices ... we have to give them the knowledge here so that they can make the change for themselves', they articulated the importance of learning opportunities beyond the classroom, involving families and the broader community as a further means to progress their students' levels of literacy to become interactive and critical. Doing so would address the multiple levels of influencing factors at the intrapersonal, interpersonal and community levels (Wharf Higgins et al., 2009).

> Have a health fair in the gym at the school where it was child centred and the children created the displays. And, invite all of the parents. That would be a positive community step. [teacher focus group]
> It would be interesting to have students keep track of their diet for a week because they are probably eating most of their food with their families. And perhaps the project could have a visual where they take a picture of their meal and also show a visual diagram of the amount of sugar or fat, or the amount of each food group they eat. From there you could make it bigger by having them research the health effects of their diet. If part of the assignment had a homework piece then they would be working on it at home and discussing food with their families. [teacher focus group]

4.5. Conclusion

As with other forms of literacy, critical media health literacy cannot be relegated to one subject or grade level; rather it is fostered throughout the cognitive developmental span and as health and media contexts and circumstances change, must continue to evolve throughout life. Our experience suggests that grade 7 offers promising place to include CMHL activities as witnessed by our students' learnings and skill development. However, to fully nurture and progress CMHL competencies (note that we were unable to find evidence of students as engaged citizens actively participating in the complexities of modern life — our final attribute and outcome in Table 4.1), students need opportunities to build on their skills past age 12 and preferably as younger learners. Based on our findings with grade 10 students, and as evidenced by their reliance on and unrelenting engagement with media, and unprecedented early onset of chronic health issues, we cannot wait until high school to introduce CMHL lessons. We further strongly advise that curricula infusion is required for teachers to be able to nurture health literacy in their students, particularly in the subjects that develop multiple forms of literacy, for example language arts (reading and media literacy), math (numeracy and document literacy), social studies (citizenship and civic literacy), computer science (digital and internet literacy). To facilitate this, health literacy learning outcomes need to be developed, cross-referenced and aligned with existing subject content and learning outcomes. Subsequently, lesson plans must be created that can be adopted and tailored for different student populations and circumstances, to be easily woven into the school day.

References

Abel, T. (2008). Measuring health literacy: Moving towards a health-promotion perspective. *International Journal of Public Health, 53*, 169–170.

Allen, K., Zolellner, J., Motley, M., & Estabrooks, P. (2011). Understanding the internal and external validity of health literacy interventions: A systematic literature review using the RE-AIM framework. *Journal of Health Communication, 16*(S3), 55–82.

Amed, S., Daneman, D., Mahmud, F. H., & Hamilton, J. (2010). Type 2 diabetes in children and adolescents. *Expert Review of Cardiovascular Therapy, 8*(3), 393–406.

Arksey, H., & O'Malley, L. (2005). Scoping studies: Towards a methodological framework. *International Journal of Social Research Methodology, 8*, 19–32.

Begoray, D., Cimon, M., & Wharf Higgins, J. (2010). *Media/ting health: The powerful role of media as adolescent health literacy educator.* New York: NovaScience.

Begoray, D., & Kwan, B. (2012). A Canadian exploratory study to define a measure of health literacy. *Health Promotion International, 27*(1). doi:10.1093/heapro/dar015

Begoray, D., Wharf Higgins, J., & MacDonald, M. (2009). High school health curriculum and health literacy: Canadian student voices. *Global Health Promotion, 16*(4), 35–42.

Berkman, N. D., Davis, T. C., & McCormack, L. (2010). Health literacy: What is it? *Journal of Health Communication, 15*(2), 9–19.

Biesta, G. J. J. (2010). *Good education in an age of measurement: Ethics, politics, democracy.* Boulder, CO: Paradigm Publishers.

Brey, R. A., Clark, S. E., & Wantz, M. S. (2007). Enhancing health literacy through accessing health information, products, and services: An exercise for children and adolescents. *Journal of School Health, 77*(9), 640–644.

Brey, R. A., Clark, S. E., & Wantz, M. S. (2008). This is your future: A case study approach to foster health literacy. *Journal of School Health, 78*(6), 351–355.

Buckingham, D. (2003). *Media education: Literacy, learning and contemporary culture.* Oxford, UK: Blackwell Publishing.

Chang, L. C. (2011). Health literacy: Self-reported status and health promoting behaviours for adolescents in Taiwan. *Journal of Clinical Nursing, 20*(1–2), 190–196.

Cinelli, R. L., & O'Dea, J. A. (2009). Body image and obesity among Australian adolescents from Indigenous and Anglo-European backgrounds: Implications for health promotion and obesity prevention among Aboriginal youth. *Health Education Research, 24*(6), 1059–1068.

Collins, J., Doyon, D., McAuley, C., & Quijada, A. I. (2011). Reading, writing and deconstructing: Media literacy as part of the school curriculum. *Explorations in Educational Purpose, 13*(1), 159–185.

Daniel, M., Moore, S., & Kestens, Y. (2007). Framing the biosocial pathways underlying associations between place and cardiometabolic disease. *Health and Place, 14*(2), 117–132.

de Leeuw, E. (2012). The political ecosystem of health literacies. *Health Promotion International, 27*(1), 1–4.

Diamond, C., Saintonge, S., August, P., & Azrack, A. (2011). The development of building wellness, a youth health literacy program. *Journal of Health Communication, 16*(3), 103–118.

European Commission. (2010). *The European platform against poverty and social exclusion: A European framework for social and territorial cohesion.* Brussels: European Commission.

Fisher, J., Cabral de Mello, M., Izutsu, T., Vijayakumar, L., Belfer, M. L., & Olayinka, O. (2011). Emerging concerns in the mental health of adolescents in resource-constrained settings. *International Journal of Social Psychiatry, 57*(1), 98–102.

Flecha, A., Garcia, R., & Rudd, R. (2011). Using health literacy in school to overcome inequalities. *European Journal of Education, 46*(2), 209–218.

Friedman, D., & Hoffman-Goetz, L. (2008). Literacy and health literacy as defined in cancer education research: A systematic review. *Health Education Journal, 67*(4), 285–304.

Frisch, A.-L., Camerini, L., Diviani, N., & Schulz, P. J. (2011). Defining and measuring health literacy: How can we profit from other literacy domains? *Health Promotion International, 27*(1), 117–126.

Ghaddar, S. F., Valerio, M. A., Garcia, C. M., & Hansen, L. (2012). Adolescent health literacy: The importance of credible sources for online health information. *Journal of School Health, 82*(1), 28–36.

Greenberg, M. T., Weissberg, R. P., O'Brien, M. U., Zins, J. E., Fredericks, L., Resnik, H., & Elias, M. J. (2003). Enhancing school-based prevention and youth development through coordinated social, emotional, and academic learning. *American Psychologist, 58*(6-7), 466–474.

Haerens, L., Deforche, B., Maes, L., Cardon, G., Stevens, V., & De Bourdeaudhuij, I. (2006). Evaluation of a 2-year physical activity and healthy eating intervention in middle school children. *Health Education Research, 21*(6), 911–921.

Hill, S. C., & Lindsay, G. B. (2003). Using health infomercials to develop media literacy skills. *Journal of School Health, 73,* 239–241.

Hobbs, R., & Frost, R. (2003). Measuring the acquisition of media literacy skills. *Reading Research Quarterly, 38*(3), 330–355.

Institute of Medicine. (2009). *Measures of health literacy: Workshop summary.* Washington, DC: The National Academies Press.

Joint Committee on Health Education Terminology. (1991). Report of the joint committee on health education terminology. *Journal of Health Education, 22*(2), 97–108.

Kaiser Family Foundation. (2010). Generation M2: Media in the lives of 8–18 year olds. Retrieved from http://www.kff.org/entmedia/mh012010pkg.cfm. Accessed on January 5, 2011.

Kelly, K. B. (2007). Promoting adolescent health. *Acta Pædiatrica, 96,* 1389–1391.

Kickbusch, I. (2008). Health literacy: An essential skill for the twenty-first century. *Health Education, 108*(2), 101–104.

Kupersmidt, J. B., Scull, T. M., & Weintraub Austin, E. (2010). Media literacy education for elementary school substance use prevention: Study of media detective. *Pediatrics, 126,* 525–531.

Kutner, M., Greenberg, E., & Baer, J. (2006). *National assessment of adult literacy (NAAL): A first look at the literacy of America's adults in the 21st Century.* Washington, DC: National Center for Education Statistics, Institute of Education Sciences, U.S. Department of Education.

Lay, S. Y., Ang, R. P., Chong, W. H., & Huan, V. S. (2007). Gender differences in adolescent concerns and emotional well-being: Perceptions of Singaporean adolescent students. *The Journal of Genetic Psychology, 168*(1), 63–80.

Manganello, J. (2008). Health literacy and adolescents: A framework and agenda for future research. *Health Education Research, 23,* 840–847.

Marmot, M. (2007). Achieving health equity: From root causes to fair outcomes. *Lancet, 370*(9593), 1153–1163.

Marx, E., Hudson, N., Deal, T., Pateman, B., & Middleton, K. (2007). Promoting health literacy through the health education assessment project. *Journal of School Health, 77*(4), 157–163.

McCuaig, L., Coore, S., & Hay, P. J. (2012). Reducing dissonance along health education fault lines: Health-literacy advocacy and the case for efficacious assessment. *Asia-Pacific Journal of Health, Sport and Physical Education, 3*(1), 2–14.

Metropolitan Area Child Study Research Group. (2002). A cognitive-ecological approach to preventing aggression in urban settings: Initial outcomes for high-risk children. *Journal of Consulting and Clinical Psychology, 70,* 179–194.

Montoya, M. J., & Kent, E. E. (2011). Dialogical action: Moving from community-based to community-driven participatory research. *Qualitative Health Research, 21*(7), 1000–1011.

Murphy, P. W., Davis, T. C., Long, S. W., Jackson, R. H., & Decker, B. (1993). Rapid estimate of adult literacy in medicine (REALM): A quick reading test for patients. *Journal of Reading, 37*(2), 124–130.

Naylor, P. J., & McKay, H. A. (2008). Prevention in the first place: Schools a setting for action on physical inactivity. *British Journal of Sports Medicine, 43*(1), 10–13.

Nutbeam, D. (2000). Health Literacy as a public health goal: A challenge for contemporary health education and communication strategies into the 21st century. *Health Promotion International, 15,* 259–267.

Nutbeam, D. (2008). The evolving concept of health literacy. *Social Science & Medicine, 67,* 2072–2078.

Paakkari, L., & Paakkari, O. (2012). Health literacy as a learning outcome in schools. *Health Education, 112*(2), 133–152.

Parker, R. M., Baker, D. W., Williams, M. V., & Nurss, J. R. (1995). The test of functional health literacy in adults: A new instrument for measuring patients' literacy skills. *Journal of General Internal Medicine, 10*(10), 537–541.

Paul, B., Salwen, M. B., & Dupagne, M. (2007). The third person effect: A meta-analysis of the perceptual hypothesis. In R. Preiss, B. Gayle, N. Burrell, M. Allen & J. Bryant (Eds.), *Mass media effects research: Advances through meta-analysis* (pp. 81–102). Mahway, NJ: Lawrence Erlbaum.

Pettman, T. H., Armstrong, R., Doyle, J., Burford, B., Anderson, L. M., Hillgrove, T., ... Waters, E. (2012). Strengthening evaluation to capture the breadth of public health practice: Ideal vs. real. *Journal of Public Health, 34*(1), 151–155.

Pietilainen, K. H., Kaprio, J., Borg, P., Plasqui, G., Yki-Järvinen, H., Kujala, U., ... Rissanen, A. (2008). Physical inactivity and obesity: A vicious circle. *Obesity, 16*(2), 409–414.

Potter, W. J. (2004). *Theory of media literacy: A cognitive approach*. Thousand Oaks, CA: Sage Publications, Inc.

Rodgers, B. L. (1993). Concept analysis: An evolutionary view. In B. L. Rodgers & K. A. Knafl (Eds.), *Concept development in nursing: Foundations, techniques and applications* (pp. 73–92). Philadelphia, PA: W.B. Saunders.

Rootman, I., & Gordon-El-Bihbety, D. (2008). A vision for a health literate Canada. Report of the expert panel on health literacy. Ottawa: Canadian Public Health Association.

Saan, H., & Wise, M. (2011). Enable, mediate, advocate. *Health Promotion International, 26*(S2), ii187–ii193.

Shields, M., & Tremblay, M. (2010). Canadian childhood obesity estimates based on WHO, IOTF and CDC cut-points. *International Journal of Pediatric Obesity, 5*(3), 265–273.

Simovska, V. (2012). What do health-promoting schools promote? *Health Education, 22*(2), 84–87.

Sorenson, K., Van Den Broucke, S., Fullam, J., Doyle, G., Pelikan, J., Slonska, A., Brand, H., & European Health Literacy Project. (2012). Health literacy and public health: A systematic review and integration of definitions and models. *BMC Public Health, 12*(80). doi:10.1186/1471-2458-12-80

Speros, C. (2005). Health literacy: Concept analysis. *Journal of Advanced Nursing, 50*(6), 633–640.

Stamatakis, E., Zaninotto, P., Falaschetti, E., Mindell, J., & Head, J. (2010). Time trends in childhood and adolescent obesity in England from 1995 to 2007 and projections of prevalence to 2015. *Journal of Epidemiology and Community Health, 64*(2), 167–174.

Stokols, D. (2000). The social ecological paradigm of wellness promotion. In M. S. Jamner & D. Stokols (Eds.), *Promoting human wellness: New frontiers for research, practice, and policy* (pp. 21–37). Berkeley, CA: University of California Press.

Strasburger, V. C., Wilson, B. J., & Jordon, A. B. (2009). *Children, adolescents and the media* (2nd ed.). Thousand Oaks, CA: Sage.

Tremblay, M., Shields, M., Laviolett, M., Craig, C. L., Janseen, I., & Connor Gorber, S. (2010). Fitness of Canadian children and youth: Results from the 2007–2009 Canadian Health Measures Survey. *Health Reports, 21*(1), 1–15.

Trickett, E. (2011). Community-based participatory research as worldview or instrumental strategy: Is it lost in translation(al) research? *American Journal of Public Health, 101*(8), 1353–1355.

Van Cleave, J., Gortmaker, S., & Perrin, J. (2010). Dynamics of obesity and chronic health conditions among children and youth. *Journal of the American Medical Association, 303*(7), 623–630.

van Sluijs, E. M. F., McMinn, A. M., & Griffin, S. J. (2007). Effectiveness of interventions to promote physical activity in children and adolescents: Systematic view of controlled trials. *British Medical Journal, 42*(8), 703–707.

von Wagner, C., Steptoe, A., Wolf, M. S., & Wardle, J. (2009). Health literacy and health actions: A review and a framework from health psychology. *Health Education and Behavior, 36*(5), 860–877.

Vygotsky, L. (1978). *Mind in society: The development of higher psychological processes.* Cambridge, MA: Harvard University Press.

Wharf Higgins, J., & Begoray, D. (2012). Exploring the borderlands between media and health: Conceptualizing 'critical media health literacy'. *Journal of Media Literacy Education, 4*(2), 136–148. Retrieved from http://www.jmle.org

Wharf Higgins, J., Begoray, D., & MacDonald, M. (2009). A social ecological conceptual framework for understanding adolescent health literacy in the health education classroom. *American Journal of Community Psychology, 44*, 350–362.

World Health Organization. (2008). *Ten facts on adolescent health.* Retrieved from http://www.who.int/features/factfiles/adolescent_health/facts/en/index.html. Accessed on March 37, 2012.

Wu, A., Begoray, D., MacDonald, M., Wharf Higgins, J., Frankish, J., Kwan, B., ... Rootman, I. (2010). Measuring health literacy of Canadian high school students. *Health Promotion International, 25*(4), 444–452.

Zimmet, P. (2011). The growing pandemic of type 2 diabetes: A crucial need for prevention and improved detection. *Medicographia, 33*, 15–21.

Appendix A.   Energy Drinks Lesson Plan

Lesson #1 — Energy Drinks — Good or Bad?

Course: Planning Ten	Unit: Health, Energy Drinks	**Lesson #1 Energy Drinks: Good or Bad?**
Learning Outcomes: *Healthy Living: Social and environmental influences on health (peers and media)* *Health Information: Analyse health information for validity and personal relevance, media literacy for health information — accuracy, bias, point of view, relevance* *Health Decisions: Evaluate the potential effects of an individual's health-related decisions on self, family and community*		

Detailed Lesson

Purposes/Teacher Considerations	Student Engagement and Activities
Activate Prior Knowledge (10 min) • Teacher shows student a collection of energy drink cans (i.e. Red Bull, AMP, Rockstar etc.) • Teacher engages students in a short discussion about energy drinks. Questions include: Has anyone tried any of these? Do you know anyone who drinks them? What are the reasons you think people drink them? What have you heard about related health factors to these drinks?	• Students reflect on their knowledge of and experience with energy drinks (Alternative: students can discuss these questions in small groups)
Activity: 25–30 min • Hand out the scenario about energy drinks. Let students know that there are two versions (female characters and male	• Students read the scenario on their own or in pairs. • After reading they engage in a discussion with a peer. They are

characters), and they can choose which one they want to read.

Teacher monitors student progress and engages in discussion when necessary. She/he should be looking for students understanding that advertisement, peer pressure and overwhelming schedules all relate to the use of energy drinks. Students should also demonstrate awareness that people commonly do negative things to their body if they see positive effects in their ability (i.e. increase in energy). Finally, students should be coming up with questions about what is in energy drinks, what do doctors and researchers say, what is the maximum number of drinks per day etc.

Closing:
• As a whole class, the teacher records all of the questions the students came up with. She/He then groups questions that are similar to produce major themes of information the main character and the students in the class need answered (Possible Themes include: information about ingredients, information about studies and what doctors say, information about usage).

provided the following discussion questions:

1) Why did the main character's friend promise that energy drinks were healthy? Where might she/he have gotten that idea?
2) Why did the main character go from drinking 1–2 drinks a day to drinking up to 4 drinks? What motivates you to drink or eat things in excess?
3) What questions should the main character ask while he/she researches energy drinks? List questions you think need to be answered before he/she continues drinking energy drinks.
4) What do you think? Are energy drinks healthy or not? Do you need more information?

• Students share their answers to questions 1–4 in groups of four.

Lesson #2 — What Is in This Stuff?

Course: Planning Ten	Unit: Health, Energy Drinks	**Lesson #2 What Is in This Stuff?**
Learning Outcomes: *Healthy Living: Social and environmental influences on health (peers and media)* *Health Information: Analyse health information for validity and personal relevance, media literacy for health information — accuracy, bias, point of view, relevance* *Health Decisions: Evaluate the potential effects of an individual's health-related decisions on self, family and community*		
Connection to Last Lesson: N/A		

Purpose/Teacher Considerations	**Student Engagement and Activities**
Introduction: 15 min • Briefly review questions compiled from previous lesson. • Discuss with students that before the main character or the class can decide if energy drinks are good or bad we need to learn more about what is actually in them. • Poses question to class: What ingredients are actually in an energy drink?	• In pairs, students create a list of what they think is in energy drinks. The pairs then form groups of four to compare and discuss their lists. Each group is then given a can of an energy drink to examine. They look at the list of ingredients and pick out two that they are unfamiliar with.
Activity: 25–30 min • Teacher monitors student research. Assists in finding appropriate websites if necessary and ensuring that students are recording the information they are finding.	• Students work in their groups researching their selected ingredients on the internet. They complete worksheet 1 together as they work. (Modification: Students can break into pairs with each pair taking one ingredient, this will save time.)

Closing: 5–10 min
• Teacher lists the ingredients for both milk and orange juice on the board or on overhead. She then engages students in a discussion comparing these ingredients with the ingredients found in energy drinks.

Lesson #3 — The Appeal of Energy Drinks

Course: Planning Ten	Unit: Health, Energy Drinks	**Lesson #3 The Appeal of Energy Drinks**
Learning Outcomes: *Healthy Living: Social and environmental influences on health (peers and media)* *Health Information: Analyse health information for validity and personal relevance, media literacy for health information — accuracy, bias, point of view, relevance* *Health Decisions: Evaluate the potential effects of an individual's health-related decisions on self, family and community*		
Connection to Last Lesson: N/A		

Purpose/Teacher Considerations	**Student Engagement and Activities**
Opening: 15–20 min Review/Wrap-up of Previous Lesson • After students have shared, teacher offers additional information about taurine and glucuronolactone (two of the most common ingredients in energy drinks). Information can be found at: http://en.wikipedia.org/wiki/Taurine	• Students will share what they discovered about their ingredients with the whole class.

and http://en.wikipedia.org/wiki/Glucuronolactone
- Teacher then leads a discussion on the following questions: Why is it important to read the labels of our foods and drinks? Why is it important to do research on ingredients we are unfamiliar with?

Introduction to Advertisement
- Teacher asks students: If energy drinks have ingredients that are not good for you, what makes them so appealing?
- Teacher discusses the fact that advertising plays a big role in this. She/He asks students: Who do you think is the targeted group of consumers for energy drinks? Why?

Activity: 35–40 min
- Teacher shows students an example of an energy drink's commercial on YouTube. The link below is a good Red Bull commercial, but there are several other options: http://www.youtube.com/watch?v=8x9iYweART4
- After showing the video twice, the teacher engages students in a discussion about the questions they were considering.
- The teacher then puts the students in groups of 3–4 and provides each group with a website of an energy drink to investigate.

- While watching the video students are to consider: Who is the ad appealing to? What does the product claim to be able to do? What means of persuasion have the advertisers used? Is there any mention of health concerns or limitations on use?
- Students complete the worksheet #2 while they are looking at the website.
- The following are websites students can go to:
  – AMP www.ampenergy.com (click on Drink)
  – Red Bull www.redbull.ca (click on Products)
  – Rockstar www.rockstar69.com
  – Hype www.hype.com

	NOTE: as content on these websites is constantly changing the teacher should review prior to lesson for appropriateness
Closing: 5 min • Teacher engages students in a brief discussion about how influential they feel advertising is on their age group and why nutritional information is commonly left out of advertising campaigns.	

Lesson #4 — School Survey

Course: Planning Ten	Unit: Health, Energy Drinks	**Lesson #4 School Survey**
Learning Outcomes: *Healthy Living: Social and environmental influences on health (peers and media)* *Health Information: Analyse health information for validity and personal relevance, media literacy for health information — accuracy, bias, point of view, relevance* *Health Decisions: Evaluate the potential effects of an individual's health-related decisions on self, family and community*		
Connection to Last Lesson: Students will be sharing what they found on the websites they looked at during the last lesson		

Purposes/Teacher Considerations	**Student Engagement and Activities**
Introduction: Previous Lesson Review/Wrap-Up • After sharing, engage students in a discussion about how many foods and drinks leave out all health and nutritional information from advertisement and instead appeal to one's desire to be 'cool'.	• Students share with the class what each of their group found on their website. At the end of sharing, each group must decide if their website made them want to buy an energy drink.

Introduction to Survey
- Teacher states: As found in our review of the advertisements of energy drinks, teenagers and young adults are the target market. At our school then we have access to their targeted group. When it comes to understanding the impact a product might have on the health of a community it is important to gather information about the people who use it and who do not use it. One way of doing this is to conduct a survey. In a moment, you will be placed in groups to complete a challenge. Your challenge will be to create a survey on knowledge and use of energy drinks to give to two classrooms in our school. Once you have given your survey, you and your teammates will compile the data and create a poster or power-point presentation to report your findings to the class.

Activity
- Teacher will divide students into teams of 4–5 for the survey challenge.
- Modifications: Teacher can give students sample survey to look at the format, types of questions used and wording. Additionally, the class can come up with the survey together and then form groups when they go out into classrooms to do the survey.
- Possible survey questions: List all of the energy drinks that you know of. Do you drink any

- Students will create a survey that would gather essential information about energy drinks, including usage (personal, friends), frequency, reasons for usage, background knowledge of energy drinks.
- Once the teacher has okayed the survey, students will conduct their survey in two assigned classrooms (pre-organized by the teacher).

drinks? If yes, how often? Do you have friends who drink energy drinks? If yes, how many friends? Why do you drink energy drinks (or why do you think other people drink energy drinks)? Why do you not drink energy drinks? Do you think they are healthy?

Closing: 5–10 min
- The teacher should leave 5–10 min each day to bring the students together as a whole class and discuss what they are finding, experiences in creating and conducting surveys etc.

- Students will then compile data and create a poster or a power-point.
- Students will need 3–4 class periods to complete this lesson.

Worksheet 1: Hey ... What is in here anyway?!?

Name of Energy Drink:_____

List the ingredients found in your drink that you guessed were in there:

_____

_____

List 2 ingredients you have never heard of:

_____   _____

For each ingredient of these unheard ingredients, find out as much information as you can about it. Including: What is it? What other foods/drinks is it in? Is it nutritional? Why is it in there?

Ingredient #1:

Ingredient #2:

Worksheet 2:

Evaluating Advertising: Does this website make me want to buy an energy drink?

1. Overall Appeal — consider the following about the website:
   - Are the images catchy? Provide example for why or why not.
   - Is the language persuasive? Provide example for why or why not.
   - Are there any gimmicks, prizes, contests being offered?
   - Is the focus of the website the product or an image?
   - What are your overall impressions of the website?

2. Who are the intended consumers (viewers of website)?

For example, male/female, age group, lifestyle. Be sure to support your reasoning!

3. Health Information

Can you find.....
   - nutritional information?
   - a list of the ingredients?
   - recommended usage?
   - any health warnings?

If you found any of these things, how hard was it to find this information?

Additional Resources:

Article debating the effects of energy drinks:
http://style.uk.msn.com/wellbeing/healthyeating/article.aspx?cp-documentid=5580378

Information regarding a common chemical in energy drinks:
http://en.wikipedia.org/wiki/Glucuronolactone

Articles regarding debate surrounding energy drinks:
http://altmedicine.about.com/od/completeazindex/a/energy_drinks.htm
http://www.nytimes.com/2005/11/23/business/23drinks.html?pagewanted=print
http://www.energysip.com

Support for energy drinks:
http://www.exploreenumbers.co.uk/energy-drink-ingredients-given-clear.html

Appendix B.   Energy Drinks Scenario

A TYPICAL DAY FOR YOUR FRIEND IS PRETTY HECTIC. YOU'VE
NOTICED THAT LATELY YOUR FRIEND HAS BEEN RELYING ON
ENERGY DRINKS (E.G., RED BULL, SHARK, JOLT COLA, SOBE
ARUSH) TO GET THROUGH SCHOOL, SPORTS PRACTICE, WORK,
AND THEN HOMEWORK.

YOU JUST GOT YOUR FIRST AFTER SCHOOL JOB AND ARE
FINDING IT DIFFICULT TO STAY AWAKE AT NIGHTS TO FINISH
YOUR HOMEWORK.

YOU MENTION TO YOUR FRIEND THAT YOU ALWAYS FEEL TIRED. YOUR FRIEND SUGGESTS YOU TRY SOME OF THE ENERGY DRINKS TOO. YOUR FRIEND PROMISES YOU THAT THEY ARE HEALTHY AND THAT MOST IMPORTANTLY THEY WILL HELP YOU STAY AWAKE.

SO YOU DECIDE TO TAKE YOUR FRIEND'S ADVICE AND START TO USE ENERGY DRINKS TO GET THROUGH THE DAY. AT FIRST, YOU STARTED WITH ONE OR TWO DRINKS A DAY, BUT ARE NOW HAVING UP TO FOUR ENERGY DRINKS A DAY.

ALTHOUGH YOU ARE EXHAUSTED BY THE TIME YOU LAY DOWN
TO SLEEP, YOU'VE ALSO NOTICED LATELY THAT YOU ARE
SOMETIMES TOO WIRED TO SLEEP.

ENERGY DRINKS OFTEN MAKE BIG PROMISES. SOME SAY
THEY'LL INCREASE ENERGY AND ALERTNESS. OTHERS OFFER
EXTRA NUTRITION, AND SOME EVEN CLAIM TO BOOST YOUR
ATHLETIC PERFORMANCE OR POWERS OF CONCENTRATION.
YOU BEGIN TO WONDER HOW THESE PRODUCTS MAY AFFECT
YOUR BODY. YOU DECIDE THAT YOU WILL LOOK INTO WHAT
EXACTLY ARE IN THESE ENERGY DRINKS, AND WHAT THEY MAY
DO TO YOUR BODY SO YOU ARE BETTER INFORMED.

Appendix C. Critical Media Health Literacy Grade 10 Lesson Plans

<table>
<tr><td colspan="2" align="center">**Lesson # 1 of 3 – Introduction to Brand and Image**</td><td rowspan="20">Health and Media Literacy – Grade 10 ⟨⟨ Planning 10 – Create an Ad</td></tr>
<tr>
<td>

Objectives, based on the BC Ministry of Education Planning 10 Prescribed Learning Outcomes for Health Living:

- C1 analyze factors that influence health
- C2 analyze health information for validity and personal relevance
- C5 evaluate the potential effects of an individual's health-related decisions on self, family, and community

</td>
<td>

Rationale:

- Consider the effect of branding on choices
- Determine why advertisers use branding
- Apply learning to advertising about products designed to be healthy choices
- Determine author/audience/purpose/omissions for sample PSAs (how was the ad designed to appeal to a particular group?)

Resources:

- Students will be provided with materials to complete a taste test including:
- 3 small disposable cups for each student
- Coke, Pepsi, and a generic brand of soda, enough for each student to do a blind taste test
- Two print ads (or video ads) for Vitamin drinks to consider the health messages linked to branding
- Two print PSA ads to critique, both related to health
- Students will be provided with examples of advertisements related to health and wellness issues/products from print and the Internet, such as from the Canadian Media Awareness site: http://www.media-awareness.ca/english/resources/educational/lessons/elementary/advertising_marketing/upload/Selling-Obesity-Lesson-Kit.pdf
- Source of the taste test idea used in this lesson: Lynda Bergsma interview, 2010
- Source of the objectives for this lesson is the Planning 10 Integrated Resource Package 2007 of the BC Ministry of Health http://www.bced.gov.bc.ca/irp/plan10.pdf

</td>
</tr>
<tr><td>**Timing**</td><td align="center">**Body of Lesson**</td></tr>
<tr>
<td>

Day 1

10 min/ 80

</td>
<td>

1)
- Let the students know what the agenda will be for today's 80-minute block.
- Ask students if they feel they are affected by branding (does term need to be defined?)
- Take a quick straw poll about which brand of soda students drink (results on board)
- What health messages have they seen or heard about drinking soda?

</td>
</tr>
<tr>
<td>

20 min/ 80

</td>
<td>

2)
- Describe the blind taste test, showing the students the brands being tested
- Discuss how the test needs to be done as a group so even their comments don't influence each other (peer/near peer influences on point of view)
- Carry out test and record results (students mark sheet with choices and hand in)
- Discuss results and ask again if students feel they are affected by advertising, particularly that advertising geared to buying a particular brand. Ask how is brand associated with image (values, lifestyles: If you drink Diet Coke are you making a more healthful choice than another brand?)

</td>
</tr>
<tr>
<td>

40 min/ 80

</td>
<td>

3)
- Show a Vitamin water ad (ask how many students have tried this and how do they feel-are they making a good choice?, What values and lifestyle images are represented with "health" products?)
- Show an ad for a "health product" and model dissecting the ad: Who was the author? Target audience? What was omitted from the ad?
- Look at the second ad and ask the students if they can spot how the advertisers try to convince the consumer of the health value of the product. Again ask the above questions, remembering to stress there are many right answers.
- Discuss what motivates advertisers to try and convince consumers of a product's value. Are all ads bad? Can an ad convince you to buy something (or take advice) you don't really need? Or are ads more concerned with trying to get you to choose one brand over another?
- List some other products available that use the health angle to attract consumers.
- Discuss how advertisers test their ads (focus groups, etc.)

</td>
</tr>
</table>

10 min/ 80	4)
	• Ask the students to reflect in a journal what they thought were the concepts they found most valuable in the class. What might life be like without advertising? Good/bad (see Messages and Meanings)
Day 2	1)
10 min/ 80	• Whole class: Check in with the group and give them the agenda for today's 80-minute block.
20 min/ 80	2)
	• Introduce the PSA concept and show some classic PSAs from earlier decades
	• Discuss audience, author, purpose, points of view and context
	• Model deconstructing a PSA (What is the agenda of the group presenting the PSA? Who was the author? Target audience? What was omitted from the ad?)
20 min/ 80	3)
	• Should anybody be allowed to create a PSA and what are the rules that apply to what is allowed to be shown on TV/movie/internet
	• Are all PSAs meant for all people?
20 min/80	4)
	• Show another PSA and have the students critique it individually (pen and paper)
	• Share critiques, writing main themes/discoveries on the board
	• Let the students know that the information will be compiled and handed back to them as a reference sheet.
10 min/ 80	5)
	• Ask the students to reflect in a journal what they thought were the concepts they found most valuable in the class.

Accommodations and Extensions:

Reflective journals can be written and/or illustrated

Check for visibility/hearing hearing issues

Assessment:

N% for Participation in class discussions

N% for journal/WIKI

N% for attendance

Evaluation will be based on the students' knowledge, thinking, and application skills to effectively:

• Apply learning/insight from the branding taste test to critiquing products advertised as healthful
• Apply learning/insight about psychographics or demographics when considering PSAs and other ads
• Reflect on author's purpose, target audiences, point of view, omissions, health messages

Moving Forward:

Dissect a PSA

PSA= Public Service Announcement: A public service announcement (PSA) or community service announcement (CSA) is an advertisement broadcast on radio or television, for the public interest. PSAs are intended to modify public attitudes by raising awareness about specific issues. Produced and programmed much like commercials, but usually not produced for profit. A PSA is aired free by broadcasters as a public service. The spots are commercials prepared by government agencies or nonprofit organizations that typically deal with noncontroversial topics, such as health and public safety.

Who was the author?

Who was the target audience?

What did the advertisers tell you? Why?

What didn't they tell you? Why?

What images, words, or sounds did the advertisers use to make you interested in watching?

How did the advertisers try to convince you that you should listen to their advice?

Advertisers and Motivation

What motivates advertisers to try and convince you, the consumer, of a product's value?

Can an ad convince you to buy something (or take advice) you don't really need?

Are most ads just really trying to get you to choose one brand over another?

Are all ads bad? What might be examples of good or bad ads?

What is a focus group?

Lesson # 2 of 3 – Create an Ad/PSA

Objectives, based on the BC Ministry of Education Planning 10 Prescribed Learning Outcomes for Health Living:	Rationale:
• C1 analyze factors that influence health • C2 analyze health information for validity and personal relevance • C5 evaluate the potential effects of an individual's health-related decisions on self, family, and community	• Apply learning from the persuasion unit *(Lesson 1 of 3)* in initial development of a product or message *about health* • Choose appropriate ads *about health* for first impressions by a *middle school* focus group • Apply learning about psychographics or demographics when choosing and defining focus group • *Determine potential ideas to* Re-design the project through analysis of focus group results **Resources:** • Student groups will be provided with materials to create an ad, including tri-fold posters, pens, magazines, glue sticks, and access to the computer lab for students who want to create a digital poster. • A journal or wiki space for each group to keep a thorough log and rationale of the whole process of creating an ad. • For warm up/group activities in Day 1, use the Accessing Media Messages resources from the Media Education Lab (Renee Hobbs, Temple University). See Identifying Media Messages and How Do You Use the Media at http://web.archive.org/web/20030402230031/archive.nandotimes.com/prof/edsvc/teach/niecurric/accessing.html • For warm up/group activities in Day 2, use questions from the Evaluating Media Messages resources from the Media Education Lab (Renee Hobbs, Temple University). See Modifying Your Position ,What is it Saying? and Values in Advertising at http://web.archive.org/web/20030214191704/archive.nandotimes.com/prof/edsvc/teach/niecurric/evaluating.html • Students will be provided with examples of advertisements related to health and wellness issues/products from print and the Internet, such as from the Canadian Media Awareness site: http://www.media-awareness.ca/english/resources/educational/lessons/elementary/advertising_marketing/upload/Selling-Obesity-Lesson-Kit.pdf • Source of the project idea used in this lesson: http://www.aml.ca/resources/item.php?articleID=379 • Source of the objectives for this lesson is the Planning 10 Integrated Resource Package 2007 of the BC Ministry of Health http://www.bced.gov.bc.ca/irp/plan10.pdf

Timing	Body of Lesson
Day 1 10 min/ 80	1) • Let the students know what the agenda will be for today's 80-minute block. • Lead a group discussion to recall the activities of lesson 1, specifically the critiques of the magazine ads and the public service announcements (PSAs). • Ask, if they have noticed ads or PSAs related to health since the class last met? • Ask about the characteristics of the ads and PSAs that the students talk about.
20 min/ 80	2) • Whole class: Introduction to "Create an Ad" assignment. Discuss the purpose of the "Create an Ad" assignment and the activity of presenting the ad to focus groups. Let the students know: - They will be presenting their ads to middle school students while taking notes about the middle school student comments and feedback during the focus group sessions - They will also have the opportunity to analyze and present their findings from the focus groups. - This activity is based on authentic industry practices, except that in this activity focus group members will not be tracked with identifying information. - This activity is designed to provides students with a clear understanding of the deep level of planning and audience/consumer research that goes into an ad campaign. • Partners: Discover what each cares about in terms of health and present back one thing learned about the partner's health concern/question. Note the topics on a projected screen.

		• Whole class: Brainstorm about more health topics, based on what students consider as "health" and add to the list. • Review the vocabulary and phrases: author, purpose/main purpose, values, lifestyles, points of view, audience, different people understand things differently, omitted, health messages
40 min/ 80	3)	• Have the students form groups of 3-4 students, such as by counting off 1 through 8 if there are 30 students in the class. Ask the groups to take 40 minutes to: • Assign one person from the group to keep a journal or wiki space for the purpose keeping a thorough log and rationale of the whole process. Let the students know this is intended to keep them organized and will effectively deepen the learning in this activity. • Determine what product or message/idea they want to promote. This decision will be based on the nature of *the discoveries made during lesson 1*, as well as their learning goals and consideration of the focus group characteristics. Consideration should be made about the age and other characteristics known about personal experiences as a middle school student. The groups may define the focus group in specific psychographic, as well as demographic, terms (see the V.A.L.S. - Values and Lifestyles descriptors). • Rough out a projected ad/s – can be video, sound, or print. This should be in a form clear enough so that the focus group can respond clearly and appropriately to it. Try to include all sound and narrative text, if applicable. In the case of video, storyboards are essential. • Provide examples of storyboards and student made videos, such as from YouTube.
10 min/ 80	4)	• Whole group: Check in with the progress of ideas for ads by asking that one student from each group tell the class what their group's ad will be about.
Day 2 10 min/ 80	5)	• Whole group: Check in with students and give them the agenda for today's 80-minute block.
50 min/ 80	6)	• Ask the students to work in their groups to complete their ads. • Check in with each group and provide support to the students as they complete their ads.
20 min/ 80	7)	• Present the process for working with the middle school students and emphasize that no names or identifying information will be allowed when collecting notes about feedback and comments from the focus groups. • Whole class: Discuss the process for working with the focus groups of middle school students and any concerns for the next steps.

Accommodations and Extensions:

Assessment:

N% for Participation in class discussions

N% for journal/WIKI

N% for attendance

Evaluation will be based on the students' knowledge, thinking, and application skills to effectively:

• Apply learning/insight from the branding taste test to critiquing products advertised as healthful
• Apply learning/insight about psychographics or demographics when considering PSAs and other ads
• Reflect on author's purpose, target audiences, point of view, omissions, health messages

Moving Forward:

Plan for the Poster Presentation on Health

Please list the names of students in your group:

1. What is the theme or central question for your presentation?

2. Who is the audience? Describe the characteristics of the audience with whom you want to communicate.

3. What is your purpose, and what format will you use for your poster? For example, you could explain an issue or you could make an argument about some action that should be taken by your audience.

4. Think about the characteristics of your audience. What language and tone will you use to appeal to your audience? What human needs, fears, or desires are being appealed to?

5. What images and colours would be helpful for this poster?
http://www.media-awareness.ca/english/resources/educational/lessons/secondary/alcohol/psa_driving.cfm

Lesson # 3 of 3 – Conduct Focus Groups and Analyze Findings

Objectives, based on the BC Ministry of Education Planning 10 Prescribed Learning Outcomes for Health Living:

- C1 analyze factors that influence health
- C2 analyze health information for validity and personal relevance
- C5 evaluate the potential effects of an individual's health-related decisions on self, family, and community

Rationale:

- Apply learning from the persuasion unit in initial development of a product or message *about health*
- Choose appropriate ads *about health* for first impressions by a *middle school* focus group
- Apply learning about psychographics or demographics when choosing and defining focus group
- *Determine potential ideas to* Re-design the project through analysis of focus group results

Resources:

- Poster materials
- Source of the project idea used in this lesson:
  http://www.aml.ca/resources/item.php?articleID=379
- Source of the objectives for this lesson is the Planning 10 Integrated Resource Package 2007 of the BC Ministry of Health
  http://www.bced.gov.bc.ca/irp/plan10.pdf

Timing	Body of Lesson
Day 1 10 min/ 80	1) • Review the focus group guide with the students. • Organize the groups for the focus group sessions. • Each of the Belmont groups will work with one group of middle school students.
60 min/ 80	2) • One student from each group presents ad projects/posters to focus groups of middle school students or an upper grade in the secondary school. • The rest of the students from each group document (anonymously) responses of middle school students to the ads
10 min/ 80	3) • Return to Belmont classroom.
Day 2 10 min/ 80	4) • Check in with the students to recall the focus group sessions, i.e., ask for general comments about the sessions. • Let the students know the agenda for today.
30 min/ 80)	5) • Ask students to work in their groups to discuss and analyze their findings from the focus groups. • Ask the students to prepare a presentation of their findings on a large sheet of paper.
40 min/ 80)	6) • Groups present to whole class • Thank you and close

Accommodations and Extensions:

Assessment:

N% for Participation in class discussions

N% for poster, based on rubric

N% for attendance

Evaluation will be based on the students' knowledge, thinking, and application skills to effectively:

- Apply learning/insight from the branding taste test to critiquing products advertised as healthful
- Apply learning/insight about psychographics or demographics when considering PSAs and other ads
- Reflect on author's purpose, target audiences, point of view, omissions, health messages

Moving Forward:

Health and Media Literacy – Grade 10

Planning 10 – Conduct Focus Groups and Analyze Findings

Guide for Conducting the Focus Group Session

Step 1 – Review the purpose of the focus group session:

Your health poster represents a public service announcement (PSA) on a health topic of interest to your group. The purpose of the focus group session is to see if the message of your health poster is effective with your target audience by asking questions about their knowledge, attitudes, beliefs, tastes and preferences. The target audience and focus group for this project is a group of students who are in grade 12. The questions you ask in the focus group are intended to help you understand if your health message is of interest to your audience and helpful for your audience to make decisions and take action in caring for their own health and well-being. The questions are also designed to help you understand how your audience is reading and understanding the messages in your poster.

Step 2 - Please list the names of students in your group (the group who created the poster):

Step 3 – Please choose roles for each person in your group.

1. Select one group member to be the leader of the focus group session. This person will introduce the group members, provide a brief description of your poster project, and ask the questions of the focus group.
2. Select one person to act as a moderator. This individual should be focused, familiar with what you need to know, a good listener, friendly, and able to keep everyone on track within the time allowed for the focus group session. A good moderator should be able to probe for more information and draw answers out of participants. He or she should also be able to diplomatically "tone down" dominant interviewees, and get shyer participants to speak up.
3. The rest of the group members will act as note-takers during the questioning. They will not be able to participate directly in the focus groups but will observe and help in interpreting and applying the information collected. You want to create an environment where people feel relaxed and comfortable discussing the issues raised by your poster project.

Step 4 – Meet with the focus group. Your group leader will:

1. Introduce your group members to the focus group.
2. Give the focus group member as brief summary of the purpose of the your poster.
3. Ask the focus group to take a few minutes to view and read the content of your health poster.

Step 5 – Your group leader will ask the following questions of the focus group, while the moderator keeps the process on track and the note takers record the comments of the focus group.

The group leader will fill in the blanks with the theme or main question from your poster. For example, if your topic is "sexually transmitted diseases", then question 1 would be, *Do you know about sexually transmitted diseases?*

1. Do you know or have you ever heard about _____?

2. Are you concerned about _____? Why or why not?

3. Do you believe this issue is important for your health? Why or why not?

4. Is the information in the poster helpful to you? Why or why not?
    For example, is there enough information provided for you to do something about the issue? What is missing?

5. If this poster was mounted in the school halls, would it attract your attention? Why or why not?

6. What would you change about this message? (e.g., content, style, colour, image)

7. What are the author's main purposes? Do you think the purpose is to inform, entertain, make money, or persuade?

8. What techniques were used to attract and hold your attention in this PSA poster?

9. What values, lifestyles or points of view were represented in this PSA poster?

10. What age groups do you think represent the target audience for this poster AND why do you think so? For example, do you think it would appeal to 2-11 year olds, 12-17 year olds, 18-25 year olds, 25-40 year olds, 40-60 year olds, 61 year olds and older?

11. What genders do you think represent the target audience for this poster AND why do you think so? For example, do you think it would appeal to females, males, or both?

12. What economic levels do you think represent the target audience for this poster AND why do you think so? For example, do you think it would appeal

to poor people, working-class people, middle class people, upper class people, and/or wealthy people?

13. How might different people understand this PSA poster differently than you do?

14. What is omitted from this poster?

15. What messages do you think are MOST important in this poster from the author's point of view? Check all that apply AND say why you think so.

16. Are there any health messages in this poster? If so, what are they?

Step 6– After the focus group session, each student will be asked to submit to the teacher a one-page reflection on his or her focus group experience. Question prompts will be provided. In addition, each group will present the notes from the focus group session in class. The group presentations should include the following:

1. An brief outline of the issue addressed by the PSA poster
2. Comments about the focus group questions
3. A summary and analysis of feedback from the focus group
4. Comments on the focus group process
5. Comments on the main health messages, based on focus group feedback
6. Ideas for improving or changing the poster to achieve the goals of the PSA

Sources:

http://www.media-awareness.ca/english/resources/educational/lessons/secondary/advertising_marketing/mtt_marketing_tactics.cfm

http://mediaeducationlab.com/messages-meanings

Name: Date:

INFORMATIONAL POSTER
for health awareness

Criteria	4	3	2	1
Content	Informative, accurate, relevant details, and to the point	Informative, relevant details, and accurate	Informative and accurate	Incomplete information or inaccurate
Graphics	High quality, carefully chosen to support information	Graphics enhance the pamphlet	Few graphics or irrelevant	No graphics
Layout	Excellent design and use of space. Well organized.	Good design and use of space. Satisfactory organization.	Adequate use of space. Some organization.	Little organization.
Conventions	No spelling or grammatical errors.	Very few spelling or grammatical errors.	Several errors. Little evidence of proofreading.	Errors make it difficult to read poster.
Overall impression	Helpful, user friendly, and concise.	Helpful and functional	Helpful	Unclear, incomplete

How does this project connect with what I have learned?

_____
_____
_____
_____

Sources:

_____
_____

Name: Date:

Written Journal
for reflection on CMHL classes

Criteria	4	3	2	1
Content	Reflective and thoughtful, includes a question	Reflective and thoughtful	Summarizes lesson	Vague or not connected to lesson
Overall impression	Has completed entries as requested and has used the journal to really reflect on the classes	Has completed entries as requested	Has made entries that do not include reflections	Has made at least 1 entry

How does this journal help me reflect on what I have learned?

_____

_____

_____

_____

Appendix D. Critical Health Media Literacy Pre- and Post-test questions

1. Who is the author of this message? Check all that apply.
   __Coca Cola __FIFA __ Fans of soccer/football __South African citizens__Soccer/football players

2. What are the author's main purposes? Check all that apply.
   __to inform __to entertain__to make money __to persuade

3. What techniques were used to attract and hold your attention in this advertisement?

4. Who is the target audience for this advertisement? Check all that apply AND say why you think so.
   a. __Males (I think this because_____)
   b. __Females (I think this because_____)

5. What values, lifestyles or points of view were represented in this advertisement?

6. Which age group do you think the authors were trying to reach with this advertisement? Check all that apply AND say why you think so.
   a. __2–11 year olds (I think this because_____)
   b. __12–17 year olds (I think this because_____)
   c. __18–25 year olds (I think this because_____)
   d. __25–40 year olds (I think this because_____)
   e. __40–60 year olds (I think this because_____)
   f. __61 year olds and older (I think this because_____)

7. Who is not mentioned in this advertisement?

8. Who do you think the authors were trying to reach with this advertisement? Check all that apply AND say why you think so.
   a. __poor people (I think this because_____)
   b. __working class people (I think this because_____)
   c. __middle class people (I think this because_____)
   d. __upper middle class people (I think this because_____)
   e. __wealthy people (I think this because_____)

9. Are there any health messages in the advertisement? If so, what are they?

10. How might different people understand this advertisement differently than you do?

11. From the author's point of view, which messages are MOST important in this advertisement? Check all that apply AND say why you think so.

    __Coke will make you feel less thirsty when you are playing sports (I think this because_____)

    __Athletes drink Coke (I think this because_____)

    __Coke will give you energy (I think this because _____)

    __Coke is liked by everyone in the world (I think this because_____)

    __Coke helps people to be friends (I think this because_____)

    __Coke tastes great (I think this because_____)

    __Drinking Coke is fun (I think this because_____)

Appendix E. Grade 7 Critical Media Health Literacy Lesson Plans

Lessons and Related Resources

Lesson: 1 - Values: What's important to you?

OVERVIEW - Project pre-test and values lesson - Students identify and rank values in order of personal importance. Then reflect on what makes it difficult to live according to their values.

GOAL - The goal of this lesson is to encourage students to think about what they think is valuable, and what they feel they *should* think is valuable and then to reflect on how this impacts the choices they make.

LEARNING OUTCOMES

analyze factors including media and peer that influence personal health decisions

demonstrate comprehension of visual texts with specialize features and complex ideas
(e.g. visual components of media such as magazines, newspapers, web
sites...advertising and promotional materials)

MATERIALS - CMHL Pre-test, 'value square' sheets, sheet for gluing values to, glue, Teen Magazines, student journals.

ASSESSMENT - Free writing, representation and discussion Class.

TIMING: 75 minutes

TIMING	BODY OF LESSON
15 min	• Write **Values** on the board and ask students to think-pair-share what they think this word means. • Ask students to comment on what they think personal values are.
20 min	• **Definition of Values**: *Values can be defined as those things that are important to or valued by someone* (**Synonyms** = utility. VALUE, WORTH, IMPORTANCE, SIGNIFICANCE, intrinsic excellence or desirability). EXAMPLE - the *value of sunlight or good books.* • Define and discuss meaning of term 'value'. Ask students to share with the class things that they think grade 7 students value/think are important. • Show Values template on the screen using LCD/Smartboard/Document Camera • Ask students to select 10 things they most value in their own lives. Ask them to choose the 10 things they really value, not what they think they SHOULD value. Arrange squares with the thing they value MOST at the bottom of the list, then working upwards. Ties are okay. Glue squares to the page. (Use back of unused squares to add values not included.) • Hand out envelopes with value options, value template, and glue):

good looks	Shopping	family	friends
money	Love	talents/hobbies	boyfriend/girlfriend
great hair	Courage	Music	computer/gaming skills
pets	sense of humour	respect from others	TV and movies
like sports	Popularity	Loyalty	intelligence
good at sports	Creativity	Kindness	self respect
being healthy	Leadership	Clothes	athletic ability
popularity	Good grades	Creativity	spirituality/religion
		Honesty	respect from others

15 min	• Teacher led discussion: e.g. **Which values made your final 10?**
	   - **Which ones did YOU not pick and why?**
	   - **Why did we ask YOU to put your most important value at the bottom of the page?** (*Because they bottom forms the base/foundation for your values*)
	   - **How have YOUR values changed since elementary school?**
	   - **What actions in the past week would show me YOUR values in action?**

10 min	• **Part B:** Teen magazine investigation. "Imagine you are from another world and you are trying to figure out what is important to teenagers. You decide to buy 'teen magazines' to find the answer."
	• Tell students you are going to give the cover of a magazine to each group of 4/5 **Show a sample** and ask students to notice, just by looking at the COVER of the magazine (written words, photos, body language, facial expressions, use of colour, size/position of words), **what is the magazine presenting as most important/valuable?**
	• Tell students they are to choose 5 from list of value squares (**there is often a mix of messages). (circle these values on the sheet and star the one you think is most important from magazines point of view)
	• Hand one magazine and another copy of the value squares to each group of 4/5 students and give them 5 minutes to do this activity
	• Teacher led discussion:
	• Introduce and define the terms – *intrinsic values and extrinsic values*
	   - **What do YOU think is MOST important from the magazines point of view?**
	   - **Why? (Take ideas from a few groups while they show their cover).**
	   - **Does your magazine reflect YOUR values?**
	   - **Which ones does it overlook?**
	   - **Is there anything wrong with wanting to be good looking, etc**

15 min	• Journal writing - What **can make it hard to live according to your own values?**

Lesson: 2 - Introduction to Media and Product Branding (1st Lead)

OVERVIEW - Introduction to Media and Product Branding (1st Lead) - Students are given a definition of media and examples of different types of media, as well as introduced to the concept of Branding in advertisement. Students will understand that in order to see through advertising strategies they must think like a detective, and the first step to figuring out an ad is to identify the product.

GOAL - The goal of this lesson is to introduce the idea that advertisements are like mysteries that can be solved when we are good media investigators.

LEARNING OUTCOMES

use speaking and listening to improve and extend thinking, by, questioning and speculating, acquiring new ideas, analysing and evaluating ideas, developing explanations, considering alternative viewpoints (e.g. (i) question and speculate on possibilities regarding the ideas and information presented

demonstrate comprehension of visual texts with specialize features and complex ideas e.g. visual components of media such as magazines, newspapers, web sites...advertising and promotional materials

write a variety of clear, focused personal writing for a range of purposes and audiences that demonstrates connections to personal experiences, ideas, and opinions, featuring clearly developed ideas by using effective supporting details, explanations, analysis, and insights

MATERIALS - PowerPoint showing various types of media, student journals, 7 copies of one ad, 1 copy of another ad for teacher, chart paper.

ASSESSMENT - Free Writing, Class Discussion, Group Work

TIMING: 75 minutes

TIMING	BODY OF LESSON
10 min	• Let students know agenda for the 75 minute block. • **Define Media** – *(noun) A way to send messages to large groups of people.* • *Have class provide examples of different types of media (referring to make sure it fits with definition)* Examples include: TV, radio, movies, billboards, the Internet, magazines, newspapers, disposable coffee cups, bottles, pop cans, t-shirts. • Show power point illustrating different types of media and check how many the class had already identified. • Ask students if they know what the term 'branding' means in relation to advertising.
15 min	Share the **definition of Branding** – *the process of developing an intended brand identity - in other words, how advertisers want customers to think, feel, and do with respect to their product. It involves making a name, term, sign, symbol or design (or combination of these) that identifies the maker or seller of a product that the customer will remember and (hopefully) be loyal to.* -OR- *- In marketing, the use of logos, symbols, or product design to promote consumer awareness of goods and services. Example: Branding has made companies like Apple successful.* • Choose a well known and popular brand (i.e. Nike, McDonalds) and ask students **how they feel or react when they see this image or logo?**

15 min	• Tell students that in order to see through advertising strategies they must think like a detective, and the first step to figuring out an ad is to identify the product.
	• Write Lead #1 – Identify the Product on a piece of chart paper or to bulletin board display (this will be added to as the unit progresses).
	• Show print ad and model answering the following questions, with student input.
	  1. What product is this ad selling?
	  2. What does this ad want you to do?
	  3. How is this ad trying to get your attention?

20 min	• Put students into groups of 3 and pass out examples of advertisements to each group of students (7 examples = groups of 3-4).
	• Ask students to look at the ad they have been given and answer the following questions
	  - Who is the author of this ad?
	  - What product is this ad selling?
	  - What does this ad want you to do?
	  - How is this ad trying to get your attention?
	Have students share their ads and what they discovered.

15 min	• Write in journals –
	  1. What's YOUR favourite ad?
	  2. How do YOU think advertisers would target you? (because of your age, interests, and sense of style).
	  3. What's one thing YOU learned during today's lesson?

Lesson: 3 - Surrounded by Ads and Target Audience (2nd Lead)

OVERVIEW – By the end of this lesson students will understand how pervasive advertising is in all of our daily lives (jingle identification activity) as well as how ads work. Students are shown ads for "health products" (i.e. Milk) and learn to dissect the ad using critical viewing strategies such as recognizing the target audience. Students will create an ad selling a 40 minute nutrition break.

GOAL - Students will begin to understand that they are surrounded by ads and that ads are effective in getting people to buy things. Students will recognize the significance of a target audience for advertisers.

LEARNING OUTCOMES

listen critically to understand and analyse ideas and information, by making inferences and drawing conclusions, and interpreting the speaker's verbal and nonverbal messages, purposes, and perspectives use speaking and listening to improve and extend thinking, by, questioning and speculating, acquiring new ideas, analysing and evaluating ideas, developing explanations, considering alternative viewpoints (e.g. ask and answer critical questions about an advertisement (e.g., "Who is the target audience for this ad? How do you know?")

demonstrate comprehension of visual texts with specialize features and complex ideas e.g. visual components of media such as magazines, newspapers, web sites...advertising and promotional materials

create meaningful visual representations for a variety of purposes and audiences that communicate personal response, information, and ideas relevant to the topic

MATERIALS - various jingles used in ads , paper or bingo card template, pencils, several print ads to show different target audiences., 'dissect and ad' handout (double side with same questions on both sides), template for creating an ad (iRT page 8), 2 You Tube ads for milk (child, adult as target audience), I print mild ad targeted at adults

ASSESSMENT - Critical viewing of advertisement (visual texts), creation of an ad.

TIMING: 75 minutes

TIMING	BODY OF LESSON
5 min	• Recap previous lesson (definitions of media and branding) and tell students we are going to continue exploring how influential ads are on our lives.
20 min	• Introduce Jingle Bingo – Tell students that they will hear a series of jingles from ads and they have to try to identify as many as they can. • When student has created a row they can call out "BINGO" and share their responses. Game can then continue on to end of playlist.
5 min	• Ask students if any of them want to change their previous answer to yesterdays question (**are they affected by branding) now?** • **What do they think of the significance of their ability to recognize so many jingles?**
5 min	• Fill in Lead #2 – 'Find the Target Audience' on the chart paper list of leads (or ad lead to bulletin board) • Activity: Find the Target Audience - show several pictures and have students share who they think target audience is and why. • Students will be tempted to say 'everyone' and will need guidance to look for specific age, gender, demographic targeting.
5 min	• Show two ads for a healthy product [MILK] (aimed at different target audiences) • Initially show one ad and then, as a group go through 'dissect an ad' sheet for the first ad
15 min	• Show a You Tube video for the other ad and then put the related print advertisement on the screen (via LCD/Smart Board/Document Camera) have students view this ad, and fill in the 'dissect an ad' sheet with their desk partner. • Collect "Dissect an ad" sheet.
20 min	• Give students a template to make their own ad for "A 40-minute nutrition break" • Students can work with same partner to fill in sheet (product, target audience, slogan) **Remind students that their ad needs to target their chosen audience.** • Tell students they are to fill in this template today and to plan their print ad They will be given a bit of time next time to finish their ad

Lesson: 4 - Ad Hooks (3rd Lead)

OVERVIEW – Students will finish the ads started in lesson 3 and are introduced to several common ad hooks (star power, fun/happy/exciting, popular or 'cool', humour, romance, bandwagon, warm and fuzzy, strong or powerful, colour, movement, sound/music). Several examples will be shared and students will be given an opportunity to spot ad hooks in advertisements.

GOAL - To introduce students to Ad Hooks

LEARNING OUTCOMES

listen critically to understand and analyse ideas and information, by making inferences and drawing conclusions, and interpreting the speaker's verbal and nonverbal messages, purposes, and perspectives

use speaking and listening to improve and extend thinking, by, questioning and speculating, acquiring new ideas, analysing and evaluating ideas, developing explanations, considering alternative viewpoints (e.g. ask and answer critical questions about an advertisement (e.g., "Who is the target audience for this ad? How do you know?")

demonstrate comprehension of visual texts with specialize features and complex ideas e.g. visual components of media such as magazines, newspapers, web sites...advertising and promotional materials

create meaningful visual representations for a variety of purposes and audiences that communicate personal response, information, and ideas relevant to the topic

write a variety of clear, focused personal writing for a range of purposes and audiences that demonstrates connections to personal experiences, ideas, and opinions, featuring clearly developed ideas by using effective supporting details, explanations, analysis, and insights

analyse factors (including media and peer) that influence personal health decisions

MATERIALS - chart paper and markers (for chart paper and for student ads), internet/TV ad clips, 15-20 print ads (x7/per class), blank paper for ads, student journals

ASSESSMENT - Creation of an ad for a 40 minute nutrition break (slogan and id target audience), critically view ads to locate ad hook features, journal writing.

TIMING: 75 minutes

TIMING	BODY OF LESSON
10 min	• Give students time to finish their ad for a 40 minute nutrition break. Students can use this time to create ad on a blank piece of paper • Have a few students share ad (slogan and target audience features)
20 min	• Fill in Lead #3 – 'Find the Ad Hooks' on the chart paper list of leads or to bulletin board display • Write the title "Ad Hooks" on a separate piece of chart paper and show students. • Have students talk with a partner sitting next to them about what companies do to make their ads memorable and enticing to their audience. • Create a list or web of students' responses, then point out some strategies not mentioned. • Marketing Strategies include: Fast pace/movement, star power (association with famous people) narrative/story, colours animation, fun/happy/exciting feeling/tone music, popular or cool feeling/tone age of characters/actors, humour romance bandwagon movement warm and fuzzy feeling/tone sound strong or powerful feeling/tone association of product with popular events
5 min	• Show students several internet/TV ads and direct them to look for the ad hooks (see next page of this document for URLS or electronic resource file.) • Ad further suggestions to list (or word web)

10 min	• Hand out 15-20 print ads to each group of 3-4 students and direct them to sort according to use of similar ad hooks (they can create labels for each section). • Monitor and redirect groups as needed (students will be tempted to sort according to the product).
5 min	• Have students re-sort using different labels
5 min	• Have students share what they sorted into each area. • Point out differences because companies use more than one ad hook. • Ask students why this is (answer = different target audiences)
15 min	• Journal writing – **Think about your favourite ads, are there certain ad hooks that YOU find more interesting and attractive? Are YOU more likely to want the things in ads that use these hooks? Why or why not?** • For example: When I am looking for a new shampoo or face wash I notice the ads for these products. If they include people who are my age, music I enjoy, or actors I really like I tend to pay attention even thought I know that these things don't really have anything to do with the actual product. • HOMEWORK: Tell students to see if they can spot the advertising hooks in ads they view and to look for any not mentioned on our list.

Lesson: 5 - Hidden Messages (4th lead)

OVERVIEW – Students will practice creating 'If, Then' statements to determine an ad's hidden messages. This will initially occur in a guided format and then students will continue to practice independently using popular magazines. Students will then take turns showing their ads to the rest of the class and describing the new Ad Hooks and hidden messages that they discovered. Students will create another Ad, keeping in mind the leads they have learned so far.

GOAL – To introduce students to hidden messages in advertisements

LEARNING OUTCOMES

listen critically to understand and analyse ideas and information, by making inferences and drawing conclusions, and interpreting the speaker's verbal and nonverbal messages, purposes, and perspectives

select and use various strategies when listening to make and clarify meaning, including: accessing prior knowledge, and distinguishing between fact and opinion (E.g. identify bias in oral texts (e.g., viewpoint, possible motivation for bias or perspective, fact vs. opinion, emotional vs. logical)

read fluently and demonstrate comprehension of grade-appropriate information texts, with some specialized language and some complex ideas, including visual or graphic materials, advertising and promotional materials (E.g. include accurate and important information from text and 'text features', including specific details from graphics)

demonstrate comprehension of visual texts with specialize features and complex ideas e.g. visual components of media such as magazines, newspapers, web sites...advertising and promotional materials

create meaningful visual representations for a variety of purposes and audiences that communicate personal response, information, and ideas relevant to the topic

analyse factors (including media and peer) that influence personal health decisions

MATERIALS - Several print ads, handouts, "Finding the 4th Lead: What is the Hidden Message, "Create your own ad Part 2""

ASSESSMENT - "Find the Hidden Message" worksheet, creation of an ad for a made up product.

TIMING: 75 minutes

TIMING	BODY OF LESSON
5 min	• Recap the first 3 Leads: 1. Finding the product in the ad, 2. Target audience, and 3. Ad hooks. Review marketing strategies (ad hooks).
5 min	• Fill in Lead #4 – 'Find the Hidden Messages' on the chart paper list of leads or add to bulletin board display • Tell students they will be looking for the fourth Lead today which is spotting the hidden message. • Ask if anyone can think of an example of a hidden message in an ad.
10 min	• Show some print examples and practice saying related "if... then.." statements. Students will require guidance to look beyond the literal meaning of the picture in order to uncover the message.
15 min	• Show students some more print ads and have them fill in the worksheet "Finding the 4th Lead: What is the hidden message?"
35 min	• Tell students they will now be given a chance to create their own ad (teachers will have suggestions for students who need them). This should be a made up product and company • Examples: magic spray, gum that could give you an accent for a day, shampoo that makes your hair longer, or a different colour, products from Harry Potter (i.e. extendable ears, Bertie Bott's every-flavour jelly bean) • Students can work with partners and use the template "Create your own ad Part 2" to plan their ads (remind students to keep all the leads learned so far in mind as they plan). • Students will create their ads
5 min	• Invite students to share ads. • Collect ads

Lesson: 6 - Missing Information (5th Lead)

OVERVIEW - Students will view several ads in order to analyze and determine what information is missing in the ad, or left out of its message. Students will view ads and look for characteristics that show "Ad Land" versus the "Real World".

GOAL - Students will be able to independently analyze an ad and will become familiar the concept of 'Ad Land' (as it compares to the 'Real World').

LEARNING OUTCOMES

listen critically to understand and analyse ideas and information, by making inferences and drawing conclusions, and interpreting the speaker's verbal and nonverbal messages, purposes, and perspectives

select and use various strategies when listening to make and clarify meaning, including: accessing prior knowledge, and distinguishing between fact and opinion (E.g. identify bias in oral texts (e.g., viewpoint, possible motivation for bias or perspective, fact vs. opinion, emotional vs. logical)

read fluently and demonstrate comprehension of grade-appropriate information texts, with some specialized language and some complex ideas, including visual or graphic materials, advertising and promotional materials (E.g. include accurate and important information from text and 'text features', including specific details from graphics)

demonstrate comprehension of visual texts with specialize features and complex ideas
e.g. visual components of media such as magazines, newspapers,
websites...advertising and promotional materials

create meaningful visual representations for a variety of purposes and audiences that
communicate personal response, information, and ideas relevant to the topic

analyse factors (including media and peer) that influence personal health decisions

MATERIALS - Several print ads with exaggerated facial expressions and body poses, a print hamburger ad, LCD projector, Word Document to show pictures to show difference between Ad Land and Real World (before and after Photoshop), chart paper, markers, and student journals

ASSESSMENT - Class discussion, role play, journal writing

TIMING: 75 minutes

TIMING	BODY OF LESSON
5 min	• Tell students they have almost all the tools they need to solve the mystery of ads. • Remind students that last time we talked about what ads are telling you, and we figured this out that by using our 4 Leads including the 'if –then' statements • Tell students that today we are going to look at what ads are telling you and not telling you. • Add "Find what's missing from the Ad" to the chart paper list of Leads, or to bulletin board display
15 min	• Have on hand a few ads that have exaggerated pictures. • Tell students we are going to do a bit of acting today. Have 2 students volunteer to come up. • Take these students to the side of the room - show one ad to the volunteers and tell them what the ad is for and that they are to examine it closely and try to copy the exact pose and facial expression that is in the ad. • Tell the rest of the class that the student volunteers are going to model the ad and that when they have finished doing the pose they can raise their hands to guess what the ad was for • Take several students guesses (they probably won't guess it – which is the point- to illustrate the discrepancy between the Ad World and Real World) • Ask questions for actors and audience **1. Were the poses they acted out ways you usually see people stand or sit?** **2. Is that the way peoples' faces look when they are eating salad?** **3. Ex. Does eating salad ever make you smile like the girl in the picture?** **4. Are you ever this excited about eating salad?** • Repeat using a couple more ads (same volunteers) and ask questions after each one to show difference between Ad Land and Real World • Introduce terms Ad Land and Real World to explain what they just saw in the activity
5 min	• Show Power Point presentation of models before and after Photoshop.
10 min	• Show one of ads from previous activity and have students point out differences between Ad Land and Real World. • Record on Chart Paper Using 2 columns: Ad Land/Real World - Go through lists and using a different colour, write what value each statement represents.

Examples from Ad Land	Examples from Real World
• People in ads have all the same body type – tall and skinny • People in ads have perfect skin • People in ads wear expensive stylish clothes • Everyone in ads in beautiful • Everyone in ads is happy • Everyone is healthy and nobody has a disability • Nobody in ads is poor	• Everybody looks different • People may have blemishes on their skin • People don't always have a great cut or their hair may need to be brushed • People are not always dressed up and may wear sweatpants, old shirts or beat up sneakers • Not everyone is beautiful or handsome • Not everyone is happy, strong, athletic, or powerful • Some people have a disability • Some people are poor • Some people are overweight • Some people have wrinkles

	• This is an interesting list – point out that what we're seeing is that some parts of real life are basically left out of Ad land. Ad land is more of a fantasy place.
10 min	• An example from Ad Land: Show a hamburger ad, and ask if the hamburger looks real? • Explain you are going to share a few facts about how ads are created • Show video clip of how burgers and fries are positioned for advertising. **Food Ad Tricks: Helping Kids Understand Food Ads on TV <http://www.youtube.com/watch?v=fUjz_eiIX8k>**

10 min	• Discuss what they've learned
	  1. Did you learn anything you didn't know before?
	  2. Did you already know how a hamburger ad was made?
	  3. Was anything surprising?
	  4. What do you think about hamburger ads, now that you have learned how they are made?
	  (students are likely to comment on how unnatural the hamburger is in order to make it look attractive – tell students they can now look for this in all ads, give some examples or ask students if they can think of examples)
	  5. What are the things that advertiser don't want you to know and why?
	  6. Who can tell me what is left out of ads for fast food?
	  (fast food hamburgers are fatty, full of calories, and aren't good for you
	  7. Are giant, fatty burgers really good for you? What are some pictures or facts you will never ever see in an ad for a fast food hamburger?
	  (obesity epidemic, fat or cholesterol or salt content of food; or long term health effects of eating fast food, like stroke, diabetes, or heart disease)
	• Remind students to ask themselves
	  1. What's not being said in this ad message?
	  2. Is there any missing information?
	  3. What got left out?

5 min	• Show students another video – This one is an image oriented clip that shows the ad photo and then the real product. • Fast Food: Ads versus Reality http://www.youtube.com/watch?v=mbCwi6EeNAE&feature=related

15 min	Journal Writing Questions – Link to values
	Show work sheet 'Ad Land vs. Real World' on overhead/smart board etc.
	Remind them to think of the values activity they did in lesson one.
	• Have student write in journals a response to the following prompts:
	  1. In the Real World, I feel good inside when I......
	  2. In the Real World, one thing that makes me unique or special is that I.....

Lesson: 7 - Ad Hooks and Unhealthy Products (i.e. tobacco and alcohol) and Introduction to the Counter-Ad

OVERVIEW – Students will independently analyze an ad in order to find the 5 Leads. This lesson will allow students to use what they have learned (the 5 Leads) to analyze how companies attempt to market unhealthy products to children like them. Students will be able to contrast ad messages with their own beliefs and experiences. Students will work in partners or small groups to design their own counter-ad poster.

GOAL - Students will review the concept of Ad Hooks as they relate to the advertisement of unhealthy products, and practice using the 5 Leads.

LEARNING OUTCOMES

listen critically to understand and analyse ideas and information, by making inferences and drawing conclusions, and interpreting the speaker's verbal and nonverbal messages, purposes, and perspectives

use speaking and listening to improve and extend thinking, by, questioning and speculating,   acquiring new ideas, analysing and evaluating ideas, developing explanations, considering alternative viewpoints (e.g. ask and answer critical about an advertisement (e.g., "Who is the target audience for this ad? How do you know?")

demonstrate comprehension of visual texts with specialize features and complex ideas e.g. visual components of media such as magazines, newspapers, websites...advertising and promotional materials

create meaningful visual representations for a variety of purposes and audiences that communicate personal response, information, and ideas relevant to the topic

analyse factors (including media and peer) that influence personal health decisions

analyse media and social influences related to substance misuse

MATERIALS - Print ad to pair with "Can you solve the Case" worksheet, Power Point presentation includes teacher modeling slides and counter ad examples, as well as ads for students to use for their counter ad projects.

ASSESSMENT - "Can you Solve the Case" sheet

TIMING: 75 minutes

TIMING	BODY OF LESSON
10 min	• Begin this lesson by having the students recap the 5 Leads (they can use the chart poster if necessary) • Tell students you are going to show them a few ads for product that targeted at children, but are not the types of products you'd expect to see children buying. The student's job is to find the 5 Leads in the ads. The first ad the teacher will support and model this (the second ad students will assess independently). • Start the lesson 7 Power point presentation (manual mode so that you can control timing of slide show) • Show and ad for an unhealthy product and invite students to find the 5 Leads in the ad.

Example : alcoholic beverage
Product – De Kuyper Pucker Razztini and Appletini
Target audience – kids
Ad Hooks – used bright colours and the bottom of the glasses are a pixie stick candy and a lollipop stick.
Hidden Message – 'Drinking martinis is fun' and 'these drinks taste like candy'
Missing Information – These drinks are alcoholic. Alcoholic beverages are for adult consumers, and are illegal for people under 19 years old.

15 min	• Tell students they are going to have a chance to find the Leads in an ad, independently • Show students an ad for an unhealthy product (McDonalds) and have them fill in page 15 "Can you solve the case?" Collect sheets • Ask students - why they think advertisers target children with adult products (to get them thinking about buying these products when they are older, to encourage under age drinking/smoking etc., to sell their product to more people) • Ask students – **"What is the advertiser's main concern when they create an ad?"** (to make money). • Ask students – **"Do the advertisers care if their product is good or bad for you?"** (no, because their concern is making money)
30 min	• INTRODUCE THE TERM COUNTER-AD • Ask students if they know what 'counter-clockwise' means. Then ask if they know what 'counter-productive' means (*something that will not help a situation but will make it worse* – for example: ripping up your homework before handing it in) • "Now that we've looked at 2 words with the word counter in front of them, **what do you think a counter-ad is**" (*a counter ad will do the opposite of what a regular ad does*). 　－ In a regular ad there are hidden messages and missing information. A counter ad is NOT trying to sell you something and there is no missing information or hidden message. • So counter ads do the opposite of what ads do, they don't want you to buy anything, the Message is right out in the open, and there's no Missing information. • Show students the ad for 'Sauce-Ems' If we investigate and use a magnifying glass you can see it says the product can cause weight gain and dizziness. **Do you think dog owners would like to know this before buying this product?** (yes) • Point out that in some ads the information is included but very small (or spoken very quickly in audio/visual ads). In some ads this information is not given at all. That's what Counter-Ads can do – give all the Missing Information you really should know before using a product. • Show examples of Cigarette Ad (Virginia Slims and go through 5 hooks) • Target audience (young women), Ad Hook (rebel/free spirit), Hidden Message (ad slogan implies if I smoke I am not ordinary, I am original, I make my own rules etc), missing information, cigarettes are addictive (if you are addicted to something this controls you and you are not free) • Then I – ask students what they think a counter-ad for this product might include? (take responses) • Then look at the Counter-Ads and have students point out what they notice … • Show a few more examples of Counter Ad • Now that students have seen a few counter ads make sure they understand how they work – They take an actual ad for Ad Land- and then change it in some way, either by adding new words, a new slogan, or a new picture – to get you to think about the original ad in a whole new way.
20 min	• Tell students that they will have an opportunity to make their own counter-ad. • Today they can choose a partner, pick an ad to use as the starting point for their counter ad and plan their counter – ad. • The next lesson will be a work block for them to create their counter ad, and then one after will offer an opportunity for all the grade 7's to share their Counter Ads with each other. • Pass out planning sheet and ads for students to choose from • Collect a list of partners and what ad they are using for their counter ad.

Lesson: 8 – Counter Ad Work Period

GOAL - Students will work on their projects.

OVERVIEW – Students will work in partners or small groups to design their own counter-ad poster.

GOAL - Students will create a counter ad based on a real ad that will expose the hidden message behind the original ad.

LEARNING OUTCOMES

demonstrate comprehension of visual texts with specialize features and complex ideas
e.g. visual components of media such as magazines, newspapers, websites...advertising and promotional materials

create meaningful visual representations for a variety of purposes and audiences that communicate personal response, information, and ideas relevant to the topic

analyse factors (including media and peer) that influence personal health decisions

analyse media and social influences related to substance misuse

MATERIALS - Print ads for students to use for their counter ad projects, poster board paper and art supplies to use for the creation of counter ads.

TIMING: 75 minutes

TIMING	BODY OF LESSON
15 min	Have student finish completing their counter ad planning sheet and show to teacher for approval before starting poster. 　　　　-　Students should use the back of the planning sheet to sketch out what they are going to create on the larger poster board or computer based counter ad.
55 min	Students will work on creating their counter ads.
5 min	Clean up. All unfinished projects assigned as homework before next class, or the designated presentation/Gallery walk day.

Lesson: 9 - Poster Gallery Walk

OVERVIEW - Students will set up their counter-ad posters around the classroom and all students (all 3 classes) will view and analyze posters. Some peer-review feedback will be included. Post-test to be completed.

Goal - Students will have an opportunity to both analyze and enjoy each other's Counter-Ads

LEARNING OUTCOMES

read fluently and demonstrate comprehension of grade-appropriate information texts, with some specialized language and some complex ideas, including visual or graphic materials, advertising and promotional materials (E.g. include accurate and important information from text and 'text features', including specific details from graphics)

demonstrate comprehension of visual texts with specialize features and complex ideas e.g. visual components of media such as magazines, newspapers, web sites...advertising and promotional materials

read and view to improve and extend thinking, by analysing and evaluating ideas and information, comparing various viewpoints, and summarizing and synthesizing to create new ideas (e.g. question the author's purpose or viewpoint (i.e., critical literacy) create meaningful visual representations for a variety of purposes and audiences that communicate personal response, information, and ideas relevant to the topic

analyse factors (including media and peer) that influence personal health decisions

analyse media and social influences related to substance misuse

MATERIALS - Student Counter-Ads, peer review sheets

ASSESSMENT - Student Counter-Ads, peer review sheet.

TIMING: 45 minutes

TIMING	BODY OF LESSON
10 Min	Set up projects, hand out peer review sheets.
25 min	Gallery Walk One Student will stand by their ad, answering questions and sharing their work for 10 minutes, then switch with their partner. This will allow both partners to present their ad and to view others. -All students will be assigned two projects to peer review according to the peer review sheet.
15 min	Journal entry – 1. **What did I like best about critical media health literacy?** 2. **What are the most important things I learned during this unit?**
5 min	Share highlights and 'big learning's' from unit

Chapter 5

Secondary Strategies for Maximizing Health Literacy of Youth

Ray Marks

As outlined in the earlier chapters, there is an enormous worldwide imperative to improve the public's ability to understand, act on and evaluate health information and health messages. To this end, the development of general literacy, during critical development periods, that is, in the context of pre-school, as well as kindergarten through grade 12, along with informal health promotion activities among toddlers, and caregivers, has been advocated. In addition, pre-school through 12th grade curricula to teach health literacy competencies across all educational disciplines has been advocated (Abrams, Klass, & Dreyer, 2009).

But what strategies or contextual factors are required to support such efforts? Firstly, in addition to better teacher preparation (Peterson, Cooper, & Laird, 2001), a whole school approach (Menzies, 2012), plus a positive culture for health in schools, can markedly facilitate the development of higher levels of health literacy (Lee, 2009). Secondly, the nature of the school, the school climate and whether the school defines itself as a health promoting school or not can provide a highly impactful framework for helping to disseminate the personal, cognitive and social skills youth need for maintaining good health (St. Leger, 2001).

That is, the Co-ordinated School Health (CSH) Model recommended by the Centers for Disease Control in the United States, which integrates eight components of the school community that can markedly influence health, along with the concept of the Health Promoting School are potentially key structural and organization factors to consider in efforts to foster the type of education and supportive environments needed to promote health literacy among school-aged youth. Since changes at the macro level including organizational practices and policies, are not sufficient for changing those individual behaviours that influence health status adversely (Lee, 2009), a school health co-ordinator responsible for managing and co-ordinating school health policies and programs, including comprehensive health education programs that assist students to take responsibility for their own well-being by encouraging and facilitating healthy choices and by establishing positive health practices are advocated to help foster the desired outcome of health literacy, which is lifelong wellness.

In addition to promote health literacy, multiple authorities now recognize the importance of teachers from different learning areas working together, as well as the importance of fostering practical, rather than basic knowledge alone. The impact of the prevailing ecology on health, the multidimensional features of health, including mental, physical and social health, plus the role of social and indigenous culture in mediating health behaviours is also being increasingly recognized as important to consider in efforts to promote health literacy in schools. Hence, several commonly applied health theories and theory-based models that incorporate an ecological approach to health promotion and that strongly stress the multi-layered array of structural and systemic as well as personal influences that can enhance or negate the development of optimal educational, social and health outcomes (Golden & Earp, 2012; Trickett & Rowe, 2012) are increasingly viewed as pathways for promoting health and health literacy attributes in children (see Figure 5.1). Based on these concepts, the levels of influence on child and adolescent health and health behaviour when envisioned from the ecological model perspective implies that all multiple overlapping layers of influence, that is those within the micro- as well as the mesosystem represented by health education classrooms, the whole school, family structure and culture and neighbourhood spheres and the exosystem and macrosystem represented by the popular culture sphere can all be deemed to be potential mediators or moderators of health literacy development among school-aged youth.

In health classrooms, for example, Lohrmann (2008) implies students can learn essential knowledge and skills they may need to employ to engage in healthy behaviours later on especially if their learning is reinforced by other school components including physical education, school counselling and school health services as well as other subjects such as science. At the same time to support this outcome, the entire school should constitute an immediate environment that reinforces students' inclinations and abilities to engage in healthy behaviours. Going beyond the school zone, we also must consider the family and neighbourhood as environments which may help or

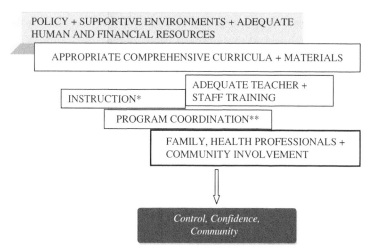

Figure 5.1: Hypothetical steps needed in the school context to promote
lifelong health literacy attributes among youth.
*Instruction should foster basic health skills, as well as higher order
interactive skills, navigational skills, decision-making skills, prolem-solving,
self- and other advocacy skills.
**Efforts to encourage collaborations to integrate health literacy efforts
across curriculum using State and National Standards are strongly
recommended.

hinder students' efforts to be healthy. Finally, the greater community
constitutes a proximal context where health-related resources for individuals,
health educators, schools and school systems, families and neighbourhoods
can further reinforce health decisions.

Popular culture too can provide the overarching values, customs and
laws, including those related to health, that can influence students' health-
related behaviours, especially through the many types of prevailing media,
and being able to examine and decide what aspects of this culture are life
affirming and which are not the obligation schools may have insofar as
helping young people to understand the impact of social and environmental
issues on their health. They also have an obligation to cover the important
topics that influence health status including relationships, safety, nutrition
and community participation.

In the United States, The National Health Education Standards
(NHES): Achieving Health Literacy report developed by a coalition of professional organizations and non-profit agencies has consequently provided
standards that can help us to identify what knowledge and skills students

should know and be able to do, in order to achieve health literacy. The NHES report has also outlined obstacles that have impeded health education programs in the past and offers 'Opportunities to Learn' recommendation standards to overcome these challenges. They have established an urgent call to action to improve the delivery of health education initiatives based on national and state health education standards so that all children and youth can achieve a high level of health literacy and advocate

- A role for *collaborative* planning among local agencies and among school personnel, students, families, community agencies and business organizations.
- Community agency *support* for creating community awareness and support for school health instruction.
- State education and health *agency collaborations* to establish health education as a core academic subject.
- *Teacher preparation* institutions that enable future teachers to make health education connections across the curriculum (McGovern, 2010).

Consequently, for school health education to be effective in influencing students to behave in healthy ways, and for helping them acquire health literacy proficiency, or improve their health literacy, the lessons they learn must be carefully selected, thoughtfully planned, evidence-based, culturally appropriate and supported and reinforced by local and state agencies and policies. In turn, the environment and ethos of the school must support the delivery of the curriculum, as well as the provision of a safe and health-affirming environment and administrators must be prepared to move beyond the curriculum and formal aspects of learning, to optimize the physical and social environment of the school, as well as advocating for support by, and involvement of the family and neighbourhood. The role of media influences, poverty, discrimination and related biases should also not be overlooked as possible mediators of health literacy development, when designing optimal strategies for the school-based venue (Lohrmann, 2008). However, even though a positive culture for health in the school is likely to be especially effective in fostering high levels of health literacy and opportunities to foster personal, cognitive and social skills (Lee, 2009), teaching the desired higher order topical skills, in addition to communication, and problem solving skills requires advanced pre-professional learning opportunities as well as integrated efforts in applying these skills across all school sectors, including the health and non-health teaching sectors. In the next section some of the elements crucial to improving school-based health literacy efforts are described.

5.1. Role of Teachers — Involve, Include, Foster, Encourage, Support

At the most basic level, a reasonable body of literature exists to support the view that teachers who are adequately prepared can help advance school-based health literacy through consistent and comprehensive efforts to

- ✔ Address a *wide* range of *locally relevant* health, developmental and social topics.
- ✔ *Engage* and *involve* all students in topics they are already learning or are *relevant* to their day to day lived experiences.
- ✔ Include *experiential* and *practical skills*, rather than simply imparting knowledge alone.
- ✔ Apply age and *developmentally appropriate* teaching strategies and materials.
- ✔ Build awareness, *self-efficacy* and interpersonal communication skills.
- ✔ *Involve* family members.
- ✔ Foster critical as well as functional and interactive health literacy.
- ✔ Create a *supportive* classroom environment.
- ✔ *Encourage* productive discussions.

According to Charlotte Hendricks, child health educational expert, the teaching approaches adopted for imparting effective health messages to young children, should be carefully considered in light of their developmental capacity, and cannot be accomplished by simply *telling* children about health and illness issues. Learning can also not be successfully accomplished or addressed adequately by exposure to only occasional health-related lessons, or a reliance on incidental learning. Children learn best if offered early opportunities to grasp key concepts in the health arena, and by affording them opportunities to practice the desired skills, behaviours or necessary competencies. Lesson plans focused on single concrete concepts, rather than multiple topics, that are supported or reinforced in several ways throughout each school day and in the context of other disciplines, including science, math, physical education, language arts, music and art, as well as in the school environment itself, such as the school cafeteria are highly recommended. Research also shows even very young children can be concrete learners, if lesson plans include simple concepts which can be individualized; and teachers are able to should determine what children at various ages need to know and are able to do.

Appropriate teaching methods as well as enjoyable hands-on activities across the curriculum should consequently assist youth of any age to develop the necessary knowledge and skills they need to lead a healthy lifestyle. A daily schedule that supports the establishment of positive health habits, plus repetition and use of appropriate resources and a healthy classroom environment can further support the application and integration of important health-related concepts.

At the same time, teachers themselves may wish to become more health literate in their day to day contexts and attempts to promote classroom-based health literacy, where the students are consumers of information, and teachers are the information providers (Peterson et al., 2001). The teacher can also try to set an example for youth by modelling good health practices, and by ensuring that the environment is safe and clean. She can also involve children in the maintenance of their environment, and foster a strong family and parental involvement component as part of her total health education program. Through regular written and verbal forms of communications, parents can be informed of the school's health goals, activities and concerns; since some health goals are best addressed and reinforced by parents (Charlotte Hendricks preface to Starting Healthy© pre-school health curriculum, National Center for Health Education, 2005).

To facilitate the teacher, especially the non-health teacher, canned curricula plus teacher training, while not always forthcoming, can be extremely helpful. This was the approach used by the highly acclaimed *Growing Healthy*® K-6 school-based health curriculum developers for many years who found the following most beneficial in promoting the teacher's confidence and skill. That is, the developers recommended support for professional development opportunities be sought and forthcoming for helping teachers to

- *Better comprehend* the link between health and learning, plus how to promote both through the curriculum
- *Identify and discuss* the objectives and goals of the curriculum
- *Set* up and review curricula materials
- *Discuss* and *practice* teaching techniques used within the program, and
- *Identify ways to integrate* the curriculum into their current schedules.

5.2. Instructional Strategies

To achieve a high level of health literacy proficiency, employing an effective evidence-based curriculum plus well-defined instructional strategies and learning experiences that are student-centred, interactive and experiential (e.g. group discussions, cooperative learning, problem solving, role playing and peer-led activities) is highly desirable (see Chapter 6). As well, learning experiences that correspond with the students' cognitive and emotional developmental levels plus learning styles, and those guided by young people themselves at all stages of their development can help to personalize the information, thereby increasing their interest and motivation, while accommodating diverse capabilities and learning styles. Carefully planned learning experiences tailored to the students cognitive and linguistic abilities plus their personal preferences and competencies, and individual needs, carried out in a safe, supportive trusting environment are deemed especially helpful for

a. Addressing key basic and controversial health issues.
b. Encouraging creative expression.
c. Sharing personal thoughts, feelings and opinions.
d. Considering new arguments.
e. Developing critical thinking skills (AAPHERD).
f. Improving spoken communication.
g. Improving self-efficacy for self-reflection and self-management.
h. Empowering youth to make healthful choices (NIHCM, 2011).

In addition, these attributes and others such as empowerment and critical thinking abilities are likely to be fostered especially if implemented by teachers who strongly believe in what they are teaching, and are knowledgeable about the curriculum content, as well as comfortable and skilled in implementing it. One curriculum specifically designed by the Canadian Public Health Association's National Literacy and Health Program for those who teach or guide youth entitled *What the HEALTH!*[©] and intended to enhance health awareness and literacy skills of youth who have trouble reading, and appears pertinent in this respect is a good example of a potentially useful canned curriculum. Divided into 10 lessons, the cover page of each provides an introduction to the lesson, followed by learning objectives, relevant websites and other resources. Although, basically simple to apply, as with other curricula, however, it is important to stress the need for ongoing professional development and training for purposes of helping teachers implement this or any other curriculum that requires new teaching or assessment skills (AAPHERD).

Benham-Deal and Hodges (n.d.) further suggest a skills-based rather than a topical instructional approach is likely to be more helpful than traditional curricula that are commonly problem-based for fostering health literacy. In this approach, the authors recommend the related instructional units be organized so as to promote health literacy around a single core concept that can be learned and practiced over time. It was further suggested by Benham-Deal and Hodges that this approach aligned well with that of Donald Nutbeam (2008) who viewed health literacy as an asset to be developed in the formative years, and that would facilitate greater decision-making ability, and empowerment as an educational outcome.

Accordingly, teachers' efforts in this respect are of utmost import and might include, but would not be limited to providing basic reading and writing skills, numeracy skills, communication skills, high end critical thinking skills as well as health-related instructions tailored to the developmental needs of students. In addition to repetition, and taking a small-steps approach, according to Greeno (1998) learning is likely to be especially optimized when classroom discussions and activities are meaningful, functional and genuine and the learners' cognitive skills are applied to personal issues and authentic activities (Darvin, 2006). Since health literacy depends on the development of basic literacy skills, including reading, speaking and writing skills, as well as the ability to understand and apply these skills, or critical literacy, integrating instruction on health issues along with basic reading and writing exercises is highly recommended for advancing critical health literacy (Benham-Deal & Hodges, n.d.).

Thus as opposed to relying solely on standardized formal health education lessons or formulae alone, to advance information uptake, and to solidify learning, and skills development need by the 21st-century citizen, lessons incorporated into the general curriculum that take the environment and individual traits of youth into account are highly recommended. This use of interdisciplinary approaches to advance health literacy might involve, but would not be limited to collaborations between English/ESL, mathematics, science, biology, arts and social studies teachers. A broader purview that tries to break down artificial silos of learning and that takes an empowerment approach appears worthy of consideration. Including families and taking into account the local culture beyond the walls of the school and its personal relevance to the target audience appears equally compelling in relation to efforts to foster lifelong health literacy skills and their potentially favourable impact on health, educational, economic, political and social outcomes (Flecha, Garcia, & Rudd, 2011).

In addition to classroom lessons, to foster the acquisition of lifelong knowledge and skills needed by youth to engage in health-affirming behaviours, given that both the school environment and its focus on academics places youth today at high risk for risky and unhealthful behaviours, instruction supplemented and reinforced by other school-based professionals and services such as the school counsellor, the school nurse, the physical education teacher, school health services and science lab class activities, along with efforts to create safe, health-affirming environments are recommended. Moreover, in light of the multidimensional nature of health literacy, as well as the multiple determinants and dimensions of health, this co-ordinated collaborative approach towards fostering school health education should employ a broad array of in class and off campus activities, for example, trips into the community, health fairs, health museums, health centres, the pharmacy, the supermarket. In addition, because including several activities rather than a single activity is commonly more effective in fostering and reinforcing any health-related behaviour change, the dosage as well as the resources needed to attain and sustain the desired health goal should be carefully considered. When such activities should commence and focusing on how these can be built on from as early as the pre-school stage through to the grade 12 stage should improve adolescent health literacy abilities. To further reinforce these efforts, encouraging parents and school staff to work together to positively influence the child's health knowledge and skill and application, applying national science, health, maths and language arts standards to the existing lessons, as well as fostering exposure of the child to positive role models and optimal health practices is highly desirable. Where indicated, efforts to foster parental literacy and to attend to issues of culture seem strongly indicated as well.

To specifically foster media literacy, as this impacts the ability to carefully weigh media messages, teachers can help provide students with opportunities to access and carefully evaluate printed and electronic sources of health information, examine causative factors that influence their health, and learn how to make careful decisions and set healthy personal goals. Helping them to understand how marketers are influencing their behaviours, how to locate information in multiple data sources, exposing them to the concept of peer-reviewed resources and showing them how to critically evaluate these resources is deemed to be very helpful in informing youth about the choices they make and should make. In addition, helping them to acquire and practice health-related skills, as well as different forms of communication in contexts where they are likely to be needed so that they can become critical thinkers and actors in the context of their health and their health choices and decisions is advocated.

To achieve e-Health literacy Paek and Hove (2012) recommend class room trainings have local and personal relevance to the adolescent. They indicate this can be attained by using social and norms-based appeals. They recommend too that adolescents should be informed about how their peers are successfully using online health resources and reinforce the message that they will be pleasing to significant others by improving their e-Health literacy skills. They carried out age-appropriate classroom trainings on topics of nutrition, and physical activity, and included personalized narratives, humerous cartoons, photographs, and images referring to local events, symbols and community members which significantly improved 182 adolescents e-Health literacy.

There were three lessons in total over a three week time period.

- Lesson One: Instructed students to evaluate research on aerobic exercise, and determine if the web-based information was reliable.
- Lesson Two: Involved an exploration of the food pyramid website to answer questions on nutrition.

- Lesson three: Involved the topic of energy balance, questions, the relevance of information and the reliability of web-based sources.

As a result of one or more of these aforementioned approaches, children exposed to one or more of these strategies in a consistent thoughtful way can be expected to be in a better position to have positive health-related attitudes and skills than their parents as a whole because the more one practices health-related literacy skills, the more advantageous this is likely to be. At a minimum, these lessons are likely to provide a platform for advancing basic health literacy skills and should include, but should not be limited to, education in ten key content areas: community health, consumer health, environmental health, family life, mental and emotional health, injury prevention and safety, nutrition, personal health, prevention and control of disease and substance use and abuse and involve teachers from different areas. Children exposed to curricula that cover these ten topics in a sequential and progressively challenging manner are expected to be able to

1. Comprehend basic health promotion and disease prevention concepts.
2. Access valid health information products and services.
3. Demonstrate the ability to practice behaviours that enhance health and reduce risks.
4. Analyse the influence of personal beliefs, culture, media, technology and other factors of health.
5. Use interpersonal communication skills to enhance health.
6. Use goal-setting and decision-making skills to enhance health.
7. Demonstrate the ability to advocate for personal, family and community health.
8. Understand how all curriculum topics are interrelated and how all affect life quality.

According to the Centers for Disease Control (2012), a state-of-the-art health education curriculum designed to attain these goals should emphasize

- The teaching of functional health information or essential knowledge.
- The shaping of personal values and beliefs that support healthy behaviours.
- The shaping of group norms that place a high value on a healthy lifestyle.
- The development of those health skills needed to foster health-enhancing behaviours.

Moreover it should

- Focus on clear health goals and related behavioural outcomes.
- Be research-based and theory-driven.
- Address individual and group norms that support health-enhancing behaviours.

- Focus on reinforcing protective factors and increasing perceptions of personal risk and harmfulness of engaging in specific unhealthy practices and behaviours.
- Address social pressures and influences.
- Build personal competence, social competence, and self efficacy by addressing skills needed to achieve desired outcomes.
  - That is, for each skill, students should be ably guided through a series of developmental steps where they
    - Discuss the importance of the skill, its relevance and relationship to other learned skills.
    - Are presented with steps for developing the skill.
  - Have an opportunity to model and practice the skill.
  - Are provided with appropriate feedback and reinforcement.

An effective curriculum should also

- Provide basic, accurate, knowledge that directly contributes to health-promoting decisions and behaviours including the 5 Core Literacy Elements of
  - Reading
  - Writing
  - Numeracy
  - Speech
  - Listening
- Use tailored strategies that help to personalize information and engage students.
- Provide age-appropriate and developmentally-appropriate information, learning strategies, teaching methods and materials.
- Cover concepts and skills in a logical sequence.
- Incorporate learning strategies, teaching methods, and materials that are culturally inclusive.
- Provide adequate time for instruction and learning.
- Provide opportunities to reinforce skills and positive health behaviours, and integrate skills application opportunities in other academic areas.
- Provide opportunities to make positive connections with influential others.
- Include teacher information and plans for professional development and training.
- Help students become familiar with the variety of services available to them in the school and wider community, and how to better understand and gain access to these services.
- Help foster students acquire confidence, control and ability to think critically about health issues (Lee, 2009).

5.3. Example of Elements of a Promising Comprehensive School-Based Curriculum for Promoting Health Literacy for Grades K-6

5.3.1. *Growing Healthy® Curriculum Components*

5.3.1.1. Growing Healthy® Curriculum Guide The Growing Healthy® Curriculum was a K-6 curriculum that covered the 10 health education topics in a comprehensive way over the duration of K-6 grades developed in the United States over a 30 year period, and serving over 1 million children. Longitudinal studies showed it had a beneficial impact on knowledge and behaviours after students had reached the eighth grade (Lammers, 1996) and its strength lay in its guide, which described the activities and orchestrated the use of corresponding multimedia materials, and a K-6 glossary of the vocabulary introduced throughout the curriculum. This element was instrumental in facilitating health education delivery.

5.3.2. *Growing Healthy® Ready-Made Teaching Materials*

Growing Healthy® produced ready-made materials for the convenience of the classroom teacher, and this may be useful as an approach to future developers. These ready-to-use classroom materials complemented the variety of instructional strategies and peripherals used in the context of the curriculum and were highly effective and time saving. Examples of ready-made teaching materials include

- Informational Charts
- Flannel Board Figures
- Graphs
- Learning Station Direction Cards
- Cooperative Learning Activity Directions
- Phase Charts
- Bulletin Boards
- Role Play Instruction Cards
- Classroom Informational Posters

5.3.3. *Growing Healthy® Peripheral Kits*

The resource rich Curriculum also utilized a variety of peripheral materials to engage and captivate students. At each grade level, a diverse assortment of books, posters, videos, games, and other multimedia materials provided the interactive stimulus to capture the imagination and provoke student participation. This approach was deemed highly promising at fostering health later on in life according to preliminary research and can serve as a helpful template in the context of any future curriculum development process.

5.3.4. *Growing Healthy*® *Glossary*

A composite glossary of the terms used in the curriculum, including definitions, would be an added feature of potential importance in any future curriculum development.

5.3.5. *Growing Healthy*® *Online Training*

Growing Healthy® Online Training provided a unique tool for introducing teachers to the curriculum, as well as an understanding of comprehensive school health education as a component of a co-ordinated school health program, which can greatly benefit non-health teachers, or teachers who do not have time or resource support for face to face trainings. That is, Online Training permits a teacher to participate in training activities through convergent technology, by melding video and web content to create an engaging, interactive experience. This approach can provide more efficient and economical preparation of teachers who are asked or desire to implement health-related curricula. In order for lessons to be easily accepted by both teachers and students, they need to be simple, while well structured. They also need to be reinforced over time.

Ultimate Goal and Approach of Growing Healthy® which can be readily adapted

- Students receive lessons related to 10 Key Health topics each year K-6 across the curriculum — each year and lesson plan should build on the other — lessons designed to be didactic and experiential and meet State standards for English, science and health at a minimum-end with a culminating project — which shows students efforts to stay well and fit — have students share what was learned with others.

Comprehensive Curricula Principles:
A well-designed comprehensive curriculum provides consistently formatted, sequenced lessons — that provides knowledge, as well as lessons that *intentionally engage* students in *personally relevant* activities.

It provides *multiple* rather than single opportunities to apply what is learned through

- Role-plays
- Learning groups

- Scenarios
- Mixing together a variety of approaches

Other modes of instruction might include (see Appendix 5.A.3 for details)

Active learning
Collaborative learning
Co-operative learning
Bookmaking
Brainstorming
Concept mapping
Debating
Demonstrations
Developing videos and films (Photovoice)*
Discussions
Dissections, can be facilitated online
Field trips
Guest speakers, celebrities
Informal class discussions
Journaling
Laboratory for exhibitions, collections, health and environmental research
Life Skills Training
Museum trips, on and offline
Presentations
Peer education
Pop Quizzes
Portfolios
Projects
Puppets
Reflections
Rhymes
Self-assessments
Service learning
Show and Tell
Simulations
Social Skills Training
Songs simple, complex, thematic, student produced
Think Pair Share
TV ads analyses
Workshops
Writing assignments

*Useful for efforts to incorporate cultural conceptions of health and wellness (see Stewart, Riecken, Scott, Tanaka, & Riecken, 2008).

Also useful for assisting youth of marginalized cultures may be an adaptation in the school of the following intervention approach discussed by Parker et al. (2012) who have proposed the use of an intervention consisting of a series of five culturally sensitive, oral health education workshops delivered over a 12 month period by Indigenous project officers to raise oral literacy among indigenous adults. Workshops will consist of presentations, hands-on activities, interactive displays, group discussions and role plays. The themes addressed in the workshops will embody oral health literacy concepts, and incorporate oral health-related self-efficacy, oral health-related fatalism, oral health knowledge, access to dental care and rights and entitlements as a patient knowledge elements. Data will be collected through a self-report questionnaire at baseline, at 12 months and at 24 months. The primary outcome measure will be oral health literacy. Secondary outcome measures will include oral health knowledge, oral health self-care, use of dental services, oral health-related self-efficacy and oral health-related fatalism.

Also in this approach, teachers need to provide feedback, so as to allow them to review what they already know and to build on this in subsequent lessons.

At the same time, teachers can also send letters home to parents, giving them an idea of what their child is learning (see samples in Appendix 5.A.4–5.A.6). This gives the parent something to talk about with their child. It can also provide activities for the students to carry out with their parents and may reinforce the desired behaviour and/or in some cases it can help to educate the parents inadvertently!

This is very important — because often the desired behaviour may not be modelled, or incorporated in the home, and may not be carried out at all, thus preventing the translation of the school lesson[s] into daily practices.

To accommodate substitute teachers or non-health teachers, who may have to teach topics they are not specialized in, the school in turn, can help by providing relevant curricula guides, materials and training that would allow the teachers to become familiar with the curriculum and its overall goals. It may also be helpful to keep in mind that

- ✔ Schools and communities are closely linked and thus members of both should be encouraged to work as partners rather than in silos to foster children's learning.
- ✔ Children need to be active participants in their own learning and may benefit from initiating a health fair, forming a local health committee, or by inviting the local newspaper in to photograph their activities — thus instilling the belief that the entire community values these attitudes and health attributes — and to demonstrate the curriculum and school effort is of significant merit.

In addition to reinforcing positive health practices in a consistent and timely manner, across the curriculum and over a protracted time frame, prevention of adverse health and societal outcomes is likely to be most effective when school lessons are reinforced by a clear, consistent social message that alcohol, tobacco and drug use are *harmful*, *unacceptable* and *illegal*. Creating a strong culture of respect and connectivity and an environment that inspires healthy practices as the norm has been shown to be very important as well.

5.4.   Integrating Health into Lesson Plans

According to the California Health Literacy Initiative Inc. (http:// www.cahealthliteracy.org) teachers in all disciplines rather than the health discipline alone are strongly encouraged to make health a part of their lesson plans.

To supplement their lesson plans teachers in different subject areas can potentially achieve this in a practical way by carrying out very simple activities within the content of their lessons such as

- Encouraging learners to become familiar with names and functions of body parts, for example, in science, biology, language arts classes
- Having them simulate the use of maps/other directives so they will know, how to obtain appointments and navigate the health system, for example, in geography, or social studies classes
- Having them practice filling out insurance and medical history forms, for example, language arts classes
- Having them practice how to communicate with others, for example, language arts classes.

    They can also

- Provide opportunities for bringing in food or nutritional services to teach a lesson on menu planning or body weight issues
- Bring in a doctor or dentist from the community to discuss health issues that affect young people
- Decorate the classroom with life-affirming messages and reinforce health living in practices such as birthday celebrations, field trips.

In addition to working with school counsellors, and nurses, they can also work with local agencies, such as the Boys and Girls club to help to raise children's health literacy, while forging a united community message.

Special attention should be given to

- Students whose first language is not English or the vernacular of the country
- Recognition of the developmental level and readiness to transition to adult care of the learner
- Respect for cultural and linguistic diversity; consideration of cultural attitudes and beliefs
- Special needs children
- Families with limited resources.

To support these aforementioned strategies and ideas a recent analysis revealed a strong need exists in the following domains:

- The need to use more comprehensive assessment approaches that move beyond readability and numeracy to address the full spectrum of health literacy factors.
- The need to apply more robust experimental studies to examine the effectiveness of health literacy interventions among individuals, communities, health-care providers and health-care systems.
- The need to explore the moderating and mediating roles of an individual's health literacy status on health outcomes.
- The need to examine long-term effects of health literacy interventions on health outcomes (Carbone & Zoellner, 2012).
- Another is the need for ascertaining the extent to which dedicated school-based efforts yield the three dimensions of health literacy proposed by Nutbeam.
- Another is for uncovering the most effective way of addressing policy makers and stakeholders and engaging communities in efforts to transform the present outmoded delivery of sporadically delivered unidimensional health-related lessons in contexts that are incompatible with health, in light of the current era of diversity, chronic disease, economic dislocations and recessions.

5.5. Summary

The majority of premature deaths and disabilities of people of all ages are predicted by poor health decisions and unhealthy behaviours or practices. The ultimate goal of school-based health education is to prevent premature deaths and disabilities by empowering children and youth with health literacy. Health enhancing practices that improve health literacy can be successfully learned in school health education programs and their use has grown increasingly necessary (Centers for Disease Control (CDC), 2012). As the health system as well as health challenges have grown increasingly complex, well-designed health education for school age children are found to enable youth to begin to acquire knowledge and to develop the capacity to practice health-affirming skills so they become active partners in the context of individual and collective decisions that affect their well-being. Students who can use functional health-related knowledge and apply personal and social skills who know how to resist social pressures will also be more likely to experience better health status and as adults will be better prepared academically and health-wise to contribute to the nation's economic challenges (Joint Committee on National Health Education Standards, 1995).

However, it is increasingly evident that in order for the school to promote health literacy effectively, the school alone cannot accomplish this and its surrounding community must be involved because the nature of the environment and culture both in the school, as well as the community can either support or impede the ability of students to engage in healthy behaviours (Lohrmann, 2008). For example, food services on school campuses may support healthy eating or foster unhealthy eating behaviours, and even if they do, factors in the family setting and wider community, including health professionals, health organizations, businesses, non-profit organizations and other potential partners, as well as policies need to be supporting the same positive practices in order to yield positive youth health outcomes. In particular, schools that provide a healthy school environment and encourage families and neighbourhoods to work alongside with them to support healthy behaviours of youth will be more able to help their students to achieve society's health promotion goals. In addition, for health-associated lessons to be effective, they must be personally and environmentally relevant, reinforced throughout the school, as well as by school principals, school policy makers, administrators, teachers and allied personnel (Lohrmann, 2008). In addition to the approach outlined by Paakarri and Paakarri in the next chapter, raising community awareness, and robust support for school health instruction, community building, building community capacity and capital and effective community organizing may provide an important bridge to the achievement of high standards of critical health literacy for youth, as well as a mechanism for improving youth health and empowerment in an indirect sense (Lohrmann, 2008).

As argued by participants in a recent Stakeholder Workshop held in the United Kingdom (Menzies, 2012), however, encouraging schools to take their pupils on a 'Health Literacy Journey' is not likely to occur simply as an outcome of curriculum changes or prescriptions for teaching. Instead this group stressed the importance of providing teachers and leaders with the skills and tools to do so in addition to the need to development a coherent methodology for teaching health literacy, along with the provision of training for teachers to enable them to implement the methodology. A clear rationale for school leaders as to why they need to foster health literacy, involvement of all stakeholders, including youth was advocated as well.

In sum, important factors that may underpin the success of a health education curriculum designed to maximize health literacy of youth include the use of

- Science and health standards-based comprehensive curricula implemented from pre-school to grade 12 by trained teachers.
- Step-by-step guidelines for each lesson plan that includes listening, speaking, reading and writing opportunities.
- Adequate training and technical assistance for instructors.
- Consistent implementation practices.
- Tailored/adapted resources in light of local contexts and populations.
- Classroom and homework assignments that provide frequent feedback and are action-oriented.
- Appropriate supportive health enhancing school policies (Perry et al., 1996).
- Multi-level school-family-community partnerships and activities that foster connections to real-world contexts (Lohrmann, Alter, Greene, & Younoszai, 2005).

5.5.1. Desirable Classroom Resources

Adequate human and material including time resources
Assessment tools*
Books, pictures, charts, CD-ROMs, items related to study units
Computers and multimedia technology
Handouts
Pamphlets and Posters
Study Guides
Text and Reference Books
Videos
Workbooks
Worksheets

*Note that: In the future tools to measure health literacy in youth may be helpful

5.5.1.1. Early Childhood Resources

- Parent/primary caregiver
- Pediatrician

- Public library
- Teacher
- Comprehensive curriculum covering [10] major health topics that focuses on *crucial life skills, personal and social well-being from preK-6 grade or higher*.

5.5.2.   Potential Outcome

- By instilling a life skills approach skills, children will be better able to tackle many other problems that may occur as they are growing.
- By having a structured, strong life skills base, children will, more often than not, be able to make the right choice when faced with a tough decision.

A high level of basic, interactive, critical, media, e-health, physical activity and mental health literacy will be achieved.

5.5.3.   Desirable K-12 Partners Needed to Meet Desired Health Literacy Outcomes

- Businesses
- Families
- Government Agencies
- Community Leaders
- Community Organizations
- Faith-based Organizations
- Health Organizations
- Health Professionals
- Politicians
- Teachers and School Personnel.

5.6.   CODA

Health literacy for all is currently not a luxury, but an imperative that should be heeded because new medicine is designed to accommodate those with high health literacy preferentially. As depicted in Figure 5.1, a well-designed and well-supported sequentially organized and co-ordinated comprehensive school-based program, is expected to have far reaching consequences in shaping a young person's health beliefs and behaviours, and their health literacy in a positive way. However, even if we engineer the environment and provide a health promoting school-the skills youth need today require more than just topical in class lessons to become innate and proficient-and environmentally independent. To achieve this goal, what is required at a minimum is appropriate and sustained leadership, policies that provide financial incentives for schools, appropriate curricula, teacher training and sufficient resources and time periods for promoting *active learning* and *problem solving. To provide a greater opportunity* for youth to become a health literate public, encouraging *families* and *communities to support these efforts, along with critical analysis, participation and interaction* is likely to improve health outcomes. While there seems to be no better way to promote health across the lifespan, other than addressing social determinants of health, the challenge lies in translating the vision of a healthy future for all into a reality, regardless of their starting point. However, taking for granted education itself will be enough to achieve this goal is no longer supported scientifically or economically. To enable youth to be productive citizens, with optimal creative and critical abilities, and to level the health and educational divide, a concerted effort by all schools, community members, government agencies, students, parents and teachers working together in and out of the classroom can surely ensure all youth have optimal chances to reach their own potential.

NOT to do this would be incongruous with a school's mission, as well as with social and cultural structures and health and educational organizations that prevail in society for purposes of the common good.

References

Abrams, M. A., Klass, P., & Dreyer, B. P. (2009). Health literacy and children: Recommendations for action. *Pediatrics, 124*, S327–S331.

American Alliance for Health, Physical Education, Recreation, and Dance (AAPHERD). (2012). Retrieved from http://www.aahperd.org/aahe/advocacy/positionStatements/upload/Comprehensive-School-Health-2003.pdf

Benham-Deal, T. B., & Hodges, B. (n.d.). *Role of 21st century schools in promoting health literacy.* National Education Association Health Information Network. Retrieved from http://www.neahin.org/educator-resources/health-literacy/benhamdeal-hodges-paper.pdf. Accessed on June 9, 2012.

California Health Literacy Initiative. *Health literacy for tutors: Your students have a right to understand.* Retrieved from http://cahealthliteracy.org/resource_center.html. Accessed on June 24, 2012.

Carbone, E. T., & Zoellner, J. M. (2012). Nutrition and health literacy: A systematic review to inform nutrition research and practice. *Journal of Academic Nutrition and Diet, 112*, 254–265.

Centers for Disease Control. (2012). *Adolescents and school health.* Retrieved from http://www.cdc.gov/HealthyYouth/CSHP/

Darvin, J. (2006). Real-world cognition doesn't end when the bell rings: Literacy instruction strategies derived from situation cognition research. *Journal of Adolescent & Adult Literacy, 49*, 398–407.

Flecha, A., Garcia, R., & Rudd, R. (2011). Using health literacy in school to overcome inequalities. *European Journal of Education, 46*, 209–218.

Golden, S. D., & Earp, J. L. (2012). Social ecological approaches to individuals and their contexts: Twenty years of *Health Education & Behavior* health promotion interventions. *Health Education & Behavior, 39*(3), 364–372.

Greeno, J. G. (1998). The situativity of knowing, learning, and research. *American Psychologist, 53*(1), 5–26. doi:10.1037/0003-066X.53.1.5.

Joint Committee on National Health Education Standards. (1995). *National health education standards: Achieving health literacy.* American Cancer Society, Inc. Available at www.cancer.org

Lammers, J. W. (1996). The effects of curriculum on student health behaviors: A case study of the Growing Healthy Curriculum on health behaviors of eighth grade students. *Journal of Health Education.* Retrieved from http://www.nsba.org/SHHC/SearchSchoolHealth/CustomSearch/

Lee, A. (2009). Health-promoting schools: Evidence for a holistic approach to promoting health and improving health literacy. *Applied Health Economics and Health Policy, 7*, 11–17.

Lohrmann, D. K. (2008). A complementary ecological model of the coordinated school health program. *Public Health Reports, 123*, 695–703.

Lohrmann, D. K., Alter, R. J., Greene, R., & Younoszai, T. M. (2005). Long-term impact of a district wide school/community-based substance abuse prevention initiative on gateway drug use. *Journal of Drug Education, 35*, 233–253.

McGovern, E. (2010, November). *Health literacy: Our children and the future.* Institute for America's health. Retrieved from http://iah.healthy-america.org/?p=616. Accessed on May 12, 2012.

Menzies, L. (2012). Charting a health literacy journey-overview and outcomes from a stakeholder workshop. *Perspectives in Public Health, 132*, 43–46.

National Center for Health Education. (2005). Formerly located at Retrieved from www.nche.org. No longer active.

National Institute for Health Care Management (NIHCM). (2011). Retrieved from http://www.nihcm.org/

Nutbeam, D. (2008). The evolving concept of health literacy. *Social Science in Medicine, 67*, 2072–2078.

Paek, H. J, & Hove, T. (2012). Social cognitive factors and perceived social influences that improve adolescent eHealth literacy. *Health Communications, 27*(8), 727–737.

Parker, E. J., Misan, G., Chong, A., Mills, H., Roberts-Thomson, K., Horowitz, A. M., & Jamieson, L. M. (2012). An oral health literacy intervention for indigenous adults in a rural setting in Australia. *BMC Public Health, 12*(1), 461.

Perry, C. L., Williams, C. L., Veblen-Mortenson, S., Toomey, T. L., Komro, K. A., Anstine, P. S., et al. (1996). Project Northland: Outcomes of a communitywide alcohol use prevention program during early adolescence. *American Journal of Public Health, 86*, 956–965.

Peterson, F. L., Cooper, R. J., & Laird, J. M. (2001). Enhancing teacher health literacy in school health promotion: A vision for the new millennium. *Journal of School Health, 71,* 138–144.

Stewart, S., Riecken, T., Scott, T., Tanaka, M., & Riecken, J. (2008). Expanding health literacy: Indigenous youth creating videos. *Journal of Health Psychology, 13,* 180–189.

St. Leger, L. (2001). Schools, health literacy and public health: Possibilities and challenges. *Health Promotion International, 16,* 197–205.

Trickett, E., & Rowe, H. L. (2012). Emerging ecological approaches to prevention, health promotion and public health in the school context: Next steps from a community psychology perspective. *Journal of Educational and Psychological Consultation, 22*(1–2), 125–140.

What the HEALTH!. (2000). Canadian Public Health Association Health Resources Center. Retrieved from http://www.cpha.ca

Appendix 5.A.1

Example of a Classroom-Based Approach to Medicine Education for Youth

SCOPE & SEQUENCE		
Grade Level	**Lesson Topic**	**Themes**
K-2	• Communicating with the Doctor • Medicine Labels • Dosages • Immunization • Medical Emergencies • Medical Forms • Medicine Safety	• What are Medicines? • What is a Pharmacist? • What is a Nurse? • Who Gives Medicine to You? • What in Your Medicine Cabinet?
3–5	• Medicine — for Children vs. Adults • Side Effects of Medicines • Drugs versus Medicines • What are Vitamins and Minerals? • What is a Dose?	• What is a Prescription? • What are Medicines used for? • Visiting the Doctor • Immunizations • Use vs. Misuse of Medicine
6–8	• Medicine Advertisements • Dietary Supplements • Herbal Medicines • Supplements • Antibiotics • Medicines From Around the World • Brand Name vs. Generic Medicines	• Internet Pharmacies • FDA • Pharmaceutical Companies (where do medicines come from?) • From Prescription Medicine to Over-the-Counter • Steroids • Communication with Health Care Professionals

Appendix 5.A.2

BASIC LESSON TEMPLATE

Title

Subtitle

Grade

OBJECTIVES

From this lesson, students will accomplish the following:

1.
2.
3.
4.

ASSESSMENT

Following this lesson, teacher will address the following:

1.
2.
3.
4.

TEACHING MATERIALS NEEDED

THINGS TO DO BEFORE LESSON

1.
2.
3.
4.

LANGUAGE DEVELOPMENT

ACTIVITIES

Smaller Groups:

Full Group:

LEARNING LOG

Journal based on the course of study/enhances student learning

Informal record of learning/not graded/allows students to review concepts in their own words

EXTENSION ACTIVITIES

Appendix 5.A.3   *Modes of Instruction*

Cooperative learning groups Cooperative learning is an approach to instruction in which students work in small groups and the teacher acts as a consultant. Each student in the cooperative learning group is held accountable for the group effort; all group members must learn the material, and everyone in the group usually receives a common grade or reward. Research shows that cooperative learning contributes benefits that individualistic models of instruction cannot provide. Cooperative learning results in higher student achievement, enhanced self-esteem, and improved attitudes towards teachers, other students and school itself.

Cooperative learning groups can be established to accomplish a number of purposes, but for four of the most common are

- To discuss issues or events
- To engage in decision-making activities
- To provide small group instruction
- To research or investigate problems or questions.

The size of the group depends on its purpose and activity. Generally, there are three to eight students per group. Groups should be large enough to be stimulating yet small enough for individual participation and personal recognition. Careful attention to the composition of student groups is critical to the success of cooperative learning activities. When forming the class into groups, consider ability, ethnicity and gender. To ensure a variety of group membership opportunities, change composition often. Keep a record of your groups so that students have the opportunity to be teammates with everyone in the class during the school year.

Cooperative learning occurs when groups of students work together to attain a common goal. Cooperative learning is facilitated when each member has an assigned task to help the group achieve its goals. Depending on the group's size and the activity, the teacher may assign the following roles to group members:

Co-ordinator (or facilitator):
Organizes and co-ordinates the group's efforts and assists group members in getting the help they need to do tasks; seeks answers to questions within the group and answers queries only if no one in the group can help.

Recorder:
Informs the class of the group's actions or decisions; reports what the students learned

Monitor:
Sets up all the materials at the learning station and replaces supplies and equipment as needed; may also be responsible for putting away materials.

Timekeeper:
Keeps the group advised of the time and on task.

Encourager/coach:
Keeps the group on task and encourages students when necessary; monitors completion of worksheets, learning logs, or other written responses.

Rotate roles on a regular basis so that all students have the opportunity to learn and practice new skills. Teachers monitor group behaviour and interaction and provide feedback o how students are conducting their roles. It is important to remember that students are learning social skills as well as academic content through cooperative learning groups.

Post the names of group members and assignments. In the upper grades, a large chart can be used to indicate the group, the activity station and the role of each child. The responsibilities expected of each role should also be posted. In the primary grades, roles can be color-coded and each child can wear a color-coded badge.

If cooperative learning with assigned tasks is new for students, they will need to learn how to work cooperatively prior to working at learning stations. Decide which norms and skills are needed for students to work successfully in the learning stations. Students rarely learn new behaviours or convictions through lecture or general group discussion alone, hence the norms and skills desired for students should be taught through exercises and games.

Before attempting a cooperative learning group effort, the teacher should discuss the roles and responsibilities of the students within the groups. They may include some of the following:

Group Members:
1. Help the co-ordinator carry out plans.
2. Share the work equally.
3. Work without disturbing other groups.
4. Ask other members to contribute ideas.
5. Act courteously and respect the ideas of others.

Co-ordinator
1. Helps everyone become a part of the group.
2. Gives everyone a turn at the 'good' jobs.
3. Seeks ideas from all members of the group.
4. Helps the group identify its job.
5. Encourages the group to decide which ideas are best.

Teachers find that cooperative learning is most successful when used as an integral part of the instructional program. The approach works best when students have opportunities to practice group interaction skills and receive feedback about how the group is working together. Commend students who perform during group efforts.

Role play Role play is an experimental learning technique that can be used easily in a learning situation. It does not involve elaborate acting skills on the part of the participants. Instead, it only requires the participants to adopt the attitudes they believe to be appropriate to the scenario.

Role play is an important teaching strategy for skills building. Through role-play, participants can

– experience the social pressures to engage in health-compromising behaviour.
– react spontaneously to the pressures.
– evaluate their reactions.
– develop persuasive and assertive techniques for resisting social pressures.

Role play provides training in life skills and skills to resist pressures to smoke, drink alcohol, or engage in other health-compromising behaviours. It provides students with new information and an awareness of health-related issues while providing teachers with a means to evaluate the effectiveness of various interpersonal skills.

When using role play, there are important factors necessary to ensure its effectiveness. Students need to be assigned lead-up tasks and exercises that will enable them to participate successfully. Teachers need to ensure that an appropriate level of empathy exists in the group and must clearly explain to students the aims and procedures of the role play activity.

Hints for successful role play:

Do:
– Inform participants of their right to withdraw at any time without explanation.
– Be alert to the actions and feelings generated, and call 'cut' if the role play is arousing too much anxiety.
– Keep the scenes short, no more than 3 minutes. This will enable participants to concentrate on impact.
– Use techniques such as 'freeze frames' or 'pause' to maximize learning and minimize unintended outcomes.
– Allow participants the opportunity to create their own scenarios to achieve greater realism and relevance.

– Maximize involvement by ensuring that the entire class is involved in the role play activity.
– Debrief participants after the role play, particularly if levels of anxiety are raised. This can be done by analyzing and discussing the role play or characters when out of role.

Don't:
Judge the role play 'right' or 'wrong'. Concentrate instead on eliciting alternative solutions or possible consequences from the behaviour involved.

– Comment during the role play. Instead, wait until it is finished, then introduce the desired changes and ensure that the students do the same.
– Cast participants in roles too close to that of their real life-roles.
– Assume a morally 'right' stance. Instead, be non-judgmental, and encourage all points of view in the debriefing period.

Before participants can be involved in role plays which involved health-related issues, they must be able to participate in other types of role play that result in 'real' learning. Often role play is seen as a 'lot of fun' or an exaggeration of the real situation. This is certainly the case when time is not spent preparing for the role. The activities' suggested aim is to develop a supportive learning environment and encourage students to assume roles and react spontaneously to situations.

Follow this procedure for role play activity:

1. Introduction or Warm-up
Acquaint participants with the scenario and establish the goal of the role play. Use an introductory exercise preparation game to focus the attention of the group.

2. Select Participants
Select an observer who will offer feedback.

3. Set the Stage
Inform participants of their assigned roles. The time, place, surrounding, others present, and position of players can be determined by the teacher and later, by the students. Videos, case studies, short scripts, or open sentences can be used to set the scene.

4. Prepare Observers
If there are observers, give them specific tasks to keep them focused on the role play and to elicit feedback.

5. Act the Role

Role players assume the roles and 'live' the situation.

6. Processing/Feedback (Debriefing)

- Ask open-ended questions and focus discussion on
  - feelings involved
  - attitudes expressed
  - what alternatives could have occurred
  - what consequences may have resulted
  - what participants learned about the character they played.

7. Re-enactment

Roles may be switched to demonstrate alternate solutions and interpretations. Other variables may be introduced, such as changing attitudes of other characters or changing outcomes. '

8. Generalizing

This is a particularly vital component. The outcomes of the role play are discussed in terms of realism and are 'stamped' with the authority of the peer group, teachers, students or others present. This sharing of experiences and outcomes involves

- constructing some general principles of conduct, relating to specific situations,
- helping participants realize their problems are shared by many others.

Learning logs   A learning log is a journal based on the course of study. *Growing Healthy*® made use of learning logs to enhance student learning. To keep a learning log, students write about the concepts covered in class. Kept regularly, learning logs improve learning and provide experience in the writing process. Learning logs are not graded. They are informal records of learning, not quizzes. Students are encouraged to write whatever they can to reinforce concepts in their own words. Spelling and grammar may be incorrect, but students will respond to the content in a meaningful way.

Entries should be made on a regular basis. Writing may follow lectures, demonstrations, discussions, assignments, cooperative learning groups or videos. A separate notebook or folder can be used to keep notes in order and in one place. The entries should be dated for future reference. Direction can be simple, for example, 'Write what you learned today' or 'Write about whatever was most interesting (unusual, confusing, important)'.

Learning logs have several advantages. Because entries follow a lesson, students are more easily stimulated to write. They experience the joy of fluency instead of the frustrations of writer's block and thereby gain confidence. Writing requires students to think about the material, recall facts, vocabulary and key concepts. The value of writing in learning logs is cumulative. As students make entries regularly, they acquire the habit of writing. As they think about concepts, they also draw conclusions.

Once students are comfortable with learning logs, their entries can be used in several ways.

1. The teacher may collect logs periodically and read entries to see how students are learning. Correction of language and mechanics is unnecessary, but the teacher may want to write marginal notes, praising good ideas or clearing up minor confusion.
2. Students may real their logs aloud to one another in groups.
3. Before beginning new material, a teacher may have students write what they know about the concept. After study, students write again. This process allows the teacher and the student to see what has been learned.

Demonstrations   During a demonstration, the teacher or another expert demonstrates a concept or life skill. For example, the teacher may want to demonstrate the proper technique for brushing teeth. Using a tooth model and a large toothbrush, the teacher demonstrates the toothbrushing method recommended by the American Dental Association. Students observe the proper technique and then practice the skill at home. When conducting a demonstration, organize materials before class; following the demonstration, discuss the skills demonstrated and answer questions.

Lecture   Lecturing is an instructional strategy involving a verbal presentation to a large number of students. It is most effective when presented with a motivational opening, a delivery of factual content and a concluding summary of the information. Using a variety of audiovisuals to support the verbal presentation enhances the factual and conceptual elements of the lecture. Any lecture will be more interesting with the addition of personal anecdotes, humor, if appropriate, and related stories.

If the lecturer follows a structure, pre-determined outline and then shares it with students, they will more easily follow the sequence and take the necessary notes. The teacher should vary physical stance, pace of speech, eye contact and movement about the classroom in order to gain and keep the attention of students.

Guest speakers   A guest speaker relays experience(s) or expertise in a specific field or with a specific health skill. A guest speaker can also demonstrate a concept or life skill while discussing personal experiences.

Lecture and discussion Lecture and discussion combines a verbal presentation with student dialogue, fostering student participation and interaction. Adding discussion to the lecture method strongly increases the likelihood that students will interact with the subject matter. As a straight lecture, include a motivational beginning, a presentation of factual content, a summary, engaging audiovisuals and personal anecdotes. Insert questions for students into your presentation and recognize and affirm their participation.

Brainstorming Brainstorming requires a variety of responses to the same question, problem or trigger statement. Teachers state the question or problem and then facilitate the brainstorming session, or students break into smaller groups to generate a list of responses. This instructional strategy helps students to make responsible decisions, think creatively, explore several options or solutions and participate in class.

Brainstorming rules

– All members share ideas; quantity is as important as quality.
– No discussion of an idea is allowed during the brainstorming.
– No evaluation of a remark, positive or negative, is permitted, as this inhibits the free flow of ideas.
– Record all ideas regardless of how ridiculous they may seem.
– Limit the session to three to six minutes.

Think-pair-share Think-Pair-Share is a simple yet effective teaching strategy that allows students an informal forum to collaborate on a mini-project or classroom activity with a partner. Students pair with a partner, work on the predetermined activity, and then share their conclusions with the full group. Think-Pair-Share allows teachers to break up a full group quickly and efficiently and to give ample opportunities for class participation.

Small groups Small group discussions provide the best opportunity for students to practice skills in effective communication. These groups should be comprised of students who are not necessarily familiar with each other. They should also allow for at least one students who has good communication skills to be in the group with one students who has fewer communication skills. When giving the students the topic to be addressed in a small group, present specific instructions to proceed, how much time is allowed, and what needs to be accomplished. Allow time for students to evaluate their communication skills in small groups.

Student presentation   A student presentation is an instruction strategy in which a student makes an oral presentation that has been fully researched. This strategy helps students develop effective communication skills and allows them to gather and evaluate important information. Before students make their presentations, it is helpful to give them the criteria on which they will be evaluated — this information can improve their performance.

Field trips   During a field trip, students visit a site outside the school to gather information or to develop a skill. A field trip might involve visiting a doctor's office, a recycling plant, or the local police station. Prepare students for the trip — clarify the reasons for the field trip and your expectations. Set guidelines for students' behaviour and explain the consequences for breaking those guidelines. After the trip, discuss what was learned, and have students write thank you notes to the individuals who participated in the field trip site and to other adults who helped with the excursion.

Multisensory projects and presentations   Multisensory projects allow a student to utilize a variety of talents and interest in order to learn, as well as to convey information to others. This methods offers opportunities to interview an expert, develop a multimedia presentation, incorporate music and present a researched topic enriched by the imagination and energy of either an individual or small group.

Multimedia technologies   Multimedia technologies incorporate computers to combine video, sounds, graphics, photography and animation into an interactive system. Multimedia technologies allow students to develop their own multimedia presentations using scanners, videos, photography and video clips. Typically, multimedia set-ups refer to a computer with a CD-ROM drive in which students can play discs which have high quality still and video, images, sound and text. Additionally, schools may have interactive laser disk systems connected to their computers, in which case instruction is provided through a still or moving video images, printed text, computer graphics and sound. Students respond to instruction and make choices using a mouse, keyboard, or lighted pen at the computer monitor.

Telecommunication technologies   Telecommunications technologies link students and teachers to each other and to others without being physically present at the same time. More specifically, through the use of cable television, satellite systems and online communication through computer networks, students and teachers can communicate regardless of location.

Additional instructional strategies Other instructional strategies can be utilized in a health-related classroom to understand a particular concept or to practice specific life skills.

Debate A debate provides the opportunity for students to recognize the importance of being highly informed and prepared to identify and defend a topic, an approach, or a solution. This instructional strategy presents an issue and requires students to research, interview and assimilate information that will support a position either FOR or AGAINST. Debate requires students to document sources and to evaluate the reliability of information.

Panel discussion Panel discussion is a strategy that allows two or more students to research and report on a topic or issue. Panel discussions allow for interaction among the panel members and the audience of students. The role of the teacher or moderator is to review and clarify information presented and to facilitate the interaction between panel members and the students.

Jigsaw In a Jigsaw learning activity, the participant becomes a teacher and learner simultaneously. Each team member becomes an expert on one aspect of the lesson content and then helps the other team members learn the material. This framework is like a jigsaw puzzle: each person contributes a piece of the puzzle by sharing the information learned with others. The Jigsaw consists of 4 steps reading, expert group discussion, teaching and home team discussion.

Directions: Have the full group count off into equal home groups (1, 2, 3, 4 etc.), depending on the size of the group and the amount of material to be read. Have participants report to their home groups. Once within the home group, count off into equal expert groups (A, B, C, D etc.) Next, have each participant report to his/her expert group — A's together, B's together and so on. Assign the reading to group members A,B, C, D etc. In the expert group, they will read the material, share their knowledge and discuss new concepts. Allow approximately 10–15 minutes for reading and discussing.

Circulate from group to group to ensure that participants are discussing the material and to answer questions. After the allotted time, have participants return to their home teams.

Now that they have become experts on their topics, have each expert report newly learned information. Allow 5–10 minutes for each expert to discuss and report to the home team.

An example:

There are 9 participants and three topics (Learning Logs, Cooperative Learning Groups, Assessment) to be discussed. Begin by dividing the full group into 3 home groups of 3 individuals each by having individuals count off 1, 2, 3. Once in home groups, have participants count off into 3 expert groups of A, B, C. The A group will read about Learning Logs, the B group will read about Cooperative Learning Groups, and the C group will read about Assessment. Now, have participants meet with their expert groups to read about and discuss their assigned topic. Upon completion, expert groups will return to their home team to share newly learned information from their other team members.

Appendix 5.A.4   *Sample Lesson Plan*

Title: Communicating With a Health Provider (K-2)

Teacher Background Information:

Learning Outcome: Students should be able to define medicine and understand what questions to ask when they visit a provider (**Basic Health Literacy; Interactive Health Literacy**).

Objectives:

Students will:

1. Identify what medicine is.
2. Where they may encounter medicines.
3. Describe the types of questions that a doctor or nurse might ask a patient.
4. Explain the importance of communicating with the doctor or nurse during a visit.
5. Practice communicating with a doctor or nurse through role-play.

Materials:
- Drawing paper
- Art supplies

Things To Do Before Lesson:

- Optional: Invite a doctor and/or nurse to speak to the class about the importance of medicines.

Language Development:

- **Clinic:**
- **Communication:**
- **Medicine:**
- **Nurse:**
- **Patient:**

Assessment:

Teacher will assess:

1. Students' ability to identify where doctors and nurses are encountered.
2. Students' ability to explain the importance of medicines.

3. Students' ability to illustrate how to talk with a provider through role-play.

Activity:

Full Group

1. Ask students, 'When do you see a doctor or a nurse?' (when you are sick, when you go for a check-up, when you need to get a shot etc.)
2. Ask students, 'Where are some places where you might visit the doctor or nurse?' (doctor's office, clinic, school nurse's office, hospital)
3. Tell students to imagine that they are going to the doctor or nurse because they are not feeling well. Ask students, 'What types of questions might the doctor or nurse ask you during your visit?'
   a. How do you feel?
   b. Where does it hurt or where do you feel sick?
   c. What does the pain feel like?
   d. When did you start feeling this way?

Sample Letter for Parents

Dear Family:

We have been discussing the importance of communication between doctors and patients. The students identified some of the questions that a doctor or nurse may ask during a visit. They also identified some questions that patients may ask a health-care provider. These included questions about their illness, medicines and procedures.

Please discuss the importance of communication with your child. At your child's next visit to the doctor, help him/her to speak to the doctor or nurse and ask questions. Have your child answer as many of the doctor's questions as possible. Likewise, let the doctor or nurse know that you are encouraging your child to communicate with them. After the visit, review what the doctor or nurse said with your child to make sure that he or she understands. Any additional questions that arise can be answered by calling the doctors office at a later time.

Remember, better communication between patients of all ages and their health-care providers leads to better overall care.

Sincerely,
Your Child's Teacher

Appendix 5.A.5 *Sample Lesson Plan*

Vitamins and Minerals (3–5)

Teacher Background Information:

Learning Outcome: Students should be able to define medicine and identify proper versus improper use of medicines (**Basic, Interactive and Critical Health Literacy**).

Lesson Objectives:

Students will:

1. Define vitamins and minerals.
2. Explain the importance of vitamins and minerals.
3. Describe how the body can obtain the vitamins and minerals it needs.

Materials:

- Poster board (1 sheet per group)
- Art supplies
- Optional: candy that resembles children's vitamin supplements (e.g. Pez®)

Language Development:

- **Vitamin:**
- **Mineral:**
- **Deficiency:**
- **Supplement:**

Assessment:

Teacher will assess:

1. Students' ability to define vitamins and minerals.
2. Students' ability to explain the importance of vitamins and minerals.

Activity:

Full Group

1. Ask students what they had for dinner the night before. Allow for several of the students to respond.
2. Ask students why it is important to eat.
   a. Remind students it is important to eat healthy foods and not a lot of foods that contain high levels of sugar, salt, or fat.
   b. Have students give examples of healthy foods. Have students give examples of foods that they should eat in moderation.
3. Ask students, 'Has anyone ever heard of vitamins and minerals? Can anyone describe what vitamins and minerals are?'
   a. Vitamins and minerals are substances found in the food that we eat. They are very important because they help the body to grow and to repair itself when injured.
   b. The body can't make vitamins or minerals on its own. It needs to get these substances from food.
4. Give students examples of vitamins and minerals, what foods they come from and what purpose they serve in the body.

Ask students what they think might happen if the body does not get enough of a particular vitamin or mineral.

5. Explain to students that sometimes people don't get all of the vitamins and minerals they need even if they eat healthy food. In these cases, people may take a vitamin or mineral supplement.
6. Ask students if they have ever taken a vitamin and mineral supplement. Ask, 'What did it look like?'
7. Tell students that vitamin and mineral supplements should be treated like medicines. Like medicines, these supplements can be very dangerous if they are not used properly. Taking too much of certain vitamins and minerals can damage the body and could even cause death.
8. Ask students to describe children's vitamin and mineral supplements again.
9. Ask students what might happen if a child mistook vitamin and mineral supplements for candy.

Small Groups

10. Divide students into small groups.
11. Tell students that they will be working in groups to create *What We Know About Vitamins and Minerals* signs.

12. Assign each group one of the following topics. Give more than one group the same topic or develop other topics if necessary.
    a. How The Body Gets Vitamins and Minerals
    b. What Vitamins and Minerals Do For The Body
    c. Vitamins Are Not Candy.
13. Tell students they will draw whatever they want to get their message across to other students. Give examples of what they can draw such as a picture of a person eating healthy food or vitamins helping a child to grow.
14. Have each of the groups present their *What We Know About Vitamins and Minerals* sign to the class. If possible, have the students present their signs and what they have learned to other classes in the school. Hang the signs around the school.

Additional Classroom Props:

• Pictures of vitamin and mineral supplements, including children's vitamins.

Other Ideas:

• Have students go on line and try to access label information on a supplement and its price.
    Require them to make a decision to purchase, Yes/No. If Yes, why would they purchase this, and where-would they purchase this?
• Have students find out more about Government Agencies that regulate supplements.
• Create a fictional person and a scenario and ask students to see if products will meet the needs of the fictional person.
• Take HOME LETTER TO FAMILY — Try require parents to show child has shared this with them.

Dear Family:

We have been discussing the importance of vitamins and minerals for the body. Vitamins and minerals are important substances because they help the body to grow and develop properly. They also support the body's immune system and assist in repairing the body after infection or injury.

Vitamins and minerals are found in foods that we eat. In most cases, when a healthy diet is followed, the body receives enough of each of the 13 vitamins and at least 15 minerals that it needs. The students heard examples of vitamins and minerals, what foods they come from and what purpose they serve. The students learned that sometimes, when people do not have healthy food to eat, they may not satisfy the body's need for vitamins and minerals.

The students recognized the resemblance of children's vitamin supplements to candy. They discussed the danger of a child mistaking supplements for candy. Combining everything they learned and discussed, the students worked in groups to create *What We Know About Vitamins and Minerals* signs. They shared these signs and their knowledge with each other and with other classes throughout the school.

Please discuss this topic with your child. Look for vitamin and mineral information on nutrition labels on foods. Read the safety warnings on the labels of vitamin and mineral supplements together. Finally, as with medicines, keep vitamin and mineral supplements in your home out of reach of children. For more information, please visit http://www.kidshealth.org and search for vitamins or minerals.

Sincerely,
Your Child's Teacher

Appendix 5.A.6 *Sample Lesson Plan*

Medicine from Around the World (6–8)

Adapt for One's Own Country

Teacher Background Information:

Learning Outcomes: By the end of the lesson, students should know the difference between prescription and over-the-counter medicines. Students should understand that medicines manufactured in the United States must be approved by the Food and Drug Administration (or their own country) (**Basic, Interactive and Critical Health Literacy**).

Objectives:

Students will:

1. Define the word 'import'.
2. Describe regulations governing imported medicines.
3. Explain the danger in taking medicines from other countries.
4. Define 'alternative medicine'.

Language Development:

- **Import:**
- **Manufacture:**
- **Traditional:**
- **Ethnic:**
- **Contaminated:**
- **Over the counter medicine:**

Assessment:

Teacher will assess:

1. Students' ability to define the words 'import' and 'alternative medicine' and give examples of each.
2. Students' ability to explain why people may take medicine from another country and why it can be dangerous.

Activity:

Full Group

1. Ask students, 'What does it mean if something is described as imported?' (An imported item is something that is brought into this country after being manufactured in a different country.)
2. Ask students to identify some items that may be imported. (cars, electronic equipment, jewellery, furniture, food etc.)
3. Tell students that sometimes medicines are imported into the United States from other countries.
4. Explain to students that sometimes people bring medicine into the United States for their own use. They may carry it with them from a foreign country or order it over the Internet.
5. Ask students, 'Why do you think people take medicines from other countries?'
   - Some countries have problems with counterfeit medicines. These medicines may look like the real thing but they are fake. Countries with this problem are those where the manufacture and sale of medicine is less regulated.
   - Counterfeit medicines may not contain any active ingredient (the part of the medicine that makes it work to treat, prevent, or cure illness), it may contain an incorrect amount of active ingredient, or it could contain different active ingredients. Counterfeit medicines sometimes contain chemicals that are poisons.
   - Ask students why counterfeit medicines are dangerous. (People are not taking the medicine they think they are.)
     a. Dangerous Ethnic or traditional remedies.
6. Tell students that around the world, including in the United States, groups of people may have different ideas about how to prevent, treat and cure illness. Some people prevent and treat illnesses without going to a doctor or taking medicine like we are familiar with.
   a. In some cases, there are people who help patients to treat their illnesses but they are not doctors like those licensed in the United States.
   b. Treatments can include taking herbal supplements or performing certain exercises.

Small Groups

Divide students into groups. Tell students that they will investigate forms of alternative medicine from around the world including the United States.

c. Assign or have students choose their topic. Some examples are listed below:

- *Acupuncture*: a therapy practiced in China for the last 2500 years involving the insertion of thin needles into specific places on the body. It is believed that the needles can treat and cure illness by encouraging the flow of energy or qi (pronounced chee) in the body.
- *Acupressure*: a therapy that originated in China 5000 years ago. Specific points on the body are pressed or rubbed with the fingers or hands to treat ailments such as headaches and stress, and to treat pain.
- *Homeopathy*: a system of treatment based on the work of German Chemist Samuel Hahnemann (1753–1843). It uses minute amounts of whatever is causing an illness to treat the illness. It is based on the idea that 'like cures like'.
- *Traditional Chinese medicine*: a system of health care that originated over 2500 years ago. It is based on the belief that illness is caused by an imbalance of qi (prounced chee) or energy flow in the body. The imbalance is remedies through the use of herbal medicine, changes in diet, acupuncture, acupressure, movement (Tai Chi exercises)
- *Ayurveda*: the traditional Indian system of medicine practiced for more than 5000 years that includes yoga, massage, meditation and changes in diet. Practitioners of ayurveda receive state-recognized training not unlike Western doctors.
- *Reiki*: (pronouned ray kee) the practice of transferring healing energy from the hands of a practitioner into the person being treated. Although associated with Japan, reiki may have origins in Tibet.
- *Yoga*: developed in India over 5000 years ago, yoga is a system of exercises that encourages the balance between the body and mind through breathing and meditation.
- *Reflexology*: the practice of putting pressure on specific areas of the feet and hands for overall health. Reflexology holds that each area of the feet and hands correspond to another area of the body. Therefore, the rest of the body can be treated by applying pressure to these areas. The origins of reflexology may date back to ancient China, India and Egypt.

d. Tell students they should research their topics and be able to present their group's topic to the rest of the class. They can create posters, brochures, or perform a newscast where they report on their topic. They should be as creative as possible.

Optional: Have students choose a country or region and research the area's major imports and exports. Have students report on their findings.

Additional Classroom Props:

- Related web sites:
    National Center for Complementary and Alternative Medicine –
    http://www.nccam.nih.gov
    National Library of Medicine—Medline Plus – http://www.nlm.nih.
    gov/medlineplus/alternativemedicine.html

Take HOME LETTER TO FAMILY:

Dear Family:

We have been discussing medicine from around the world. The students learned that all medicine that is brought into the United States must be approved by the Food and Drug Administration (FDA). Some people buy medicines from other countries because they may be cheaper, they may not be available in the United States, or because they are a traditional or ethnic remedy. However, the students learned that it is not advised to take medicine from other countries. In many cases there is little regulation. This can lead to the manufacture of unsafe medicine. In addition, counterfeit or fake medicines are a problem in some countries. These medicines sometimes do not contain the active ingredient of the medicine, they contain the wrong amount, or they contain other ingredients that can be dangerous. Medicines from other countries should also be avoided when their use in the United States requires a prescription. Such medicines require the supervision of a doctor. Finally, certain traditional or ethnic remedies can be dangerous because they may contain poisonous chemicals such as lead. If complications arise while a person is taking a medicine from another country treatment may be delayed.

The students learned that around the world, people treat illness with other types of remedies. These remedies are referred to as alternative medicine in the United States. In some cases, people have been using these remedies, such as acupuncture and Chinese herbal medicine, for thousands of years. Alternative medicine treatments are being studied in the United States to determine whether or not they are effective.

Talk to your child about the proper use of medicines. If your family takes medicine from other countries, check with a local pharmacist to ensure that it is safe. Allow your child to describe to you what he or she has learned about medicine from other countries and alternative medicine. For more information about alternative medicine please visit http://www.kidshealth. org/parent/general/sick/alternative_medicine.html.

Sincerely,
Your Child's Teacher

Chapter 6

Future Directions: How to Organize Classroom Practices to Support the Development of Holistic Health Literacy

Olli Paakkari and Leena Paakkari

6.1. Introduction

Schools as institutions receive considerable public attention and there are various expectations citizens have about the role of the school in fostering youth wellbeing. Marton, Runesson, and Tsui (2004) have aptly pondered how school personnel often encounter situations where they are expected to carry out 'less whole-class teaching', 'more problem-based learning' and 'more peer-learning', but rarely do these arguments extend to truly pondering the question 'for what purpose'. What are we intending to achieve through these various approaches? Too often the discussions begin with the teaching methods, even though the starting point should be in the learning objectives. Yet, only by starting with the learning objectives may we truly ponder what kind of methods are needed to attain the desired objectives. The same argument can apply to any intention to develop health literacy among the pupils. That is, if our aim is to foster an individual's health literacy from a basic to a more advanced level, we need to be clear about our objectives, and we need to clearly define what components of health literacy we are addressing in order to develop any appropriate learning objective.

As the prior chapters of this book show there are various ways of defining or viewing what health literacy is and what it does. In our view, this discussion of health literacy should also constantly take into account the broader context in which we are immersed as this frames the demands that we should be able to respond to. Here, however, is where we believe the school itself does not make a difference. This is because the role of the school is to equip the pupils with the kinds of competencies that will enable them to meet the demands of current and future society. Thus, in defining what aspects of health literacy should be taught, it seems reasonable to suggest we should try to think ahead, and anticipate the type of world our pupils will be part of, as well as the future demands that may be made on their overall competence, and this is the same regardless of school setting. In preparing youth for future citizenship, Wagner (2008) has argued that certain skills should be taught. These skills include critical thinking and problem-solving skills, the ability to access and analyse information, and having the ability to collaborate, as well as having intrinsic curiosity, imagination and initiative, to mention a few. In addition, the present emphasis in schools on lifelong learning skills also assumes people will need to be able to self-reflect and assess themselves as learners. However, at the same time, we believe we agree with others in the field as regards the need to see pupils as citizens in their own right, within their *current* surroundings (see Hill, Davis, Prout, & Tisdall, 2004; see also Barrow, 2010), and to consider their more immediate expectations and demands as crucial elements in efforts to foster the development of their health literacy related skills.

We also believe that too often the definitions of health literacy have not taken into account these specific perspectives, and hence, we have tried to look beyond the existing definitions and to add some new insights to the discussion. This chapter is based on the previously published paper called '*Health literacy as a learning outcome in schools*' (Paakkari & Paakkari, 2012). In the following paragraphs we describe our way of understanding health literacy and its constituent components. Then, we provide some examples of various types of teaching–learning events, which we believe will support the development of school-based health literacy efforts.

6.2. Health Literacy — An Ability to Understand Oneself, Others and the World Beyond

Reports in the literature suggest that very often we may consider health literacy largely as an individual's competency that focuses on personal issues only, or even, on issues that a person should gain or receive *without* personalizing them. However, our view is that health literacy is far more than that. That is, it involves literacy about oneself, others and the world beyond. It is about being able to construct one's own views on health matters (see Nutbeam, 2008; cf. Rubinelli, Schulz, & Nakamoto, 2009), while understanding and also taking into consideration the perspectives of others and the collective (Paakkari & Paakkari, 2012). If we consider health literacy as an ability to make sound health decisions, these decisions should also be made in relation to others, as well. After all, as members of various societies people cannot merely think solely about what is good for 'me' and 'contextualize health knowledge for his or her own good health' in isolation (Rubinelli et al., 2009, p. 309).

We thus provided the following definition for health literacy that we feel is relevant in this chapter as follows (Paakkari & Paakkari, 2012):

> Health literacy comprises *a broad range of knowledge and competencies that people seek to encompass, evaluate, construct and use*. Through health literacy competencies people become able to *understand themselves, others and the world in a way that will enable them to make sound health decisions, and to work on and change the factors that constitute their own and others' health chances*. (cf. Abel, 2007; Zarcadoolas, Pleasant, & Greer, 2005) (p. 136)

This definition suggests that individuals should become literate not only about themselves but also about the broader environment in which they are immersed broader context they are part of. Thus, we recently proposed that as a learning outcome to be addressed by schools, health literacy should consist of five core components: theoretical knowledge, practical knowledge, critical thinking, self-awareness and citizenship skills (Paakkari & Paakkari, 2012). These components may overlap somewhat, or may even be inclusive, and not necessarily entirely hierarchical (but cf. Nutbeam, 2000). Moreover, although separating these components may be artificial, it is through this separation that we aim to highlight the foci of these various health literacy components and the critical differences between them.

However, even though we understand health literacy as a phenomenon that constitutes the five core components listed above, we agree with other authors that basic reading, writing and speech skills are also vital to the development of pupils' health literacy (see Borzekowski, 2009; Mancuso, 2009; Nutbeam, 2000; Parker, 2000; von Wagner, Steptoe, Wolf, & Wardle, 2009; Zarcadoolas et al., 2005). Similarly, as an example, we do not separately perceive social skills as a core component of health literacy (cf. Mancuso, 2009; Nutbeam, 1998, 2008; Nutbeam & Kickbusch, 2000), since we see that social skills are implicitly included in various aspects of the core components. In addition, although we regard motivation, self-esteem, self-respect, tolerance and perceived self-efficacy as important factors that can give support to, result from, and/or evolve in parallel with the enhancement of health literacy, in our view they do not represent *core* components of health literacy (Paakkari & Paakkari, 2012). Thus, if a pupils' health literacy has to be evaluated and graded, these aspects should not be included within the grading rubric.

6.3. Learning for Theoretical Knowledge

Theoretical knowledge, which has been described as something explicit, factual, formal and declarative (see Bereiter & Scardamalia, 1993, p. 45; Tynjälä, 2008a, 2008b), is commonly seen as useful for providing a comprehensive education on health matters. Moreover, declarative knowledge as described by Scardamalia and Bereiter (2006) refers to knowledge *about* something, such as basic knowledge about what constitutes healthy eating (e.g. the content and structure of the food pyramid). Gaining theoretical knowledge enables pupils to develop a broader understanding of different health issues, and helps them to identify similarities and differences between them. Theoretical knowledge thus forms a necessary basis for the other core components of health literacy. However, it is seldom sufficient for helping people to take health-promoting actions or to change their health habits. Among the lower level thinking skills implicitly acknowledged within this knowledge category are recalling, listing, describing or naming, because knowledge and experiencing that knowledge cannot be separated (Paakkari & Paakkari, 2012).

Thus learning theoretical knowledge can be achieved through memorizing or reproducing the health knowledge, but this does not include those higher order skills such as application, critical thinking or reflection (see Paakkari, Tynjälä, & Kannas, 2011). The main aim in schools is often simply that pupils should be able to repeat what they have read from a book or other source and to remember what the teacher said earlier in the lesson. The teacher functions as an expert, who chooses the health content that will be covered during the lessons. The pupils' role is mainly to obtain knowledge from the teacher, and not to actively process or assess the knowledge (Paakkari, Tynjälä, & Kannas, 2010a). This means that the knowledge dealt with will be seen as non-complex and as taken for granted, and acquisition of this knowledge can be judged on simple tests as being either right or wrong. To the extent that there may be question-and-answer sessions, pupils may become slightly more involved (van Rossum & Hamer, 2010, p. 10). Such an approach to learning may well increase pupils' factual knowledge capital, and may support the ability to remember the health information, which is important in problem-solving and other more complex

---

Box 6.1.   Theoretical Knowledge

Goal   • to gain more information about current health topic
       • to memorize and repeat the main aspects
How   • receiving information from the teacher and from books or
         other materials
       • activities focusing on rote-learning (e.g. tests)
       • teacher-led discussions

---

tasks (Mayer, 2002). However, 'traditional educational practices' that focus on knowledge delivery alone have only a limited potential in responding to the expectations raised for today's youth (Scardamalia & Bereiter, 2006) (Box 6.1).

6.4.   Learning for Practical Knowledge

Practical knowledge can also be referred to as *procedural knowledge* or skills-based knowledge (Bereiter & Scardamalia, 1993, p. 45; Tynjälä, 2008a). It can be seen as a competency or capability to do something, that is having the capacity to put theoretical knowledge into practice (Paakkari & Paakkari, 2012). In the context of health literacy, practical knowledge includes the basic health-related skills pupils need to acquire in order to be able to behave in health-promoting ways. The practical knowledge needed to behave in a health-promoting way may include a variety of practical skills or techniques, for example the ability to take care of one's hygiene (e.g. hand and teeth washing), resist requests to participate in health-harming behaviours, follow safety traffic regulations, search for and navigate health services, gather health information, give first aid, and to clearly communicate one's ideas and thoughts to other people.

When the objective of teaching–learning events is to develop a pupils' practical knowledge this demands conditions that allow the learner the ability to *apply* the health knowledge to various situations. This type of learning must be supported through the provision of up-to-date examples, cases from real life and teacher-led/-dominated discussions (van Rossum & Hamer, 2010, p. 11). Similarly, this type of learning process could be termed learning by doing, and it is essential for pupils to gain mastery over what is practiced at one particular time or another (see World Health Organization, 2003). However, at this point, when the teaching only supports the development of health skills for *hypothetical* situations, that is *for later*

```
┌─────────────────────────────────────────────────────────────────────┐
│ Box 6.2.   Practical Knowledge                                        │
│                                                                       │
│ Goal      • to apply theoretical knowledge in practice                │
│ How       • practical exercises                                       │
│           • role-play                                                 │
│           • hands-on exams                                            │
└─────────────────────────────────────────────────────────────────────┘
```

use only (cf. Marton, Dall'Alba, & Beaty, 1993), the knowledge acquired during these learning situations stays more or less non-complex; it is also something that will only be received and used on some indefinite future occasion (Paakkari et al., 2011). It is nevertheless practical and concrete (Paakkari, Tynjälä, & Kannas, 2010b). When approached in this way learning has strong similarities with the concept of *token participation* (see Simovska, 2000, 2004; see also Jensen & Simovska, 2005). Token participation could be characterized as fairly active involvement in exercising various health skills and in the making of health-related choices. However, the content of the learning is something that has to be accepted and utilized (ready-planned outcomes), and this will be treated in isolation from the broader, real-life context. Thus, in this scenario, the teacher may be seen as an organizer and the pupil (in the best case) as an active participant (Paakkari et al., 2010a) (Box 6.2).

6.5.   Learning for Critical Thinking

Critical thinking has been described as an individual's ability to think clearly and rationally. In schools this means, for example that pupils are able to search for the logical connections between health ideas, to detect inconsistencies, to solve problems, to argue, to draw conclusions and generalizations and maybe to create something new (cf. Biggs, 1996; Biggs & Collis, 1982, pp. 17–28; Ohlsson, 1996). The acquisition of individual critical thinking skills not only allows pupils to understand life and health issues in a deeper way and to make sound health decisions, but also to participate as active members in society (ten Dam & Volman, 2004). In addition, critical thinking serves as a crucial tool for managing large amounts of knowledge. On the other hand, pupils need theoretical and practical knowledge for think critically; if they know about more than one aspect of a phenomenon, they may be able to create links between these or evaluate these if all the significant aspects have been taking into account. Pupils need to also have some practical knowledge, such as skills for information retrieval, in order to be able to locate valid sources of information.

It seems that traditional school culture is not enough to support critical thinking skills, however. Pupils have difficulties with the open-ended questions and unstructured task assignments, and it is rather common that knowledge sharing among pupils is uncritical and the topic in question will not be discussed very deeply (Arvaja, 2005; Rasku-Puttonen, Eteläpelto, Arvaja, & Häkkinen, 2003). That is why the whole teaching–learning process needs some reassessment. Creating an effective atmosphere for critical thinking is undoubtedly a very demanding task for a teacher. He or she should encourage pupils to be curious, distrustful and to have an investigative attitude, and to be open to multiple and differing perspectives (see Baxter Magolda, 2004). Moreover, teacher should increase pupils' 'ability and willingness to attend critically to another's argument' (Kuhn, 2010, p. 816). After all, health as a phenomenon is multidimensional and it can be understood differently in different contexts. Also knowledge should be seen as complex and uncertain. When pupils are encouraged to raise doubts and to test the certainties, it is crucial that there truly be room for various interpretations and the creation of new ideas (Paakkari et al., 2010a). Similarly, the atmosphere during the lessons should be safe and accepting.

Pupils live their lives today in complex environments where they receive health information from numerous sources like family, peers, Internet, newspaper, school and health care. In this case their picture of health issues can remain fragmented. Hence, pupils should individually be able to find and understand the connections between the various health ideas or the broader phenomena. Thus, the lessons should be organized around complex tasks and situations that are derived from the pupils' everyday life.

Health knowledge is also changing over time. It is thus important to have skills that can be readily adapted, especially where new knowledge contradicts older knowledge or there is generally contradictory knowledge on the topic in question. Thus learning situations in the classroom should include opportunities for students to identify and critically evaluate arguments related to the health debate: as well as to evaluate how trustworthy or untrustworthy the source of the knowledge is, what purpose the text or the picture serves, how the authors are possibly trying to influence us, and what is a scientific fact and what is not. The teacher can facilitate the pupils' critical and creative thinking skills by using open-ended questions such as 'could this situation be understood another way?' (Paakkari & Paakkari, 2012). They can also be facilitated by being provided with enough time to ponder questions or problems (see Potts, 1994). Here, the use of a variety of conceptual frameworks to promote conceptual understandings may be helpful. Being subject to prejudice, partiality, and bias, such frameworks are never neutral or objective, though (Milligan & Wood, 2010), and may serve

---

Box 6.3.   Critical Thinking

Goal	• to have control over knowledge
	• to create links, to have new perspectives and to build up coherent pictures
	• to assess topics from various perspectives, to evaluate knowledge and sources of knowledge
How	• mind-mapping, concept-mapping
	• debating, round-table discussions, conflict situations, evaluating arguments, justifying claims
	• systematic analysis of texts and pictures
	• collaborative ranking and listing, collective problem-solving
	• pupil data-gathering and synthesis

---

as very adequate teaching–learning devices in efforts to promote critical thinking (Paakkari & Paakkari, 2012).

In addition, if the teacher's role is perceived as a facilitative one instead of merely as the expert transmitting the knowledge, then the pupils' role may need some rethinking as well. Pupils still tend to think that teachers always have the right answers and their role is to repeat the facts. Pupils should be active and take responsibility for own their learning, and also learn to tolerate feelings of uncertainty and navigate their own paths in open-ended learning tasks (Rasku-Puttonen et al., 2003). Similarly, the interaction between the pupils is very important (Potts, 1994): it allows pupils to get new insights, and to evaluate and transform one's own thinking (Box 6.3).

6.6.   Learning for Self-Awareness

Being aware of whether we are behaving in a health-promoting manner as well as how we are perceiving various health issues are essential components of health literacy. These self-perceptions make possible the personal contextualization of health issues. That is, they are linked and allow the individual to view health topics from their own perspective and in the light of their own goals (see Rubinelli et al., 2009), and to examine reasons for their behaviour and specific ways of thinking. Hence, being aware of health makes it possible to attribute personal meaning to health issues. Self-awareness, as understood in this context, is about the ability to self-reflect. It covers the capability to inquire, assess and become aware of one's thoughts, needs, feelings, behaviour, experiences, attitudes and values (Grant, Franklin, & Langford, 2002; Lund, 2009), and to relate these to one's own ways of behaving, hopefully in a health-enhancing way. In addition, it covers the ability to identify and understand the physical and psychological messages that the body is sending. Reflection may help pupils make their own implicit routines explicit, that is, they may become conscious of something they have not realized before, such as the many culturally bound ways of behaving they have learned through socialization.

Self-awareness focuses not only on the self in general, as was described above, but also on the self as a learner. This mode of self-reflection, referred to as *metacognitive knowledge*, is also called self-regulatory knowledge (Bereiter & Scardamalia, 1993). Self-regulatory knowledge helps pupils to recognize how they have to study, if they want reach the learning objectives. Hence, it is about understanding how to set about attaining goals. This particular form of knowledge is a significant component of lifelong learning skills (Zimmerman, 2002).

We believe that when teachers want to develop pupils' self-awareness, the learning should be truly situated within the pupils' experiences. Pupils should be challenged to think of various 'how' and 'what' questions linked to their lives (descriptive reflection) (see Paakkari et al., 2011). Questions such as 'how do I understand these health issues and how do they relate to my life' and 'what is my current way of behaving with regard to the learning content' increase pupils' understanding about themselves in general. The questions 'how have I proceeded in my learning task', and 'in what way could I learn more effectively' strengthen their understanding about themselves as learners. Questions such as 'why do I behave or think as I do' relate to critical reflection, and critical reflection allows pupils 'to recognize the underlying assumptions and values of their ways of behaving and thinking, and/or to strengthen their own opinion' (Paakkari et al., 2011). Pupils need descriptive reflection when starting to *develop* their own health meanings, and critical reflection in the process of *changing* their ways of thinking. In this process other pupils' differing thoughts may serve an important mirror for one's own perspectives (Paakkari et al., 2011).

This way of approaching the development of pupils' health literacy regards knowledge as something complex or problematic. After all, through relating the objects of learning to pupils' experiences, the knowledge becomes personal, and similarly, does not only include aspects of factual knowledge (see Baxter Magolda, 2004; Paakkari et al., 2011). Teachers serve as mentors or facilitators who support pupils so they can test their own opinions, wishes, preferences and ways of behaving against theoretical knowledge and the perspectives of others. This mode of learning calls for an atmosphere that is trusting and accepting (Paakkari et al., 2010a). Learning metacognitive knowledge takes place in the context of learning other components of health literacy, and this process calls for learning events

---

Box 6.4. Self-Awareness

Goal
- to reflect on health matters from the perspective of one's own life
- to critically examine one's own thoughts and ways of behaving
- to set learning goals and monitor learning processes

How
- learning diaries
- portfolios
- self-evaluations
- letters of opinion

---

where pupils' are encouraged to reflect on their beliefs about learning, set learning goals for themselves, plan strategies for how to reach these goals, and reflect on the actual learning process. At the beginning, teacher's support and feedback will be crucial, but subsequently pupils' should assume a greater role in monitoring their own learning processes (Paakkari & Paakkari, 2012). Also, Lin (2001) has argued that when a teacher asks a pupil to explain him/herself (to fellow-learners) or how they have ended up in a particular situation when solving a given problem — that is, what kinds of decisions were made and why — this may help pupils to identify what they do and do not understand, and hence, to learn more the content domain more deeply. Lin with her colleagues have also used virtual learning environments when helping pupils to develop their understandings of self as a learner; here pupils are allowed to help 'virtual-kids' to develop their metacognitive knowledge by equipping 'kids' with varying personalities, for example knowledge, attitudes, self-beliefs and creating supportive social environments (Lin, Schwartz, & Holems, 1999, as cited in Lin, 2001). At its best the development of knowledge about oneself leads to 'a habit of mind', rather than to a specific activity and occasional task-related activity (Lin, 2001) (Box 6.4).

6.7. Learning for Citizenship

By citizenship we refer to the ability to act in an ethically responsible way and to having the ability to take social responsibility for one's actions. This highlights the importance of pupils being able to understand what kind of rights and responsibilities they have, and also to be aware of the effects of their thoughts and actions on other people and the world at large. In this context Tuana (2007) ponders about moral literacy, which constitutes a set of knowledge and skills for making ethically sound decisions. She argues that pupils should learn to assess if a situation at hand involves ethical issues, to identify the values and moral virtues like honesty underlying that situation, and to ponder and recognize morally correct or best solution. Citizenship as a core component of health literacy includes also an ability to argue in favour of something, such as to persuade the school principal to plan and administer changes in policy for tobacco-free schools (World Health Organization, 2003). The point is that pupils should be able to consider health matters beyond their own perspective: to think of what *other people* or *we* (as a group or as a society) regard as important, what could be done to improve *their* or *our* health and well-being (Paakkari & Paakkari, 2012). Baxter Magolda (1999) refers to more complex forms of meaning making, which allows people 'look at society as a whole, to reflect on the meaning of its organization for all of us, rather than look at it only from our own perspective and its meaning for us personally' (p. 272). Ethical reflection skills enable pupils to evaluate the effects of their ways of behaving and thinking on other people. In addition, these skills make it possible for pupils to ponder the appropriateness of a variety of health-related practices and to show empathy when trying to understand something from the point of view of others. However, at this point it is crucial that pupils' have been able to become aware of themselves (i.e. self-awareness as health literacy component). As Alexander (2005) argues, 'one cannot engage views different from one's own without understanding one's own orientation or respect the other without respecting oneself' (p. 14). Thus, schools should serve as a learning context where there is a possibility to take part in ethical discussions on various health issues and 'to expose to multiple conceptions of good' and 'to attitudes and orientations with which one may not be inclined to agree' (Alexander, 2005, pp. 14–15).

In addition, since citizenship in its personal and cultural aspects covers the idea of belonging to a society, schools need to encourage dialogue (i.e. collective reflection; cf. De Lawter & Sosin, 2000) conjoined with peer collaboration (cf. Osler & Starkey, 2003). Collective reflection enables participants to define their responsibilities and to decide upon the best actions to carry out for their communities or society (see Osler & Starkey, 2003). This calls for conditions in which knowledge and meaning are seen as mutually constructed and in which all participants' view points are accepted as valuable. Moreover, it calls for a tolerant atmosphere, which supports pupils and enables them to share and expose their own personal, even sensitive reflections to collective and critical inquiry (Zdenek & Schochor, 2007). The teacher participates, together with the pupils, in putting people's conceptions together and in considering both the evidence and experience in constructing knowledge (Baxter Magolda, 1999, p. 28).

Changes in pupils' and teacher's roles and the social learning environment have been argued to be linked to improvements in pupils' understanding of the self as a learner including their understanding of their cultural-self, that is, 'who am I within the socio-cultural context I am part of' (Lin, 2001). The crucial element here is *genuine participation* (see Simovska, 2000, 2004) because genuine participation fosters pupils' meaning making for the actions they are taking part in. Simovska (2004) argues that in genuine participation 'the process of the creation of meaning is taking place while they [pupils] actively search for common ground with other participants in culturally organized activity' (p. 203). However, pupils should be allowed to exert influence as citizens in their own right, and thus to place their views on the agenda (see Hill et al., 2004; King & Occleston, 1998; Osler & Starkey, 2003). Moreover, learning opportunities should be available in the context of 'extended classrooms', both within and outside the school. Arthur and Davison (2002) even argue that classroom-based learning is far from the ideal leaning environment for learning citizenship. In this regard, learning should preferably occur within those sites where pupils feel valued and respected, such as in schools, parks, shopping centres, community centres or libraries (Osler & Starkey, 2003). Hence, teaching strategies should include opportunities to carry out various real-life scenarios or projects should be assigned that can help pupils' to ponder and solve real-life problems, keeping in mind that any desired achievements or changes should be realistically attainable (Davies & Evans, 2002). Lakin and Littledyke (2008) have reported a good example of such a project where pupils' were genuinely and actively involved in decision-making (e.g. with school personnel and parents) about improving school meals into a healthier and ethical direction (Box 6.5).

Box 6.5. Citizenship

Goal
- to evaluate the consequence of one's behaviour on others
- to evaluate individually and collectively the appropriateness of various health issues for people in general (ethical reflection, collective reflection)
- to argue in favour of something

How
- drama
- panel discussions
- role-playing
- projects
- peer assessment

6.8. Summary

In this chapter we have aimed at highlighting the fact that when teachers are aiming to develop health literacy among their pupils, they should have an idea of the kind of health literacy and corresponding learning outcomes they are striving for. After all, not all teaching supports the kind of learning that will bring about self-awareness, the ability to think critically or the ability to take ethically responsible actions. Figure 6.1 summarizes the essential aspects and main differences between the various learning conditions. Similarly, it shows how the conditions for learning can be organized into an inclusive hierarchy where the more complex or more sophisticated conditions may include aspects of less complex or less sophisticated conditions, but not other way around. To provide an example, we propose conditions for developing self-awareness could be seen in this context as more complex than those promoting critical thinking, and even though both options include critical inquiry, the former 'adds' self-reflective elements to this scheme.

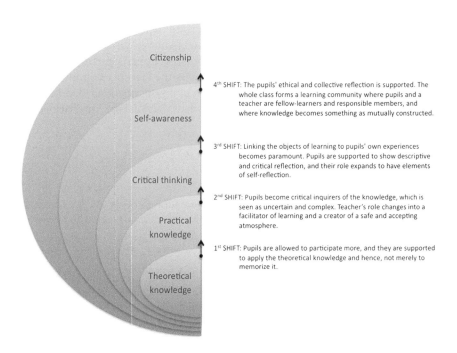

Figure 6.1: Inclusive hierarchy of the conditions for learning health literacy, described in terms of the critical differences.

We could also say that the second shift between the conditions for supporting the development practical knowledge and critical thinking could be seen as a watershed because at that point the teaching–learning events may move from being more or less teacher-focused or content-focused towards being pupil-focused or learning-focused (cf. van Rossum & Hamer, 2010). Similarly, in the first two conditions the learning of health contents is an end in itself, whereas in the last three conditions the focus is on learning about oneself, others and the world *through* learning about the contents (see Paakkari et al., 2011). Even, one could see elements of growth as a person as pupils learn about themselves, others and the world (see Paakkari et al., 2011); every time a pupil undertakes an ethical thinking process, he or she may change as a person (cf. Kwak, 2007; Williams, 1985). Finally, the second shift is designed to allow for the emergence of the constitution of, first, personal meaning, and later, collective meaning, which is lacking in the first two conditions for learning that focus mainly on acquiring, memorizing or applying knowledge (cf. Marton et al., 1993).

These descriptions of the various ways of supporting the development of health literacy are examples that can be used as tools in planning for the future, and in evaluating current teaching–learning situations where the aim is to enhance pupils' health literacy. We did not ponder the conditions from the perspective of one particular age group; hence it is natural that the conditions may acquire additional characteristics when teaching health issues in primary schools, secondary schools or upper general education. Nevertheless, for pupils in different age groups the learning conditions may well include aspects of each of the learning components described here. In the best possible situation all the components should be intertwined to achieve the highest level of health literacy.

References

Abel, T. (2007). Cultural capital in health promotion. In D. V. McQueen & I. Kickbusch (Eds.), *Health and modernity: The role of theory in health promotion* (pp. 43–73). New York, NY: Springer.

Alexander, H. A. (2005). Education in ideology. *Journal of Moral Education, 34*(1), 1–18.

Arthur, J., & Davison, J. (2002). Experiential learning, social literacy and the curriculum. In D. Scott & H. Lawson (Eds.), *Citizenship education and the curriculum* (pp. 27–44). Westport, CT: Ablex Publishing.

Arvaja, M. (2005). *Collaborative knowledge construction in authentic school contexts.* Research reports. Institute for Educational Research 14. Jyväskylä: University of Jyväskylä.

Barrow, W. (2010). Dialogic, participation and the potential for philosophy for children. *Thinking Skills and Creativity, 5*, 61–69.

Baxter Magolda, M. B. (1999). *Creating contexts for learning and self-authorship: Constructive-development pedagogy.* Nashville, TN: Vandervilt University Press.

Baxter Magolda, M. B. (2004). Evolution of a constructivist conceptualization of epistemological reflection. *Educational Psychologist, 39*(1), 31–42.

Bereiter, C., & Scardamalia, M. (1993). *Surpassing ourselves: An inquiry into the nature and implications of expertise.* Chicago, IL: Open Court.

Biggs, J. (1996). Enhancing teaching through constructive alignment. *Higher Education, 32,* 347–364.

Biggs, J. B., & Collis, K. F. (1982). *Evaluating the quality of learning.* New York, NY: Academic Press.

Borzekowski, D. L. G. (2009). Considering children and health literacy: A theoretical approach. *Pediatrics, 124*(Suppl. 3), S282–S288.

Davies, I., & Evans, M. (2002). Encouraging active citizenship. *Educational Review, 54*(1), 69–78.

De Lawter, K., & Sosin, A. (2000, April 24–26). *A self-study in teacher education: Collective reflection as negotiated Meaning.* Paper presented at the Annual Meeting of the American Educational Research Association, New Orleans, LA.

Grant, A. M., Franklin, J., & Langford, P. (2002). The self-reflection and insight scale: A new measure of private self-consciousness. *Social Behavior and Personality, 30*(8), 821–836.

Hill, M., Davis, J., Prout, A., & Tisdall, K. (2004). Moving the participation agenda forward. *Children & Society, 18,* 77–96.

Jensen, B. B., & Simovska, V. (2005). Involving students in learning and health promotion processes: Clarifying *why? what?* and *how? Promotion and Education, XII*(3-4), 150–156.

King, P., & Occleston, P. (1998). Shared learning in action: Children can make a difference. *Health Education, 98*(3), 100–106.

Kuhn, D. (2010). Teaching and learning science as argument. *Science Education, 94*(5), 810–824.

Kwak, D.-J. (2007). Re-conceptualizing critical thinking for moral education in culturally plural societies. *Educational Philosophy and Theory, 39*(4), 460–470.

Lakin, L., & Littledyke, M. (2008). Health promoting school: Integrated practices to develop critical thinking and healthy lifestyles through farming, growing and healthy eating. *International Journal of Consumer Studies, 32*(3), 253–259.

Lin, X. (2001). Designing metacognitive activities. *Educational Technology Research and Development, 49*(2), 23–40.

Lin, X. D., Schwartz, D., & Holems, J. (1999). *Preparing adaptive learners for different learning settings.* Paper presented at the Annual Fellow Meeting of the Spencer Foundation. Pittsburgh, PA.

Lund, I. (2009). An exploration of self-awareness among shy people. *Young, 17*(4), 375–397.

Mancuso, J. M. (2009). Assessment and measurement of health literacy: An integrative review of the literature. *Nursing and Health Sciences, 11,* 77–89.

Marton, F., Dall'Alba, G., & Beaty, E. (1993). Conceptions of learning. *International Journal of Educational Research, 19*(3), 277–300.

Marton, F., Runesson, U., & Tsui, A. B. M. (2004). The space of learning. In F. Marton & A. B. M. Tsui (Eds.), *Classroom discourse and the space of learning* (pp. 3–40). Mahwah, NJ: Lawrence Erlbaum Associates.

Mayer, R. E. (2002). Rote versus meaningful learning. *Theory into Practice*, *41*, 226–232.

Milligan, A., & Wood, B. (2010). Conceptual understandings as transition points: Making sense of complex world. *Journal of Curriculum Studies*, *42*(4), 487–501.

Nutbeam, D. (1998). *Health promotion glossary*. Geneva: World Health Organization.

Nutbeam, D. (2000). Health literacy as a public health goal: A challenge for contemporary health education and communication strategies into the 21st century. *Health Promotion International*, *15*(3), 259–267.

Nutbeam, D. (2008). The evolving concept of health literacy. *Social Science & Medicine*, *67*(12), 2072–2078.

Nutbeam, D., & Kickbusch, I. (2000). Advancing health literacy: A global challenge for the 21st century. *Health Promotion International*, *15*(3), 183–184.

Ohlsson, S. (1996). Learning to do and learning to understand: A lesson and a challenge for cognitive modeling. In P. Reimann & H. Spada (Eds.), *Learning in humans and machines: Towards an interdisciplinary learning science* (pp. 37–62). Oxford: Pergamon.

Osler, A., & Starkey, H. (2003). Learning for cosmopolitan citizenship: Theoretical debates and young people's experiences. *Educational Review*, *55*(3), 243–254.

Paakkari, L., & Paakkari, O. (2012). Health literacy as a learning outcome in schools. *Health Education*, *112*(2), 133–152.

Paakkari, L., Tynjälä, P., & Kannas, L. (2010a). Student teachers' way of experiencing the teaching of health education. *Studies in Higher Education*, *35*(8), 905–920.

Paakkari, L., Tynjälä, P., & Kannas, L. (2010b). Student teachers' ways of experiencing the objective of health education as a school subject: A phenomeno-graphic study. *Teaching and Teacher Education*, *26*, 941–948.

Paakkari, L., Tynjälä, P., & Kannas, L. (2011). Critical aspects in of student teachers' conceptions of learning. *Learning and Instruction*, *21*(6), 705–714.

Parker, R. (2000). Health literacy: A challenge for American patients and their health care providers. *Health Promotion International*, *15*(4), 277–283.

Potts, B. (1994). Strategies for teaching critical thinking. *Practical Assessment, Research & Evaluation*, *4*, 3. Retrieved from http://PAREonline.net/getvn.asp?v=4&n=3

Rasku-Puttonen, H., Eteläpelto, A., Arvaja, M., & Häkkinen, P. (2003). Is successful scaffolding an illusion? Shifting patterns of responsibility and control in teacher-student interaction during a long-term learning project. *Instructional Science*, *31*(6), 377–393.

Rubinelli, S., Schulz, P. J., & Nakamoto, K. (2009). Health literacy beyond knowledge and behaviour: Letting the patient be a patient. *International Journal of Public Health*, *54*, 307–311.

Scardamalia, M., & Bereiter, C. (2006). Knowledge building: Theory, pedagogy, and technology. In K. Sawyer (Ed.), *Cambridge handbook of the learning sciences* (pp. 97–118). New York, NY: Cambridge University Press.

Simovska, V. (2000). Exploring student participation within health education and health promoting schools. In B. B. Jensen, K. Schnack & V. Simovska (Eds.), *Critical environmental and health education* (pp. 29–43). Copenhagen: The Danish University of Education.

Simovska, V. (2004). Student participation: A democratic education perspective: Experience from the health-promoting schools in Macedonia. *Health Education Research, 19*(2), 198–207.

ten Dam, G., & Volman, M. (2004). Critical thinking as a citizenship competence: Teaching strategies. *Learning and Instruction, 14*, 359–379.

Tuana, N. (2007). Conceptualizing moral literacy. *Journal of Educational Administration, 45*(4), 364–378.

Tynjälä, P. (2008a). Connectivity and transformation in work-related learning: Theoretical foundations. In M.-L. Stenström & P. Tynjälä (Eds.), *Towards integration of work and learning: Strategies for connectivity and transformation* (pp. 11–37). Dordrecht: Springer.

Tynjälä, P. (2008b). Perspectives into learning at the workplace. *Educational Research Review, 3*, 130–154.

van Rossum, E. J., & Hamer, R. (2010). *The meaning of learning and knowing.* Rotterdam: Sense Publishers.

von Wagner, C., Steptoe, A., Wolf, M. S., & Wardle, J. (2009). Health literacy and health actions: A review and a framework from health psychology. *Health Education & Behavior, 36*(5), 860–877.

Wagner, T. (2008). Rigor redefined. *Educational Leadership, 66*(2), 20–24.

Williams, B. (1985). *Ethics and the limits of philosophy.* Cambridge: Harvard University Press.

World Health Organization. (2003). *Skills for health-skills-based health education including life-skills: An important component of a child-friendly/health-promoting school.* Information Series on School Health, Document 9. Geneva: WHO.

Zarcadoolas, C., Pleasant, A., & Greer, D. (2005). Understanding health literacy: An expanded model. *Health Promotion International, 20*(2), 195–203.

Zdenek, B., & Schochor, D. (2007). Developing moral literacy in the classroom. *Journal of Educational Administration, 45*(4), 514–531.

Zimmerman, B. J. (2002). Becoming a self-regulated learner: An overview. *Theory into Practice, 41*(2), 64–70.

Afterword: The Health Literacy Report Card

Health Literacy: Ideas for a Dynamic Future

It is over a decade since I wrote a paper in *Health Promotion International* about health literacy and schools (St. Leger, 2001). After examining the chapters in this book, which provide a very comprehensive overview of many of the issues about Health Literacy, and re-reading my own paper, I believe most of the challenges faced by schools at the turn of the century are still present today, and we have some new ones as well. However, there is now a much stronger evidence base to underpin school health promotion and education and more clarity about the priorities for action.

It is important to remind ourselves that schools are places that seek to achieve educational outcomes and to provide an environment for the growth of the social and emotional health of young people. They are not able to solve societal dilemmas in the health field. They can develop in students a number of competencies (mainly cognitive) that can empower them to be healthier individuals and to make contributions throughout their lives to improving the health and well-being of their communities.

My 2001 paper argued that the framework and goals of Health Literacy and the Health Promoting School (HPS) were entirely compatible. In fact, the HPS is actually an evidence-based approach to facilitate better health and educational outcomes for students. It is how high levels of Health Literacy can be achieved.

What we now have in the second decade of the 21st Century is a very strong evidence base about what works and what doesn't in school health, better access to this evidence, and clarity about it in ways that schools and systems can understand.

Two factors have emerged in the last decade or so to underpin school health initiatives. One has emerged from the education sector — the other from the health sector.

Benjamin Bloom chaired a group of eminent researchers and educators which produced a book in 1956 entitled "*Taxonomy of Educational Objectives: The Classification of Educational Goals: Handbook I*" (Bloom, Englehart, Furst, Hill, & Krathwohl, 1956). This publication shaped how teacher training institutions, curriculum designers and writers, and evaluators thought about the learning outcomes of students in all subject and topic areas of the curriculum, including health. Its influence was international and it became known as Bloom's Taxonomy. It had three domains, namely, Cognitive, Affective, and Psychomotor — although it was the cognitive domain that received most attention. The cognitive domain delineates six levels of competency in its hierarchy, each becoming more complex, namely, Knowledge, Comprehension, Application, Analysis, Synthesis, and Evaluation. For many years school health education focused primarily on the lower categories.

One of the original authors of Bloom's 1956 publication, David Krathwohl, combined with Lorin Anderson and six others to produce a new Taxonomy of Learning, Teaching and Assessment, where they revisited Bloom's famous taxonomy (Anderson & Krathwohl, 2000). This document also had six components: Remembering, Understanding, Applying, Analyzing, Evaluating, Creating, with more research-based descriptors for each than the 1956 original. The many action verbs associated with both hierarchies for the six domains are actually the detailed components and signposts for Health Literacy.

Let us leave this first educational factor, that is, Anderson and Krathwohl's new Taxonomy of Learning, and examine the other main influence of the last decade from the health sector. These are the evidence-based Guidelines for School Health Promotion and the summaries of the evidence of effectiveness about school health approaches and outcomes (IUHPE, 2007, 2010).

The Ottawa Charter for Health Promotion (1986) changed the way we thought about school health. Internationally we began to embrace the concepts of empowerment for young people and started to think about how schools, their students, teachers, parents, and the local community can take action to promote health and well-being, not only in the school but also in the local community. The framework of the HPS is derived directly from the Ottawa Charter. The six elements of the HPS as identified in the IUHPE publications are based on the five elements of the Ottawa Charter, with the "create supportive environments" split into two, that is, physical environment and social environment. The six elements are: Healthy school policies; The school's physical environment; The school's social environment; Individual health skills and action competencies; Community links; and Health services.

These elements provide a framework to operationalize school health initiatives. One sees these six elements in action in quality school health initiatives across the globe, even though their generic headings may be Comprehensive School Health, Coordinated School Health, Integrated School Health, in addition to HPSs.

The old way we thought about school health was changing. The number of research and evaluation studies which sought to understand what worked, what didn't, and why grew considerably through published papers, books, and reports. Following requests from teachers, and health and education officials, the IUHPE with financial resources from the Center for Disease Control and Prevention (CDC) in the United States used the considerable body of evidence to inform and produce two documents for practitioners and policy makers. These documents took five years to develop and involved considerable interrogation of the literature and wide international consultation with the field to ensure they were meaningful and usable. They drew on the large body of evidence about school health and the 35 years of solid evidence from the education research literature about effective schools, and learning and teaching approaches. These documents (now in nine languages) provided key groups with succinct guidelines and facts that are now changing practice in school health (IUHPE, 2007, 2010).

These two factors — one a rigorous and widely accepted and used hierarchy of Learning Outcomes, and two, accessible and comprehensive evidence about effective school health promotion and education — now provide us with a strong platform to advocate for school health as an essential component of all schooling.

They are two of the most significant developments of the last 12 years, which strengthen the case for action on health literacy in schools.

I claimed in the 2001 paper that health literacy is identical to the HPS approach. After examining the chapters in this book I feel even more confident about this claim. The various authors have explored the different elements of HPS and are writing about similar outcomes, for example, ensuring students attain a set of action competencies based on sound knowledge which equip them to take action about their own health and that of the community. The more community-oriented school health promotion of today goes a long way to address Level 3 (Critical Health Literacy) of Don Nutbeam's benchmark 2000 paper (Nutbeam, 2000).

Nutbeam deliberately used the word "literacy" to ensure we connected both health and education concepts and principles and to support the attainment of action competencies in students through our school health initiatives. (Action competencies are defined as "students gaining age related knowledge, understandings, skills and experiences, which enable them to build competencies in taking action to improve the health and wellbeing of themselves and others in their community and that enhances their learning outcomes" — IUHPE, 2007.) After all, a literate student in the original sense has their own set of action competencies; that is, they can read and write.

In my 2001 paper I used the popular health topic of nutrition to put some specifics on the concepts and framework of Health Literacy. To conclude this paper, I have provided a brief map which uses the learning hierarchy of

Anderson and Krathwohl (the educational dimension) and the school health evidence based summaries and HPS guidelines from the IUHPE publications and those of WHO (the health dimension) to show how one can address health literacy in this area. I have not called it "nutrition" as before, but moved to the current nomenclature "Healthy Eating" which reflects the contemporary action approach to school health.

Anderson and Krathwohl's learning hierarchy	HPS elements
Remembering – that one needs a variety of food each day from certain food groups	*School health policies* – a policy which prohibits the availability of high sugar drinks on school premises
Understanding – how food contributes to a healthy diet	*The school's physical environment* – facilities to wash hands and a place to sit and enjoy meals with others
Applying – using knowledge of food and its purpose to develop a daily meal profile for a family	*The school's social environment* – using food and eating to connect students and explore different cultures
Analyzing – collecting data about the food eaten by class members over a week; representing this in some form such as charts, diagrams, graphs	*Individual health skills and action competencies* – teaching students to grow and harvest food, purchase food for balanced meals, and prepare meals
Evaluating – making judgments on (say) healthy eating guidelines about food consumed over a period of time by a family	*Community links* – working with food suppliers to link students to retailing and food sources in the community
Creating – designing a healthy meal schedule for eating at the school for a certain student age group, taking into account the evidence of healthy eating guidelines and the realistic facilities available in the school	*Health services* – collaborating with health officials and practitioners about food standards and using health practitioners to inform curriculum development

Health Literacy and its conceptual and practical developments will continue to grow in the next 15 years. There is a very solid body of evidence and a current discourse to facilitate this growth. Health literacy and all the many school health models, frameworks, and initiatives (e.g., HPS) across the world are all directed at one outcome — enhancing young peoples' health and well-being by enabling them to achieve high levels of competence to take action about their own and others health.

Lawrence St. Leger

References

Anderson, L., & Krathwohl, D. (Eds.). (2000). *A taxonomy of learning, teaching, and assessing: A revision of Bloom's taxonomy of educational objectives.* New York, NY: Allyn & Bacon.

Bloom, B., Englehart, M., Furst, E., Hill, W., & Krathwohl, D. (1956). *Taxonomy of educational objectives: The classification of educational goals; Handbook I: Cognitive Domain.* New York, NY: Longmans, Green.

International Union for Health Promotion and Education. (2007). *Achieving Health Promoting Schools: Guidelines for promoting health in schools.* Paris: IUHPE.

International Union for Health Promotion and Education. (2010). *Promoting health in schools: From evidence to action.* Paris: IUHPE.

Nutbeam, D. (2000). Health literacy as a public health goal: A challenge for contemporary health education and promotion strategies into the 21st century. *Health Promotion International, 15,* 259–268.

St. Leger, L. (2001). Schools, health literacy and public health: Possibilities and challenges. *Health Promotion International, 16,* 197–205.

World Health Organisation. (1986). *Ottawa charter for health promotion.* Geneva: WHO.

Resources for Promoting Health Literacy in Schools

Health Literacy

What is Health Literacy-What we Know.
Excellent user-friendly overview provided by the Centers for Disease Control, United States: **http://www.cdc.gov/healthcommunication/Audience/Health Literacy.pdf**

Teachers Resources

Beyond Blue
National initiative of the Australian, state and territory governments with a key goal of raising community awareness about depression and anxiety, and reducing stigma associated with the illness. Works in partnership with health services, schools, workplaces, universities, media and community organizations, as well as people living with depression, to bring together their expertise around depression: http://www.beyondblue.org.au/index.aspx?

Building Wellness™
A youth health literacy curriculum targeting low-income youth from 3rd grade to 8th grade in order to prepare the youth to be active, educated participants in their healthcare. Lessons focus on asthma, obesity and overweight, accidental injury, and drug and alcohol use. Curriculum development was based on qualitative and quantitative assessment of the target population. The preliminary findings from the pilot project show an increase in knowledge, improved healthy behaviors, and enthusiasm from participants and facilitators. The development of the pilot project is described, with a suggestion for future development of youth health literacy assessment tools.

Diamond, C., Saintonge, S., August, P., & Azrack, A. (2011). The development of Building Wellness™, a youth health literacy program. *Journal of Health Communication*, *16*(Suppl. 3), 103–118.

GUIDELINES FOR SCHOOL HEALTH PROMOTION NUTRITION PROGRAMS (1996). June 14, Volume 45, pages 1–33. MMWR Journal. For paper copy contact: Superintendent of Documents, U.S. Government Printing Office (GPO), Washington, DC 20402-9371; telephone: (202) 512-1800. Contact GPO for current prices.

Excellent overview of educational and policy strategies for schools in context of nutrition

Health Literacy Website
Centers for Disease Control: http://www.cdc.gov/healthliteracy/

Comprehensive website on topic housing information on concept, as well as practical advice on how to meet health literacy goals and challenges

Health Teacher
http://www.healthteacher.com/

K-12 teachers will find the lessons useful, **regardless of whether they have professional preparation as a health educator**. Health educators involved in homeschooling, community based health and mental health centers will also find it helpful. It can **stand alone** as a school's only health curriculum, or it can **support an existing curriculum**. Health teacher addresses the **top six health risk behaviors** identified by the U.S. Centers for Disease Control and Prevention.HealthTeacher.com delineates knowledge and skill expectations that are **consistent with the Assessment Framework and National Health Education Standards** for each grade level.

Health Literacy for Tutors
Slide show of facts about health literacy for youth: http://cahealthliteracy. org/powerpointhtmls/hlpowerpoints2/patientself-advocacyfortutors_files/ frame.htm

California Literacy, Inc., USA

Health and Nutrition Plans: K-5
Friendly lessons: http://lesson-plans.theteacherscorner.net/health/

Help Prevent Underage Drinking
Resources from the United States Substance Abuse and Mental Health Services Administration to educate fifth and sixth graders about underage drinking. Free materials: http://store.samhsa.gov/product/Help-Prevent-Underage-Drinking-Kit-Teaching-Guide-and-Poster-Bonus-Worksheets-and-Family-Guide/SMA09-4406

Know Your Body, PreK-12
The **Know Your Body (KYB)** curriculum addresses all of the health education content areas recommended by the Centers for Disease Control. Through its cross-curricula matrix, **KYB** can easily be integrated into the classrooms in disciplines such as science, math, social studies, language arts, and physical education. The **Know Your Body (KYB)** health program has been rigorously evaluated and shown to be successful in changing children's health-related knowledge, attitude, behavior, and biomedical risk factors by using a combination of developmentally appropriate health instruction as well as cognitive and behavioral skill building. Five life skills that form the core of the curriculum are practiced and reinforced throughout each content area. Controlled scientific studies have shown that **KYB** has a significant positive impact on smoking knowledge, attitudes and behavior: *http://www.kendallhunt.com/kyb/*

Lesson Plans for Teachers: K-5
Excellent resources for K-5 health lesson plans: Texas State Department of Health.
http://www.dshs.state.tx.us/kids/lessonplans/default.shtm

Life Skills Training, Grades 6-9
Botvin *LifeSkills Training* (LST) is a research-validated substance abuse prevention program proven to reduce the risks of alcohol, tobacco, drug abuse, and violence by targeting the major social and psychological factors that promote the initiation of substance use and other risky behaviors. This comprehensive and exciting program provides adolescents and young teens with the confidence and skills necessary to successfully handle challenging situations.

Developed by Dr. Gilbert J. Botvin, a leading prevention expert, Botvin *LifeSkills Training* is backed by over 30 scientific studies and is recognized as a Model or Exemplary program by an array of government agencies including the U.S. Department of Education and the Center for Substance Abuse Prevention: *http://www.lifeskillstraining.com/*

Lions Quest Skills for Adolescence
Houses K-12 bullying prevention lessons, K-8 Drug Information Guide, updated rationale and media resources: http://www.lions-quest.org/

Media Literacy Project
Free Download providing handout, appropriate for ages 11 to adult, and discusses different concepts and skills to help build your media literacy knowledge. Provides free educational materials for use in schools, community settings, or professional development trainings: http://medialiteracy project.org/resources/introduction-media-literacy

Michigan Model, K-8

The *Michigan Model for Health*® is a comprehensive and sequential K-12 health education curriculum that aims to give school-aged children (ages 5–19 years) the knowledge and skills needed to practice and maintain healthy behaviors and lifestyles. It provides age-appropriate lessons addressing the most serious health challenges facing school-aged children, including social and emotional health; nutrition and physical activity; alcohol, tobacco and other drugs; personal health and wellness; safety; and HIV. The *Michigan Model for Health* facilitates learning through a variety of interactive teaching and learning techniques. Skill development through demonstration and guided practice is emphasized resulting in the development of positive lifestyle behaviors for students and families.

The *Michigan Model for Health* is based on the Adapted Health Belief Model, a merging of several behavior change theories including the Social Cognitive Theory, Social Influence Theory, and Social Behavioral Theory. A key principle of the Adapted Health Belief Model is that a health education program is more likely to impact behavior change if it includes <u>all</u> of the following components: knowledge, skills, self-efficacy, and environmental support. The *Michigan Model for Health* is designed for implementation as a component of the core school curriculum, with each of the lessons lasting 20–45 minutes in length. The lessons may be integrated in various disciplines such as language arts, science, social studies, etc. Furthermore, some lessons include activities to facilitate parental and family involvement beyond the classroom. The curriculum can be implemented in public, private, or alternative schools: http://www.emc.cmich.edu/mm/default.htm

Teaching Kids About Health

Resources from Proctor and Gamble on teaching kids about various health topics. Individual teaching resources include classroom ready materials for downloading. Some information can be ordered directly by school: http://www.pgsschoolprograms.com

Team Nutrition

United States Department of Agriculture Nutrition Website – see Educators and Resources links: http://www.fns.usda.gov/tn/

Teenage Health Teaching Modules

Teenage Health Teaching Modules (THTM) is a successful, nationally used, and independently evaluated comprehensive school health curriculum for grades 6 to 12. It provides adolescents with the knowledge and skills to act in ways that enhance their immediate and long-term health. The evaluation of THTM concluded that the curriculum produced positive effects on students' health knowledge, attitudes, and self-reported behaviors: http://www.thtm.org/

Teen Health Curriculum: Uniquely For Girls
Free interactive program for classroom: *http://www.uniquelygirl.com/HealthEd*

The Contemporary Health Series
http://www.nsba.org/SHHC/SearchSchoolHealth/CustomSearch/The ContemporaryHealthSeries.txt

What the HEALTH!
What the HEALTH! Summarised by Harvard School of Public Health, May 13, 2010, in an article entitled 'A Literacy and Health Resource for Youth' Available at: *http://www.hsph.harvard.edu/healthliteracy/practice/what-the-health/index.html*. Retrieved August 30, 2012.

What the HEALTH! is designed by the Canadian Public Health Association's National Literacy and Health Program for people who teach or guide youth in a variety of settings: literacy programs, schools, community centers and health care centers. Development of the *What the HEALTH!* curriculum was guided by young people at all stages and provides useful and easy-to-use tools to engage teens in learning about their own health, understanding healthy behaviors and improving health decision-making skills. Youth are able to reflect on their own experiences, as well as linking their experiences to a wider social context and identifying follow-up actions for themselves and their communities. While the intended use of the curricula is to enhance health awareness and literacy skills of youth who have trouble reading, *What the HEALTH!* applies to all young people and gives them a participatory opportunity to learn more about health.

What the HEALTH! is 210 pages, and is divided into 10 lessons, each of which focuses on a health topic defined as important by youth. Examples of health topics are: Feelings, Safer Sex, Drug Abuse, Living Environments and Healthy Eating. Lessons are broken down into 6 elements, each of which is an action: Highlight, Explain, Analyze, Learn, Try and Help. The cover page of each lesson gives a brief introduction to the topic, with the next page offering learning objectives, relevant web sites and other resources. The entire curriculum is in loose-leaf format, so that pages can be easily photocopied and users can order lessons as they feel appropriate: http://www.thtm.org/.

To view a sample lesson [in PDF Format] on smoking from *What the HEALTH!*, click *http://www.hsph.harvard.edu/healthliteracy/files/smoking.pdf*. © Canadian Public Health Association, 2000.

What the HEALTH! is available in English and French and can be purchased from the Canadian Public Health Association (CPHA) Health Resources Centre for about $10. For more information, or to order *What the HEALTH!*, contact CPHA: Tel: (613) 725-3769, Fax: (613)

725-9826 or email: hrc@cpha.ca More information is also available at http://www.cpha.ca

Youth
Real-Life Stories about Adolescent Health

BeSmartBeWell.com   **http://www.besmartbewell.com/spotlight-newsletter/ youth-in-control/index.htm**

Kids Health
KidsHealth is more than just the facts about health. As part of The Nemours Foundation's Center for Children's Health Media, KidsHealth also provides families with perspective, advice, and comfort about a wide range of physical, emotional, and behavioral issues that affect children and teens: *http://kidshealth.org/*

Youth Health Literacy Initiative
Organization aggressively addressing health literacy as a disparity in low-income communities in and around the DC Metropolitan Area. Has trained thousands to find and evaluate health information amassed in electronic medical libraries: *http://www.piadvocates.org/Pages/YouthHealthLiteracy.aspx*

TEEN HEALTH FACTS
Online resource for teens: http://www.teenhealthfx.com/
http://www.teenshealth.org

Health Improvement Service NHS Durham and Darlington. Retrieved June 10, 2012.
Comprehensive site providing information on drugs, health eating, physical activity and other topics.

a. Children and Young People
   The Children, Young People and Families team contribute to reducing health inequalities and achieving improved outcomes in children and young people's health and well-being, with a focus upon the priority areas of: healthy weight, emotional health and well-being, smoking, alcohol, substance misuse and teenage conceptions.

b. Library and Knowledge Service
   Access to evidence-based high quality resources to support health improvement, health management, learning and professional development is provided by the Health Improvement Library, which is at Enterprise House in Darlington.
   http://www.health-improvement.cdd.nhs.uk/index.cfm?articleid=14743

c. What is in Cigarette Smoke
   http://www.health-improvement.cdd.nhs.uk/index.cfm?articleid=5406

Health Literacy and Youth Employment Experiences
How youth can explore health literacy through their employment experiences:
http://skillspages.com/blog/?p=552

Books at Amazon.com

Children and Teens Afraid to Eat. Berg, Frances M. (2001). Healthy Weight NetworkHettinger, ND.

TEACHERS can benefit from understanding how to spot weight problems in athletes and best address body image and self-esteem.

Nutrition, Physical Activity, and Health in Early Life. Parizkova, Jana. 2010. Taylor and Francis, Boca Rotan, FL.

Our Overweight Children: What Parents, Schools, and Communities Can Do to Control the Fatness Epidemic. What parents, schools, and communities can do to control the fatness epidemic. Dalton, S. (2004). Regents of the University of California. University of California Press Ltd: London, England.

Overcoming Childhood Obesity Thompson, Colleen & Shanley, Ellen. (2004). Bull Publishing Company, Boulder, Co.

Other Resources

NUMERACY IN PRACTICE: TEACHING, LEARNING, AND USING MATHS. (2009). Department of Education and Early Childhood Development, Victoria, Australia. *Numeracy in Practice: Teaching, Learning and Using Mathematics* is a research and policy-based resource for teachers of numeracy in Years P–10.
http://www.eduweb.vic.gov.au/edulibrary/public/publ/research/nws/Numeracy_in_practice_Paper_No_18.pdf

PREVENTING CLASSROOM BULLYING
Wright, Jim. (2004). *What Teachers Can Do* provides guidelines to help school staff to better understand and manage the problem of bullying in school settings.
http://www.interventioncentral.org

Other

Title: Health literacy: A prescription to end confusion

Author/Editor: L. Nielsen-Bohlman et al.

Publisher: Institute of Medicine.

ISBN-10: 0-309-09117-9

Title: Health literacy studies: Teaching patients with low literacy skills

Author/Editor: C. Doak et al.

Publisher: Harvard University

Price: Free

ISBN 0-397-55161-4

Title: Advancing Health Literacy: A Framework for Understanding and Action

Author/Editor: C. Zarcodoolas et al.

Publisher: Jossey-Bass

Organizations

Center for Health Promotion
http://www.healthliteracypromotion.com/default.html

- Research organization that develops, tests, publishes and continuously improves health education content, materials and curricula for programs and clients.
- Provides technical assistance for health literacy promotion.
- Houses health literacy definitions among other tools.

Centre for Health Promotion, CYWHS
Fosters health promotion in education-very comprehensive site.

Better health
Schools as settings
Case studies
Links and resources

*Virtually Healthy-Newsletter
No. 41, Term 3, 2006=Health Literacy: Empowering children to make healthy choices
http://healthpromotion.cywhs.sa.gov.au/Content.aspx?p=154

Health Literacy Education 4 Kids
This is an organization founded in 2007 by Sonja Mitchell. HLE4Kids focuses on educating disadvantaged children and underserved low-income families in the inner cities of Northeast Florida and beyond, on the importance of developing a healthy spirit, mind, and body. This is achieved through HLE 4Kids quality programs and services in the areas of health and wellness, drug prevention, literacy enhancement (tutoring), and mentoring HLE4Kids mission is to enhance the quality of life and skills for the future of our children affected by today's environment by encouraging student-parent, and community collaboration, towards a healthy, safe, drug-free lifestyle to achieve the goal of academic and life success: *http://hle4kids.org/ www.amazon.com*

Pediatrician and Provider Related Resources
Excellent Comprehensive Resource located at:
*https://www2.aap.org/commpeds/htpcp/Training/Health_Literacy_Handout-1.pdf*Notes

Notes

Appendix A

Examples of a Preschool Health Curriculum Lesson Topics and Lesson Plan, plus Parent Resources.

Appendix A1 – Topics that can be Taught in Pre-K

Growth and Development	Mental and Emotional Health	Personal Health	Family Life and Health	Nutrition
Body height and weight	Being kind	Brushing teeth	My family is important	*Soda is not food*

Disease Prevention and Control	Safety and First Aid	Substance Use and Abuse	Community and Environmental Health Management	Communication
I wash my hands properly	• I don't get into fights	*Say no to drugs*	• I look after my environment	• I explain things to my family

Appendix A2

Appendix A2-Sugary Foods and Drinks (Basic Health Literacy)
Nutrition

Objectives

Children will:
1. Discover that nutritious foods and drinks help keep our body healthy.
2. Recognize the difference between nutritious foods and sugary snacks and drinks.
3. Conclude that it is better to eat fruits and vegetables and drink low fat milk or water than soda pop.

Materials

Bananas (3-4)
Water
Plastic knife
Small disposable cups (1 per child)
Paper plates (1 per child)
Poster depicting FoodPlate

Paper towels
Choose 1-2 items:

FoodPlates

Assessment

Teacher observes children choosing correct foods and drinks

Things to Do Before

1. Display the poster of the MyPlate.
2. Optional: Slice bananas and fill small cups with water before lesson.

Language Development

balanced diet:
soda:
nutrient:
Nutrition:
sugar:
vitamin:

Group Activity

1. Ask children, "What are some of your favorite fruits and vegetables?"

2. Ask children, "Who thinks candy and sweets taste really good?" Ask children, "Does anyone know some of the ingredients that make these foods taste so good?"
    *   sugar, butter, fats

3. Explain that it is not nutritious to eat candy, fats, and sweets all of the time. Even though these foods taste good, we must limit how many fats and sweets we eat.

4. Ask children, "Do you know what kind of foods have fat in them?"
    *   butter, cheese, oil, bacon, ice cream, pizza, fried foods

5. Ask, "Can you name some foods that have sugar in them?"
    *   cake, donuts, cookies, candy
    *   soda, juices, other soft drinks

6. Point to the MyPlate and review the five food groups.

7. Tell children why people need to eat a balanced diet.

8. Help children to understand why sugary drinks are not healthy.

Learning Activity

1. Show children the importance of healthy snacks, have children cut up other healthy foods such as apples, oranges, and cheese to enjoy with their water.

Have children recall why it is important to eat and drink healthy.

Optional: Make a different sweet snack that's good for you:
*   2 boxes O-shaped cereal
*   1/4 lb sesame seeds
*   1 box dried apple chips
*   2 cans raisins

Have children make their own trail mix by spooning each of the ingredients into a small plastic bag. They can enjoy this and other healthy foods at snack time.

2. Do a FoodPlate activity or demonstration.

3. Show how many spoons of sugar are in a can of soda.

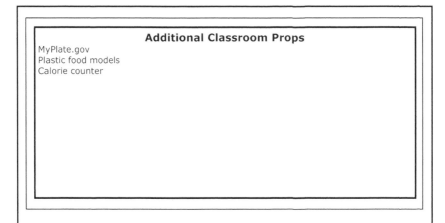

Additional Classroom Props

MyPlate.gov
Plastic food models
Calorie counter

Music, Movement, and Poems

Poems
"Pat-A-Cake, Pat-A-Cake" (Traditional)

Books

The Berenstain Bears and Too Much Junk Food by Stan Berenstain,Jan Berenstain
   (Random House, Inc., 1985)
Curious George Goes to a Chocolate Factory by Margret Rey (Houghton Mifflin, 1998)
Candy Corn by Kelly Asbury (Penguin Putnam Books for Young Readers, 2001)
The Candyland Mystery by Cynthia Alvarez (Random House Inc., 1994)
Fats and Sweets by Helen Frost (Capstone Press, 2000)
If I Owned a Candy Factory by James Walker Stevenson (HarperCollins Children's
   Books, 1989)

Letter Home

Dear Family:

Today in our health program your child learned about sodas and sweets. We learned that foods such as butter, cheese, oil, bacon, ice cream, fried foods, and pizza have fat in them, and foods such as cake, donuts, cookies, candy, and soda have sugar in them. We discussed the suggested daily portions on the MyFood Plate and learned that sweets are not good foods.

Encourage your child to eat a balanced diet, one that includes all the different kinds of food that the body needs to stay healthy and grow, and encourage them to drink water. And low fat milk.

Thank you for your participation!

Sincerely,

Your Child's Teacher

Appendix A3

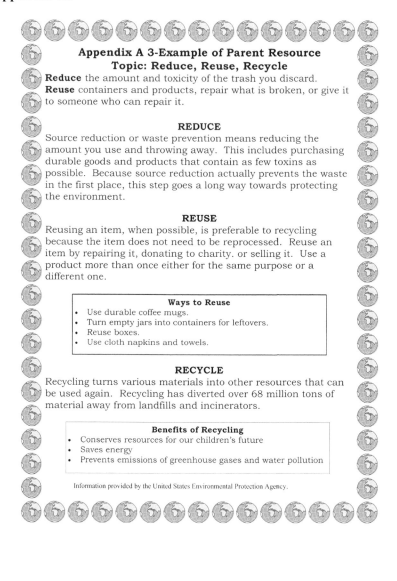

Appendix A 3-Example of Parent Resource
Topic: Reduce, Reuse, Recycle

Reduce the amount and toxicity of the trash you discard.
Reuse containers and products, repair what is broken, or give it to someone who can repair it.

REDUCE

Source reduction or waste prevention means reducing the amount you use and throwing away. This includes purchasing durable goods and products that contain as few toxins as possible. Because source reduction actually prevents the waste in the first place, this step goes a long way towards protecting the environment.

REUSE

Reusing an item, when possible, is preferable to recycling because the item does not need to be reprocessed. Reuse an item by repairing it, donating to charity. or selling it. Use a product more than once either for the same purpose or a different one.

Ways to Reuse
• Use durable coffee mugs.
• Turn empty jars into containers for leftovers.
• Reuse boxes.
• Use cloth napkins and towels.

RECYCLE

Recycling turns various materials into other resources that can be used again. Recycling has diverted over 68 million tons of material away from landfills and incinerators.

Benefits of Recycling
• Conserves resources for our children's future
• Saves energy
• Prevents emissions of greenhouse gases and water pollution

Information provided by the United States Environmental Protection Agency.

Appendix A4

Appendix A 4-Parent Related Resource Example
How to Wash Your Hands Correctly

Here are 4 simple steps for eliminating germs. Demonstrate this routine for your child or wash your hands together with your child so he/she learns how important this good habit is.

1. Wash your hands in warm water, which kills germs better than cold water. Make sure the water isn't too hot.

2. Use soap and lather for about 15 to 20 seconds (about the time it takes to sing "Happy Birthday"). Anti-bacterial soap is not necessary, any soap will do. Make sure you scrub in places like between the fingers and under the nails. Don't forget the wrists!

3. Rinse and dry well with a clean towel.

4. You and your child should wash hands often, especially:
   - before, during, and after eating and cooking.
   - after using the bathroom.
   - after cleaning around the house.
   - after touching animals, including the house pets.
   - when somone in your house is sick.
   - after blowing one's nose, coughing, or sneezing.
   - after being outside (playing, gardening, walking the dog, etc.).

Don't underestimate the power of hand washing! The few seconds you spend at the sink with your child could very well save you trips to the doctor's office.

This list compiled with information from the
Centers for Disease Prevention and Control and the Neumors Foundation.

Appendix A5

Appendix A 5-Sample of How to Construct a School Newsletter for Youth, Parents and Communities Newsletter

Volume		Date

Inside this issue:

Look for the icon below for tips on effective communication and community involvement!

Two-way Communication Between School and Home:

Effective two-way communication between families and schools is critical to student academic achievement. Without excellent communication between teachers and families, children lose out on the benefits of having the parent-teacher team involved in their learning experiences. Although parents and teachers may share the common goal of academic success for students, there may be circumstances that make communication challenging, such as personal values and attitudes. As health educators and people who work with children, we try our best to work around and within these circumstances so that children get the most out of their school experience.

Two-way communication implies that the two parties involved have an interpersonal, open flow of ideas and information. As one party talks or writes, the other listens or reads and will later have the opportunity to respond. When communication exists without the opportunity for the other to respond, it is one-way communication. A popular example of one-way communication is the parent newsletter. Although parents are being informed of activities happening within the school, they are not given the chance to provide their input and opinion. Many two-way communication techniques exist for educators to employ to ensure parent involvement in their child's learning experience. These include parent-teacher conferences where concerns and action plans are discussed among all parties; letters requesting a response; folders of school work sent home requesting parent comment; parent newsletters including mini-surveys about various school-related topics such as homework or discipline; informal meetings; and if possible, home visits.

Whatever method(s) you choose for communication with your

TIP #1: Personalized positive telephone calls are a low-cost, direct form of two-way communication between teachers and parents that also encourage students to keep up the good work!

Why Should My Family Get Involved

There are tons of reasons why your family should get involved in community service and volunteerism. For starters, it feels good. Isn't it satisfying to know that you're devoting your time and energy towards something you believe in or are passionate about? Also, volunteers provide important services at little or no cost to those who need it. When a community is healthy, so are its members. Third, volunteerism saves money. All the work done by volunteers is less money taxpayers have to pay the government to do something. Also, being a volunteer teaches us useful skills. Lastly, volunteering as a family brings its members closer together. If these aren't enough reasons for you and your family to start volunteering soon, here are a few more... When kids volunteer, they learn what it means to make and keep a commitment, be on time, do their best and be proud of their work. Volunteering is a wonderful, empowering message that informs kids that they can make a difference as individuals. Kids learn the importance of sacrifice and the virtue of tolerance. Volunteering provides young people with job skills that will be helpful in the future. Also, volunteering occupies your child's spare time wisely. That's a pretty lengthy list of reasons why we should all give some of our time and energy into community service!

This article was taken from:
www.kidshealth.org/PageManager.jsp?dn=KidsHealth &lic=1&ps=107&cat_id=168&article_set=21709

 TIP #2: Need volunteer suggestions? Foodbanks or soup kitchens are always great places to do service and they always need extra hands. Help plant flowers or trees, help with housing repairs & renovations for low-income residents, garbage pick-up at the park, playground or beach... the list is endless.

Using School Bulletin Boards to Stimulate

The Health Department in Milford, CT. has started using school bulletin boards to display information on various health topics to its students. The desire for a more innovative way of relaying health messages to students triggered school nurses to come up with the idea of using bulletin boards which are already prominently located throughout the district's schools. The creation of the age-appropriate displays is a collaborative effort between the school nurses, students, and health educators. School officials recognize the importance and efficacy of having peer-developed material on the bulletins for other students to read. Health topics will include the flu, asthma, and obesity. More sensitive topics such as sexuality and abstinence will be displayed at the high school and middle school levels. Perhaps this practical yet innovative approach to relaying information can initiate a more creative, health-conscious approach to health education in all schools.
Source: "Schools to Post Health Info" by Manuela Da Costa-Fernandes, New Haven Register, Jan. 6.

 TIP #3: Employ REFLECTIVE LISTENING, also called ACTIVE LISTENING, techniques. Repeat what you think your child is feeling and saying using different words, to be sure you're getting the message accurately.

ACTIVITIES

MAKE A HEALTHY SNACK! Try making these easy, healthy snacks at home with your kids.

Fruit Smoothies: Blend one cup of milk (or soy milk), ice cubes, your favorite fresh fruit or any combination of fruits, a dash of vanilla, cinnamon and nutmeg in a blender. Enjoy!

Homemade Ices: Pour 100% fruit juice into small plastic cups and freeze. You could add fresh fruit, like a whole strawberry, to the cup. Insert a popsicle stick into the juice before it freezes completely.

Hummus: This easy-to-make, tasty dip goes with anything: baked chips, fresh veggies, pretzels, or breads. You'll need 1 can (19 oz.) of chickpeas, rinsed and drained; 1/4 cup fresh lemon juice; 1/4 cup sesame tahini; 1/4 cup of water; 1 Tbs. olive oil; 1 garlic clove, finely minced; 1 tsp. of salt. Combine all the ingredients in a food processor fitted with metal chopping blades and pulse to puree. Recipe yields 2 cups.

As a family, try participating in a fundraiser, such as a walk, to raise money for AIDS research, breast cancer or leukemia. There are plenty of fundraisers to choose from. Choose the one that your family is most interested in and would have the most fun doing together. It will not only help to raise money for important health conditions, but it's a healthy and fun way to get exercise!

How many words can you make out of the big word COMMUNICATION?
_____
CAT
_____
_____
_____
_____
_____
_____
_____

LET'S COMMUNICATE!

Try to find the words below hidden in the word puzzle. Some answers may be backwards.

ASK
DISCUSS
EXPLAIN
FEELINGS
HEAR
LISTEN
RESPECT
SHARE
SPEAK
TALK
TRUST
TELL
UNDERSTAND

```
Q H U K S S R R S G
S G N I L E E F S K
C K D I J A L F U T
C B E L A L T B C S
U V R A E L Y E S H
L I S T E N P S I A
R L T C A S P X D R
A A A H E E I Y E E
E K N R A T S U R T
```

ONLINE RESOURCES FOR PARENTS

Below is a list of helpful online resources for parents and teachers to access for more information on different health topics and tips on how to communicate with your children about issues that may be difficult to talk about.

Community Service Opportunities

Resources for Parents and Educators
When Talking With Children About Terrorism and War

Publications and Resources

The National Association of State Boards of Education (NASBE) has updated and expanded

Upcoming Events

Youth Parents and Communities Newsletter   page 7

TIP #4: All kids want to have fun. Why not let them have fun and benefit from it simultaneously? Organized sports offer kids exercise, enhanced self -esteem and increased confidence. They also learn self-discipline, teamwork, leadership and cooperation skills. It's important to match your child with the proper sport, so ask them what THEY want to play...

www.umc-cares.org/health_info/child_sport.asp

UNIQUE OPPORTUNITIES!!!

Funding Opportunities

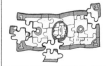

LOCAL EVENTS

TIPS

TIP #4: Take advantage of time during car rides or standing in line at the grocery store to have a conversation with your child. Ask questions that go beyond "yes" or "no" answers to prompt more developed conversation.

www.kidshealth.org/PageManager.jsp?dn= KidsHealth

&lic=1&ps=107&cat_id=171&article_set=21377

Address

Appendix B

Guidelines and Samples of a Mental Health Curriculum Approach to Heighten Mental Health Literacy

Appendix B1 — Integration Strategies for Mental Health Related Topics

Without taking away from classroom academics, here are some suggested strategies for integrating mental and emotional health (MEH) education lessons into the daily curriculum. We suggest that lessons be taught in a manner that allows students to be excited to experience lessons about MEH. Instructions in MEH education need not be separate from traditional academic learning. There are several strategies a teacher can use to successfully integrate MEH education into other parts of the daily curriculum.

The most basic incorporation strategy is to supplement existing lessons on MEH skills or other health topics. These new lessons can be considered a new topic area that either enhances existing curriculum or replaces lessons in need of update. Students who regularly attend structured Health Education class can easily participate in lessons as part of their health program.

Within the general curriculum, when appropriate, lessons can be used as motivating transitions into an academic unit, which increase readiness for learning. For example, a lesson, which addresses conflict resolution, can introduce a unit about wars. Starting with a topic that students can relate to and drawing a comparison to world conflicts can add depth to existing lesson topics.

Just as mental and emotional lessons can be used at the beginning of units on academic subjects, they can also be used at the end of units as a reward for completion. When used in this manner, discussing war in a broad sense through learning about a major world conflict can be tied to the student's life by learning to apply lessons of world conflict to personal conflict.

Lessons can also be used as a reward in and of themselves after students complete their academic work. Importantly, the lessons should logically follow academic content. For example after students complete a spelling lessons about colors, they can have a lesson about feelings and moods, which addresses colors and includes the use of drawing as an outlet for expression of feelings.

MEH education does not always have to be part of traditional academic time; lessons can be used at times when students are generally receiving enrichment. These portions of the day include special after-school programs for children that are designed specifically for students with a need for this type of curriculum as well as general after school programs. Lessons could also be taught during lunchtime for students who participate in enrichment programs during this time, or in programs that are designed for students who come to school early.

These lessons do not need to be taught by the classroom teacher alone; they can (and at times, should) involve other adults besides the teacher; for example, MEH lessons can be utilized as a learning center in the classroom, taught by either a mental health professional or by a classroom volunteer. Also, lessons can be referenced in response to specific situations in the classroom, which address the emotional or mental health needs of students who are involved in a crisis. Lessons which address topics in which a mental health professional can offer valuable insights or where a mental health professional can be asked to join the lesson to discuss their role in a mental health crisis allows students to more clearly understand the job of a mental health professional and gives them a chance to see a real mental health professional outside of television depictions. This can allow for less stigmatization of talking to mental health professionals, especially if they regularly interact with all students. Lessons can also be used by substitute teachers or other adults who come into the classroom as an opportunity for students to continue to practice MEH skills.

Overall, MEH education can actually impact on classroom academic learning. Recent findings with third- and fourth-grade participants support this idea (Malecki & Elliott, 2002, http://casel.org/wp-content/uploads/2011/04/T3053c01.pdf). The investigators found a positive association between prosocial behaviors (cooperation, assertion, responsibility, empathy, and self-control) and academic achievement (outcomes on standardized test assessing fundamental reading and quantitative skills). Thus, the emotional development that MEH fosters in students can make it easier for them to concentrate on academic subjects, and achieve school success.

Appendix B2 — Mental and Emotional Health Curriculum: Sample Lessons Topics

The following lessons may not apply to all or most children, but teachers will be able to utilize them whenever they feel appropriate.

<u>Kindergarten:</u>

1) **Personal Safety and Safe Behavior:** Abuse Prevention

<u>Grade One:</u>

1) **Self-Direction and Regulation:** Coping with Death: Pet
2) **Social and Working Relationships:** Being a good friend when someone loses someone
3) **Personal Safety and Safe Behavior:** Getting help for abuse

<u>Grade Two:</u>

1) **Self-Direction and Regulation**: Coping with friends leaving, moving.
2) **Personal Safety and Safe Behavior**: Getting help for abuse

<u>Grade Three:</u>

1) **Self-Direction and Regulation**: Coping with divorce/separation/under-standing diverse family dynamics.
2) **Self-Direction and Regulation**: Coping with long-term, chronic illness (self)
3) **Self-Direction and Regulation**: Coping with illness in others (adults): mental illness

<u>Grade Four:</u>

1) **Self-Direction and Regulation**: Coping with long-term, chronic illness and grandparents/other relatives moving in
2) **Responsibility and Integrity**: Courage to ask for help for abuse, whom/when to ask.

<u>Grade Five:</u>

1) **Self-Direction and Regulation:** Coping with illness in others (friends): long-term, chronic illness
2) **Self-Direction and Regulation:** Coping with death: Family Member
3) **Self-Direction and Regulation:** Coping with substance abuse in others

Grade Six:

1) **Self-Direction and Regulation:** Coping will illness in others (adults): mental illness
2) **Self-Direction and Regulation:** Coping with death: Friend

Grade Seven:

1) **Self-Direction and Regulation:** Coping with suicide
2) **Self-Direction and Regulation:** Coping with substance abuse in others
3) **Self-Direction and Regulation:** Coping with illness in self: mental illness
4) **Personal Safety and Safe Behavior:** Suicide Prevention for self and others

Grade Eight:

1) **Self-Direction and Regulation:** Coping with illness in others (friend): mental illness

Appendix B3 — Sample Lesson for a Mental Health Curriculum to Promote Mental Health Literacy

Decision Making

Social and Working Relationships

Grade 6

Objectives

Students will:

1. Distinguish between internally and externally influenced decisions.
2. Explain why a decision is internally or externally influenced.
3. Select what internal or external factors influence their decisions.

Assessment

Teacher will:

1. Observe students' ability to determine when a decision is influenced by internal or external factors.
2. Observe students' ability to explain why a decision is influenced internally or externally.
3. Observe students' ability to select what factors influence their own decisions.

Teaching Materials

Internal or External Decision worksheet (one per student)
Internal or External Decision answer key (one copy)
Letter to parents (English and Spanish)

Things to do before

1. Photocopy *Internal or External Decision* worksheet.

Language Development

internal: located, acting, or effective within the body
external: acting or coming from the outside.

Activities

Full Group:

1. Ask students to describe some of the decisions they have already made today (what to eat, what to wear, how to get to school).

2. Explain to students that each day we make hundreds of decisions. Some of the decisions are easy to make, some are more difficult.
3. Ask students to explain why they made some of the decisions they described making today.
   a- How did you choose what to eat?
   b- How did you choose what to wear? Etc.
4. Discuss internal influences on decisions. Use the following statements and questions to guide discussion:
   a- Some decisions are based entirely on our own feelings or beliefs. These decisions are based on internal influences.
   b- Internal decisions are based on knowledge and facts, curiosity, interests, desires, or fears.
   c- An example of an internal decision is choosing to order a pineapple pizza because you are curious about how it tastes.
5. Discuss external influences on decisions. Use the following statements and questions to guide discussion:
   a- Some decisions are made based on outside influences. These are called external decisions
   b- External decisions are based on influence from media/advertising, legal restrictions, setting/location, culture, parents/family/relatives, peers/friends/other teens, or role models outside the family.
   c- An example of an externally influenced decision is choosing to eat at a particular restaurant because your favorite movie star was seen eating there.
6. Explain that neither decisions made by external influences or internal influences are necessarily better, but that it is important to maintain a balance when making choices. Make decisions for yourself as well as recognize when you are making decisions based on outside influences.
7. Explain that the most influential factor when making a decision that is the right choice for yourself should be whether or not you can be satisfied with the consequences of the decision you make.
8. Have students work in pairs to complete the *Internal or External Decision* worksheet.
9. Review answers as a class.
10. Remind students that just because someone they know or see on television makes a particular decision, it does not mean that that decision is right for them.

Learning Logs

1. Have students keep track of 15 decisions they make throughout the rest of the day and ask them to determine whether these decisions were made based on internal or external influences. Have students to explain in

writing why they determined the decision to be internally or externally influenced.
2. Have students determine individually whether most of their decisions were made using external or internal influences.
3. Review some of the decisions students recorded and what the influences on those decisions were.

Extension Activities

1. Have students create a plan for when they will make decisions based on internal influences and when they will make decisions based on external influences. Ask students to list and rank sources of advice for making tough decisions when they need outside advice.
2. Have students create a plan for resisting external influences on decisions. Include external factors that each individual student relies on most often and alternative choices for those decisions.
3. Have students examine television and magazine advertisements for messages that may be influencing their decision making.

Dear Family,

Today in your child's *Mind it!* program, we examined some of the decisions your child makes every day and examined how each individual makes decisions based on both internal and external influences.

During adolescence teens make increasing numbers of decisions based on external influences, especially those of peers, role models, and advertising. Making them aware of these influences allows teens to think about how they are making decisions. When your child has the ability to recognize what is influencing his or her choices, your child will subsequently be able to make smarter and healthier choices for himself or herself.

You can help counterbalance the negative external factors that influence your child by encouraging him or her to make decisions based on knowledge, likes, believes, value, or desires. It is also important to remind your child that you are always available to help make decisions.

Sincerely,

Your child's teacher

Estimada familia,

Hoy durante la clase del programa de *Mind it!* evaluamos las decisiones que su hijo/a toma cada día, y el hecho de que cada persona toma decisiones basadas tanto en influencias internas como externas.

Durante la adolescencia los jóvenes toman muchas decisiones basadas en influencias externas, especialmente en las de sus pares, modelos, y la publicidad. Es importante concientizar a los adolescentes que piensen sobre cómo y por qué están tomando ciertas decisiones. Cuando su hijo/a tenga la capacidad de reconocer qué está influyendo sus decisiones, será capaz de tomar decisiones más acertadas y saludables para él o ella.

Usted puede ayudar a contrarrestar los factores externos negativos que influyen a su hijo/a alentándolo a que tome decisiones basadas en conocimiento, gustos, creencias, valores, o deseos. Es importante recordar a su hijo/a que usted está disponible para ayudarlo/a a tomar esas decisiones.

Atentamente,

La maestra de su hijo/a

Internal or External Decision
Read about the following decisions. Determine whether the decision was made because of internal influences or external influences. Then write what category of internal or external influence made you choose internal or external. Write your answers on the blank space.
Internal: knowledge, curiosity, interests, desires, fears
External: media/advertising, legal restrictions, setting/location, role models, culture, parents/family/relatives, peers/friends/others.
Ex: Ezra bought the house because of its location near the water. **External Setting/Location**

	Internal	*External*
1. Joan would not ride the Ferris Wheel because she is afraid of heights.		
2. Ravi will not eat beef because the cow is sacred in his culture.		
3. Ali climbed the fence because he wanted to find out what was making the piercing noise.		
4. Victor wore the blue suit to his grandfather's funeral because his grandmother asked him to.		
5. Priya chose fish for dinner because she does not like beef.		

6. Milo chose a banana rather than ice cream because he knows that fruit is an important part of a healthy diet.		
7. Clay bought a new toothbrush because the advertisement said it would make his teeth feel cleaner.		
8. Phoebe adopted a kitten because she wanted the feeling that something loved and needed her.		
9. Omar chose this picnic spot because of the view.		
10. Josefina saw the movie because her friends recommended it.		
11. Gail bought this perfume over that one because she had heard her favorite singer uses it too.		
12. Rhane buckles her seatbelt when she gets in the car because there is a law that says she will have to pay a fine if she is caught without one.		

Internal or External Decision Key

Read about the following decisions. Determine whether the decision was made because of internal influences or external influences. Then write what category of internal or external influence made you choose internal or external. Write your answers on the blank space.

Internal: knowledge, curiosity, interests, desires, fears

External: media/advertising, legal restrictions, setting/location, role models, culture, parents/family/relatives, peers/friends/others.

Ex: Ezra bought the house because of its location near the water. **External Setting/Location**

	Internal	*External*
1. Joan would not ride the Ferris Wheel because she is afraid of heights.	**Fears**	
2. Ravi will not eat beef because the cow is sacred in his culture.		**Culture**

	Internal	*External*
3. Ali climbed the fence because he wanted to find out what was making the piercing noise.	Curiosity	
4. Victor wore the blue suit to his grandfather's funeral because his grandmother asked him to.		Family
5. Priya chose fish for dinner because she does not like beef.	Interests	
6. Milo chose a banana rather than ice cream because he knows that fruit is an important part of a healthy diet.	Knowledge	
7. Clay bought a new toothbrush because the advertisement said it would make his teeth feel cleaner.		Media
8. Phoebe adopted a kitten because she wanted the feeling that something loved and needed her.	Desires	
9. Omar chose this picnic spot because of the view.		Setting/location
10. Josefina saw the movie because her friends recommended it.		Peers/friends
11. Gail bought this perfume over that one because she had heard her favorite singer uses it too.		Role models
12. Rhane buckles her seatbelt when she gets in the car because there is a law that says she will have to pay a fine if she is caught without one.		Laws

Appendix B4 — Sample Lesson Plan for Improving Mental Health Literacy — Grade 7

Cultural Background/Awareness

Self-esteem/Self-image

Grade 7

Objectives

Students will:

1. Identify someone in their family they admire, and talk about why they think highly of that person.
2. Examine cultural background as a source of pride.
3. Recognize cultural commonalities and differences.

Assessment

Teacher will:

1. Observe class presentations and group discussion.

Teaching Materials

Celebrating Family and Culture: Interview Sheet worksheet (one per student)
Podium for the presentations.

Things to do before

1. Distribute the *Celebrating Family and Culture: Interview Sheet* worksheet at least two days in advance.
2. Ask the class to choose someone in their family (an adult) that they value, admire, and respect.
3. Have students conduct interviews for homework, explaining to them that they will be presenting their findings to the class for a special in-class celebration. Encourage students to bring in photos, memorabilia, music, a special dish, or article of clothing that will help bring the person to life for the class.
4. Obtain a podium for the presentations.

Language Development

culture: the beliefs, customs, practices, and social behavior of a particular nation or people
values: things or ideas that people believe are important.

Activities

Full Group:

1. Explain to the class that we all belong to many cultures. Since we live in the United States, we all share the US culture. Everyone here also shares the middle school culture.
2. Ask the class to describe "middle school culture": (homework, classes, sports, foods, clothing, changing classes).
3. Because we share these aspects of our culture, it is important to celebrate the ways in which each one of us has unique cultural characteristics.
4. Explain that every family develops its own set of traditions that sets it apart from other families. Explain that aside from Native Americans, almost everyone else's family originated in a country or place other than here and that the people in the United States are a combination of many different cultural and ethnic backgrounds. For example, even if two families are white, one family may be Italian and Roman Catholic and the other could be German and Episcopalian.
5. Discuss Thanksgiving or birthdays — what are some different ways we celebrate the same holiday? (Note: If you have students that are members of Jehovah's Witness, you may want to omit this discussion.)
6. Reiterate to the class that the point of the day's presentations is to celebrate the ways in which we are all different. (You may want to start by sharing a part of your own cultural heritage.) There are no wrong answers or wrong ways to present. Simply having the courage to speak in front of the class about your chosen person for three to five minutes will earn you an "A" for the day.
7. Ask for student volunteers to begin presentations. If no one volunteers, choose names randomly, or go in alphabetical order, etc. Explain that because of time constraints, students should not read from their papers, but try and present an overview of what they learned.
8. After all of the presentations have been completed, ask the class to reflect on all the stories they have just heard. Ask the class if they are thankful that we are made up of so many diverse cultures, and explain the ways in which diversity makes our lives so much richer.

Extension Activities

1. Encourage students to participate in an Intergenerational Oral History Project or Poetry Exchange with a local nursing home or senior citizens community center.
2. Organize a school-wide multicultural day with food, music, art, dance, and guest speakers.

Celebrating Family and Culture: Interview Sheet

Name of the person being interviewed: _____

Age of person: _____

Relationship to you: _____

- -

Before you begin the interview, take 10–15 minutes to reflect and, in your own words, describe your person's strengths (intelligence, personality, interpersonal skills, abilities, talents, etc.). What is it about the person that you value so much?

- -

Questions

1. How would you describe your cultural background?

2. Where were your parents and grandparents born?

3. Discuss an important event in your life, explaining why it was so important.

4. Please tell me about any special achievements.

5. Please describe a special trip you have taken in your life, and explain why it was special.

6. Could you describe your childhood and your relationship with your parents, siblings, and friends when you were my age?

7. Please describe an important experience that happened to you in school.

8. What is an important value that you feel you have communicated to your family?

9. What about yourself and your cultural background make you proud?

10. Do you have any other memories you would like to share?

11. Do you have any photos, memorabilia, music, special clothing, or recipes that I can share with my class that reflect who you are?

Appendix B5 — Sample Lesson Plan for Improving Mental Health Literacy — Grade 8

Anger Management/Impact of Self on Others

Self-Direction and Regulation

Grade 8

Objectives

Students will:

1. Identify and control feelings within themselves that may lead to violence.
2. Identify situations that suggest they may need help to control anger in a dating situation.
3. Identify what is not acceptable behavior in a relationship.

Assessment

Teacher will:

1. Observe class discussions and group work.
2. Review **Learning Log**.

Teaching Materials

Triggers worksheet (one per group)
Identifying Abuse in a Romantic Relationship handout (one per student)
Chart paper (one sheet per group)
Markers (for one recorder per group)

Things to do before

1. Photocopy *Triggers* worksheet and *Identifying Abuse in a Romantic Relationship* handout.
2. Obtain chart paper and markers.

Language Development
aggravated: something made more severe or intense especially in law; incited, especially deliberately, to anger.

Activities

Small Groups:

1. Divide the class into groups of three or four students. Hand out the *Triggers* worksheet and ask each group to answer the questions, and to place their responses on a piece of chart paper (ask one student to serve

as recorder). If necessary, you may elicit the following types of responses for Question #1:

a- feeling taken for granted, betrayed, or taken advantage of (your best friend tells someone else your secret; your sibling breaks something of yours)

b- witnessing or experiencing something unfair (your mom accuses you of something you didn't do)

c- feeling embarrassed (someone throws a spitball at you in class)

d- being picked on or made fun of

e- being left out (not invited to a party)

f- losing or doing poorly in something (a game, competition, or grades).

For Question #2, you may want to elicit the following types of responses that represent the different levels of anger intensity that can correspond to different situations or behaviors:

a- Annoyed

b- Irritated

c- Frustrated

d- Disgusted

e- Aggravated

f- Mad

g- Furious

h- Enraged

Or, students may write down physical feelings such as:

a- Tense muscles

b- Faster heartbeat

c- Sweaty palms

d- Raised voice

Full Group:

1. Post the chart paper responses of each group around the room and discuss the various "triggers" and corresponding feelings and behaviors.

2. Emphasize the positive ways that show respect for the self and others such as:

a- pillow punching

b- leaving the room

c- playing music

d- telling a joke or finding humor in the situation

e- counting to ten backwards

f- exercising

g- talking to a friend

h- taking a walk

i- deep breathing

j- visualization

3. Remind students that everyone feels angry at one time or another. It's your ability to control your anger and use it constructively instead of destructively that shows maturity.

Learning Log

1. Have students write independently on the following topics:
   a- A situation that always makes me angry is _____.
   b- When this happens, I usually show my anger by _____.
   c- The negative consequence of this is _____.
   d- The next time this situation occurs, instead of growing angry, I will control my emotions by _____.
   e- The positive consequence of doing this will be _____.

Full Group:

1. Explain to the class that experiencing positive, healthy relationships with friends, family, or dates are only possible when you can CONTROL your anger. You don't need to eliminate anger, only express it properly.
2. Tell the class that, according to the Centers for Disease Control and Prevention, 25% of 8th and 9th grade male and female students admit to having been a victim of dating violence.
3. Distribute the Identifying Abuse in a Romantic Relationship handout and review it with the class.
4. Ask the class why they think dating abuse is such a widespread problem. Elicit and discuss the following:
   a- Victims of abuse may believe they are responsible and accept blame for causing the abuse.
   b- Many victims stay silent and don't tell anyone. They feel violence is normal or are afraid of what their parents will think.
   c- Many have been taught to take a boyfriend or girlfriend's jealous feelings as a sign of how much he or she loves you.
   d- Many people can't deal with their emotions. When they feel angry or scared or hurt, they resort to violence because they think that's what everyone does.
   e- Displacement of emotions
   f- It is not uncommon to make excuses for someone's behavior because you care about them. However, this may lead to the violence becoming a cycle.
   g- Many may fear being alone if they end an abusive relationship. They believe they have no choice but to stay in the relationship.

5. Explain to the class that the abused person can be either male or female. Females are more likely to abuse verbally than physically; however, verbal and emotional abuse may actually be harder to stop than physical abuse.

Small Groups:

1. Divide the class into groups of three students.
2. Have the groups imagine scenarios in which someone might get angry while on a date or with a date. "Rewrite" the ending. (An example: Dean wants to take Heather to a party. She doesn't want to miss her curfew, and is ready to go home. He loses his temper and starts screaming that she's his date and she'll do what he says, or else. Rewrite: Dean is disappointed that he can't go to his friend's party, but respects Heather's wishes, and takes her home).

Full Group:

1. Discuss scenarios with the class.
2. Ask the class how they can prevent dating violence. Elicit the following:
   a- Go on dates in public places.
   b- Don't leave a party or event with someone you don't know well.
   c- Don't go out with anyone who puts you down, pressures you, or tries to control you.
   d- Accept no as a final answer, not a challenge.
   e- Know that rape is a violent crime with serious consequences.
   f- Get counseling if you have violent, aggressive feelings toward the opposite sex.

Extension Activities

1. Conflict is an essential element in almost any story. Have students analyze the ability of characters in novels and/or short stories to deal with anger properly. Students can write letters to the characters, giving them advice on how to handle the conflicts more effectively or how to better manage their anger.

Triggers

Read the following questions, and write your responses on the provided chart paper.

1. *Create a list of words, behaviors, situations, and types of body language that can cause you to feel anger.*

2. *How do you feel when you're angry?*

3. How do you react when you're angry? What do you do?

Identifying Abuse in Romantic Relationships
There are several different types of dating abuse:

Emotional: Extreme jealousy and possessiveness; suspicious accusations, put downs, trying to control what you feel, think, what you wear and who you see, humiliates you, threatens to hurt themselves or others if you break up with them.

Physical: Any act that physically hurts or frightens you: hitting, slapping, pushing, kicking, using a weapon to hurt or scare you, breaking things, stalking.

Sexual: Making you do sexual things that you don't want to do through force, pressure, threats, bribery, or manipulation; not stopping when you ask.

Verbal: Screaming and shouting at you; using abusive language, making negative comments about how you look.

Remember!

It is against the law for anyone to:

– Hurt you
– Try to hurt you
– Force you to have sex
– Threaten you with weapons
– Harass you on the phone or through the mail
– Stalk you
– Destroy your property

It is never appropriate for someone to abuse you. **No one** deserves abuse!

Appendix B6 — Sample Lessons Designed for School Mental Health Professionals

Number of Lessons: 7

Grade 5 (1)	Grade Six (2)	Grade Seven (3)	Grade Eight (1)
Self-Direction and Regulation **Coping with death**	*Self-Direction and Regulation* **Coping with death**	*Self-Direction and Regulation* **Coping with suicide**	*Personal Safety and Safe Behavior* **Prevent Abuse/ Neglect**
Family Member	**Friend**	**Feelings: Expression, Identification, Management**	**Getting help Prevent Physical Abuse Prevent sexual abuse**
Feelings: Identification, Expression, Management	**Feelings: Identification, Expression, Management**	*Students will describe how they (would) feel if/ when someone they know took their own lives*	**Prevent verbal (Emotional) abuse** *Students will* **learn to identify dating violence situations and learn about dating violence prevention**
Students will describe the emotions caused by the death of a family member, and discuss ways to handle these feelings	*Students will discuss feelings associated with the death of a friend and examine how this experience has changed how they view their own lives*	*Students will discuss ways to handle these emotions and understand the importance of expressing them for their mental health*	*Students will review who are the school mental health professionals they go to for help.*
Students will recognize the importance of expressing these emotions for their mental health (1)	(1)	(1)	(1)

	Mental Illness		
	Life changes and mental illness Coping with death Feelings: Expression,	**Coping with illness Self Mental Illness**	

Identification, Management

Students will understand the importance of expressing feelings about how the death of a loved one affects them	*Students will examine how they would feel before/ during/after a diagnosis of a mental illness*
Students will discuss the emotional consequences these feelings (and not releasing them) have on their mental health	*Students will explore coping strategies to handle the diagnosis process*
This lesson is to be used in conjunction with the contingency lesson (1)	(1)

	Personal Safety and Safe Behavior
	Suicide Prevention Self and others
	Students will recognize the warning signs of suicide Students will discuss how to get help for suicide threats (1)

Appendix B7 — Guidelines for Assessing the Student's Knowledge
WRITTEN COMPONENT

Style
1. Student has strong grasp of grammar, spelling, and vocabulary. 5 POINTS

2. Student makes occasional mistakes with grammar and vocabulary. 3 POINTS

3. Student has poor sense of sentence structure and limited vocabulary. 1 POINT

Follows Directions
1. Student follows directions completely. 5 POINTS

2. Student follows most directions; misses some details. 3 POINTS

3. Student follows few directions. 1 POINT

Thoughtfulness
1. Student explores many ideas and writes with great detail. 5 POINTS

2. Student explores some ideas and leaves out detail. 3 POINTS

3. Student shows little concern for ideas or detail. 1 POINT

Organization
1. Student has well-organized ideas, excellent paragraph structure. 5 POINTS

2. Student is somewhat organized, but needs to improve. 3 POINTS

3. Student is disorganized. Ideas are scattered and confused. 1 POINT

Willingness to Take Chances
1. Student is willing to state new ideas and use new words. 5 POINTS

2. Student takes some writing risks. 3 POINTS

3. Student plays it safe, stays with the familiar. 1 POINT

TOTAL POINTS: _____

GRADE:

22–25 POINTS "A"_____   18–21 POINTS "B"_____

14–17 POINTS "C"_____   10–13 POINTS "D"_____

VERBAL COMPONENT

Clarity
1. Student presents information in a clear, confident voice. 5 POINTS

2. Student hurries parts of the presentation, stumbles over some details. 3 POINTS

3. Student mumbles, is inaudible, and/or races through the presentation. 1 POINT

Organization
1. Student presents information logically and sequentially. 5 POINTS

2. Student is a little scattered, but information is easy to follow. 3 POINTS

3. Student is disorganized; presentation is difficult to follow and understand. 1 POINT

Thoroughness
1. Student presents all the pertinent information and ideas in the project. 5 POINTS

2. Student leaves out some information but covers the main points. 3 POINTS

3. Student omits important information, uses little detail. 1 POINT

Response
1. Student answers questions accurately and with detail. 5 POINTS

2. Student answers questions with some hesitation and lack of detail. 3 POINTS

3. Student has difficulty answering questions and offering details. 1 POINT

TOTAL POINTS: _____

GRADE:

22–25 POINTS "A"_____   18–21 POINTS "B"_____

14–17 POINTS "C"_____   10–13 POINTS "D"_____

INDIVIDUAL PROJECT COMPONENT (IF APPLICABLE)

Clarity
1. Project is clear, organized, and easily understood. 5 POINTS
2. Project is somewhat disorganized, sloppy, and confusing. 3 POINTS
3. Project is difficult to decipher and understand. 1 POINT

Creativity
1. Project shows a high degree of originality and creativity. 5 POINTS
2. Project is somewhat derivative and clichéd. 3 POINTS
3. Project is unoriginal and poorly constructed. 1 POINT

Connection to Subject
1. Project specifically and directly relate to the scope of the lesson. 5 POINTS
2. Project references the lesson indirectly and incompletely. 3 POINTS
3. Project makes no obvious or logical connection to the lesson. 1 POINT

Scope of Effort
1. Project shows considerable time and effort on the part of the student. 5 POINTS
2. Project is the result of some serious work but could have been pushed. 3 POINTS
3. Project is obviously the result of little effort and time. 1 POINT

TOTAL POINTS: _____

GRADE:

17–20 POINTS "A" _____   13–16 POINTS "B" _____

10–13 POINTS "C" _____   7–10 POINTS "D" _____

PARTICIPATION

Group Participation
1. Student actively participated and took on a leadership role. 5 POINTS
2. Student participated somewhat in the discussions. 3 POINTS
3. Student participated very little or not at all. 1 POINT

Attitude

1. Student has a positive attitude and is actively engaged in the lesson. 5 POINTS

2. Student is somewhat engaged and interested in the lesson. 3 POINTS

3. Student is indifferent to the lesson and barely participates. 1 POINT

Behavior

1. Student was respectful and cooperative. 5 POINTS

2. Student was somewhat respectful and could have been more cooperative. 3 POINTS

3. Student was disrespectful and uncooperative. 1 POINT

TOTAL POINTS: _____

GRADE:

17–20 POINTS "A" _____   13–16 POINTS "B" _____

10–13 POINTS "C" _____   7–10 POINTS "D" _____

OVERALL

Grasp of Subject Matter

1. Strong grasp of the subject matter, above-average ability to apply knowledge to personal experience, and active participation in class discussions. 5 POINTS

2. On-grade understanding of the subject matter, average ability to apply knowledge to personal experience, and somewhat active participation in class discussions. 3 POINTS

3. Weak understanding of the subject matter, had difficulty applying knowledge to their own experience, and did not participate in class discussions. 2 POINTS

4. Very little understanding of subject matter, did not apply knowledge to their own experience, and did not participate in class room discussions. 1 POINT

TOTAL POINTS : _____

GRADE:

5 POINTS "A" _____   3 POINTS "B" _____

2 POINTS "C" _____   1 POINT "D" _____

Appendix B8 — Selected Mental Health Related Resources
Books

For parents and teachers — Social emotional learning, adolescence

Burkett, L. (2003). *All about talent: Discovering your gifts and personality.* New York: David C. Cook Publishing Company.

Capello, D. (2000). *Teen talks: Parents must have with their children about violence.* New York: Hyperion.

Cartledge, G., & Milburn, J. F. (Eds.) (1988). *Teaching social skills to children: Innovative approaches.* (2nd ed.). New York: Pergamon Press.

Charney, R. S. (1992). *Teaching children to care: Management in the responsive classroom.* Greenfield, MA: Northeast Foundation for Children.

Cohen, J. (Ed.). *Educating minds and hearts: Social emotional learning and the passage into adolescence.* New York, NY: Teacher's College Press, Alexandria, VA: ASCD, co-publisher.

Demetriades, H. A. (2002*). Bipolar disorder, depression, and other mood disorders (Diseases and People).* Berkeley Heights, NJ: Enslow Publishers, Inc.

Dryfoos, J. G. (1998). *Safe passage: Making it through adolescence in a risky society.* New York, NY: Oxford Press.

Elias, M. J., & Zins, J. E. (Eds.) (2004). *Bullying, peer harassment, and victimization in the schools: The next generation of prevention.* New York, NY: Haworth Press.

Gaetano, R., Grout, J. & Klassen-Landis, M. (1990). *Please talk with me.* Kendall/Hunt Publishing Company.

Gelman, A. (2000). *Coping with depression and other mood disorders (Coping).* New York, NY: Rosen Publishing Group.

Hawkins, J. D., Catalano, R. F., & Associates. (1992). *Communities that care: Action for drug abuse prevention.* San Francisco, CA: Jossey-Bass.

Hyde, M. O. & Forsythe, E. H. (2002). *Depression: What you need to know (Health and Human Diseases).* New York, NY: Scholastic Library Publishing.

Madaras, L. & Madaras, A. (2002). *My feelings, my self: A growing up journal for girls* (2nd ed.). New York, NY: Newmarket Press.

Marx, E., Wooley, S., F., & Northrop, D. (Eds.). (1998). *Health is academic: A guide to coordinated school health programs.* New York, NY: Teachers College Press.

Peacock, J. (2000). *Bipolar disorder (Perspectives on mental health).* New York, NY: Lifematters Press.

Schrumpf, F., Freiburg, S. & Skadden, D. (1993). *Life lessons for young adolescents: An advisory guide for teachers.* Illinois: Research Press.

Smith, L. W. (2000). *Depression: What it is, how to beat it (Teen Issues)*. Berkeley Heights, NJ: Enslow Publishers, Inc.

Weissberg, R. P., Gullotta, T. P., Hampton, R. L., Ryan, B. A., & Adams, G. R. (Eds.). (1997). *Enhancing children's wellness*. Thousand Oaks, CA: Sage Publications.

For students and teachers — Mental illness

Greenberg, J. (1989). *I never promised you a rose garden*. New York, NY: Signet.

Hautzig, D. (1999). *Second star to the right*. New York, NY: Puffin.

Hayden, T. L. (1983). *Murphy's boy*. New York, NY: Avon Books.

Hesser, T. S. (1999). *Kissing doorknobs*. New York, NY: Random House.

Hyde, M. O., & Forsyth, E. H. (1996). *Know about mental illness*. New York, NY: Walker & Co.

Hyland, B. (2002). *The girl with the crazy brother*. Xlibris corporation.

Neufeld, J. (1999). *Lisa, bright and dark: A novel*. New York, NY: Puffin.

Olson, L. S. (1994). *He was still my daddy*. Portland, OR: Ogden House.

Seago, K. (1998). *Matthew unstrung*. New York, NY: Dial Books.

Videos

A Different Journey. Albuquerque, New Mexico: Parents for Behaviorally Different Children Video Project.

Straight talk about mental illness. Arlington, Virginia: National Alliance for the Mentally Ill.

Day for night: Recognizing teenage depression. Baltimore, Maryland: Depression and Related Affective Disorders Association.

My (Claire's) Story. Cuyahoga Falls, Ohio: Mental Health Association of Summit County.

Howard, R. (2001). *A Beautiful Mind*.

Websites

For teachers, students and parents — Information on health and mental health

Nemours Foundation. *Teens Health*. http://www.kidshealth.org

National Institute of Mental Health. *Child and adolescent mental health*. http://www.nimh.nih.gov/healthinformation/childmenu.cfm

Center for Mental Health in Schools. *UCLA school mental health project*. http://smhp.psych.ucla.edu/

Substance Abuse and Mental Health Services Administration (SAMHSA). *National mental health information center.* http://www.mentalhealth. samhsa.gov/

Discovery school. *Lesson plans library.* http://school.discovery.com/ lessonplans

Health in mind. http://healthinmind.com/

National Mental Health Association. http://www.nmha.org/

About the Authors

Christine Beer is a Ph.D. student in the Department of Curriculum and Instruction at the University of Victoria, BC, Canada. With expertise in education and communications, Christine's doctoral research examines the digital health literacy of adolescent students in Republic of the Union of Myanmar.

Deborah Begoray, Ph.D., is a professor of language and literacy in the Department of Curriculum and Instruction at the University of Victoria, BC, Canada. Deborah has experience in literacy teaching and research in a variety of contexts and with a wide range of learners including students, teachers and clinical professionals in K-12 language arts, in other school curricula (such as literacy in mathematics), and health literacy in schools, and in other health contexts such as clinics and in nursing education.

Amy Collins, M.Ed., is a research assistant in the Department of Curriculum and Instruction at the University of Victoria, BC, Canada. Amy also teaches in the grade 7 language arts curriculum in the Victoria public school system.

Janie Harrison, M.Ed., is a research assistant in the Department of Curriculum and Instruction Instruction at the University of Victoria, BC, Canada. Janie is a literacy expert working with reading challenged adolescents and adults, and an experienced teacher in the public school system.

Joan Wharf Higgins, Ph.D., is a professor and Canada research chair (Health & Society) in the School of Exercise Science, Physical and Health Education at the University of Victoria, BC, Canada. Joan's research and teaching interests include health literacy, social marketing, healthy living, and community-based research to advance the health of citizens and communities.

Ray Marks is an award winning professor and educator; an expert on health promotion and disease prevention, health policy, school health education, health literacy and ethics; a director, Center for Health Promotion, City University of New York, York College, New York, US; an adjunct professor of health education, and a CEPH accreditation coordinator, Columbia University, Teachers College, New York, US; former associate director, National Center for Health Education, New York, US.

Leena Paakkari is a senior lecturer in health education teacher training within the Faculty of Sport and Health sciences at the University of Jyväskylä, Finland. Leena's current research interests relate to school subject health education teacher training, school health education, pupils' and teachers' personal epistemology, and health literacy as an educational and health phenomenon. The questions such as "what are the qualitatively varying ways of seeing teaching and learning in health education," "how do pupils and teachers see knowledge and knowing in health education," and "what are the ethical aspects in teaching and learning in health education" interest her. In addition, Leena is currently involved in assessing health literacy as a learning outcome among the secondary school aged children. Leena has experience in qualitative research methodology and especially in phenomenography as an educational research tradition.

Olli Paakkari is a senior lecturer in health education teacher training program within the Faculty of Sport and Health sciences at the University of Jyväskylä, Finland. Olli has also worked as a health education teacher and a physical education teacher in basic education and in general upper secondary school. Some of Olli's research interests are the development of pupils' critical thinking skills and assessment of pupils' learning in health education. Olli has also published health education schoolbooks for upper secondary education.

Lawrence St. Leger (BA, MEdSt, PhD, TSTC, FAHPA) began his working life as a teacher in rural and urban schools in Victoria, Australia. He was officer-in-charge of the health and human relationships unit in the Ministry of Education and then was appointed as deputy manager of health promotion in the Health Department. Lawry then joined Deakin University to teach and research health promotion. He was appointed as head of the School of Nutrition and Public Health and held the position of dean of the Faculty of Health and Behavioural Sciences for seven years.

In the last nine years Lawry has led international teams examining the evidence of effectiveness of school health initiatives. Two major documents have emerged from this work: *Guidelines for Promoting Health in Schools*, which is in nine languages, and *Promoting Health in Schools – From Evidence to Action*. He was also the lead author on the World Health Organisation guidelines for school health. Lawry has also evaluated many community-based initiatives and published widely on school health and community based programs.

He has worked for the World Health Organisation in Cambodia, Mongolia, and the Western Pacific region and has advised health and education ministries in Australian states, New Zealand, Canada, Hong Kong, and Singapore as well as being an invited speaker to many national and international conferences.

Currently he is a chair of the Council of Cabrini Institute, a medical research and education organization that is part of Cabrini Health, one of Australia's biggest health organizations. He is on the board of the Heart Foundation, a Trustee of the International Union of Health Promotion and Education (IUHPE) and on the advisory committee to the State Trustees Australia Foundation.

Lawry continues to advise governments, NGOs and individual organizations about Health Promotion and School Health as well as conducting evaluations and professional development programs.

Subject Index